GROWING UP IN TRENGGANU

Awang Goneng was born at an early age in the house where he grew up in Kuala Trengganu. He was pushed into Sekolah Melayu Ladang where his father's teacher friend rather than his so-called precociousness got him a place as an underage pupil. This experience aged him quickly in time for proper school, first at the Sultan Sulaiman Primary School (SSPS)—where he nearly burned his class and classmates while trying to do a magic trick

involving a box of Swedish *tandstickor* that were on sale in Trengganu at that time—and then later at the SSSecondaryS.

Then his parents moved to Kuala Lumpur and he to another school known as the Victoria Institution where he and a schoolfriend (who later became a judge in Singapore) involuntarily broke the school's medium distance record while fleeing a gang from a rival school near the Merdeka Stadium.

With this newfound talent for power running, Awang Goneng proceeded swiftly into subsequent chapters of his life: first through the doors of the London School of Economics and Political Science (LSE) where he took a Law degree (from the Academic Registrar's office one night when the door was left open), and then through an academic career (briefly) and journalism (less briefly) during which time he interviewed, among others, Anthony Burgess ... Cartland and Adnan Khashoggi. He now lives in London as a fr

T0159437

By the same author

Selangor: A Celebration
(by Wan A. Hulaimi with photographer K.C. Loo)

GROWING UP IN TRENGGANU

Awang Goneng

monsoon

monsoonbooks

Published in 2007
by Monsoon Books Pte Ltd
52 Telok Blangah Road
#03-05 Telok Blangah House
Singapore 098829
www.monsoonbooks.com.sg

ISBN-13: 978-981-05-8692-8
ISBN-10: 981-05-8692-2

Front cover photo © Picture Library Sdn Bhd/S.K. Chong
Back cover photo © Awang Goneng
Illustration on page one © Lat

Printed in Singapore

12 11 10 09 08 07   1 2 3 4 5 6 7 8 9

To Cik and Ayah
Who taught me more than they knew. Alfatihah.

To the lovely ladies in my life:
Zaharah Othman,
Rehana & Nona

And the lovely lads:
Hafiz & Taufiq

A Note on Trengganu

Trengganu did exist once, as Terengganu does now. I grew up in the former and live now outside the latter, so in the title of this book and in the writings herein it is Trengganu for me, *tra-la-la*. If I want to be an argumentative sort of fellow (which I'm not) I will say that no one pronounces Terengganu Te-reng-ga-nu, as it is spelt. In that sense, the Jawi spelling is more faithful to the tongue, T- r-ng-ga-nu. In our family we just say Teganung, others say Teganu, while others still merely go for Ganu or Gganu, so it makes arguments about Trengganu or Terengganu sound rather academic, doesn't it? And so it does to these fellows, engaged in what was once known to men and elephants as the trunk call:

'*Guane mung di Teganung?*'
('How are you in Teganung?')

'*Ggitulah sökmö!*'
('As always, for evermore!')

Introduction:
The Man by the Door

If you're reading this in a bookshop while exchanging uncertain glances with the bookseller sitting there by the door, I'd advise you, in the language of Trengganuspeak, to take this book to the counter and *beli selalu*, a gesture that will be regarded as friendly by writer, bookseller and their starving families (though you may want to take a second look at that person by the door).

This book took shape over many years (I grew up very slowly), was written in many places and spent a good few years as rough drafts on the Internet where it was discovered by a handful of people who very kindly sent me emails or left comments that confirmed, corrected or added to what I'd written there. It is tempting, therefore, to put all this down to one ugly word: a *blook*, a book sired by a blog—well yes, so it is, yes and no.

Many writers I have spoken to have likened the writing of a book to the act of childbirth: slow, painful and driven by anxiety; but as they're all men I am reluctant to take them too seriously except in one aspect, and that is your book, once finished, is nothing less than your own child. The association doesn't just end there for me. I have used my blog notes of things that I suddenly remembered, that I wished to look at again and use later in a book that I had vaguely in mind, of my Trengganu childhood, to pass on to my children to remind them of a world that they never knew and in which their father grew up. I wrote it on the fly, often in internet cafés, sometimes very laboriously into the Palm PDA they gave me for my birthday, and which thankfully only crashed after I'd transferred the bulk of its information to my PC. This is my world as I knew and as I remember it now, a journey travelled through the mind's eye, of places lived through and been to and many, sadly, now vanished.

Growing Up in Trengganu as a fascicule first appeared on 29 October 2003, numbered #306, followed by another on 27 November, numbered #9513. The last, at the time of publication of this book, had reached the lofty height of six digits, #373,123, reproduced here as *Bits of Old Paper* on page 221. The system of numbering was both spurious and purposeful: to escape the bother of having to remember all the numbers that had gone by and, more importantly, to signal that this was growing up *ad libitem*, *ad nauseam*. Of my small coterie of readers only one, a nice young man named Abidin, was puzzled enough to ask if there was method in this madness so, Abidin, this, for you, is the answer.

As I progressed through my writing, and as the numbers reached even more ridiculous digits, the wife of a prominent figure in Malaysian society wrote in with a confession: that she'd been following my numbers with great interest and had been throwing away money on the three-digit lottery based on my digits. Which is a good point now for me to ask if you're still reading this from an uncomfortably upright position in a little bookshop somewhere. If so, then I'll let you know that I don't mind that at all as I'm now living very comfortably (thanks to the confessions of that society lady) from the proceeds of blackmail. But while I'm living comfortably from the earnings of that VIP husband and his guilt-ridden lady, I want you to cast a thought to that bookseller by the door throwing a furtive glance at you, and to his starving family. So if you go now and buy this book, perhaps I too may be able to stop living off the proceeds of blackmail and go back once again to a life of abject probity.

While recording the first draft in blogs I have been fortunate to have had so many people write in with their views. Many wore the cloak of anonymity but many more came under their *noms de guerre*. I love and value them all. Of these, two deserve special mention: Md. Adib Noh (Abedib) who started me blogging, and Pök Ku (Tengku Ali Bustaman), fellow blogger and talented writer; a man who knows more about Trengganu than I do. There are others too, like Maya, who kept urging me to 'do a book', and now that it is here, on her head now be it. Another person too deserves mention: Long Ladang, a true blue Trengganuer and a wanderer, I suspect, like me. He first made his appearance in my blog pages on 9 May 2005 and continued to add his amusing, insightful and occasionally sad footnotes to my blogs for a short time. Then he disappeared completely, and his 'reappearance' was a day of tears. Please go to page 236 to read why.

Finishing a book relieves some burdens but increases others, and my debt spans the world: in Canada, to Chung Chee Min for the photograph on page 165; in New York, to John Storm Roberts for the Besut photos on pages 181, 182 and 183; in Malaysia to Wan Abdul Rahim Kamil for photos from the family album; Yahaya bin Mohd. Nor for the Al-Yunani photos, pages 73, 202 and 203; Wan Adnan Md. Noor and Athirah Azmi for the mausoleum photo on page 58; Dato Md. Noor Khalid (Lat) for the caricature of me; and to Adzakael for his Megat Panji Alam on page 139. In Britain I'm indebted to Kak Teh for her encouragement; to Dato' Yunus Raiss of Sels College, educationist extraordinaire, for those long conversations on Englishness and English grammar; and to Frederick Lees for his very comments. In New Zealand there's Nor Zarifah Maliki who occasionally helped with the identification of *ubis* and plants.

The contents of this book appeared as a first draft in my blogged notes over a few years (2004–June 2007). I have corrected many mistakes, rewritten many sentences and smoothed out many hurriedly written phrases. My bread and butter preoccupations—and laziness—meant that my notes were left out there to dry in cyberspace without the benefit of another look, and my readers were too polite to point out many mistakes to me.

A million thanks finally to Philip Tatham of Monsoon Books who, from out of the blue, sent me an email to ask 'if there's a book there'; to my editor Natalie Thompson for her patience and helpful suggestions; and to Blogspot.com for hosting my first drafts. I have already mentioned my wife and children in the dedication but I shall mention them again now with my love and thanks for their understanding and support and for their endless supply of shortbread and tea.

Please go quietly now to the man by the door and think of the starving families.

Awang Goneng
London 2007

A Community
on the Shore

Hanging From the Rafters

AT SOME POINT IN HER LIFE, Mother must've looked up to the rafters and decided that something was amiss. She ordered the best *lempok* that ever was stirred on this planet earth, put the whole big clump in a metal pot and hung it from a beam up there. This was a traditional Trengganu house which we lived in, and like other traditional Malay houses, it did not have a ceiling. So a view of the rafters, with the strutting beams, and the Senggora tiles that made the roof was clearly visible to a child lying below on a *mengkuang* mat. In some houses, a few tiles would have been taken out and replaced by a sheet of clear glass so that a beam of light could shine through into the house at any time of day. I remember waking in the night to the silvery glow of the moon shining through the skylight—an eerie thought considering that we'd been regaled daily with stories of nocturnal ghostly shapes emerging with legs straddling the beams above.

This encapsulates for me the essence of my Trengganu childhood: sweetness and light, *lempok* in the pot, pane in the sky.

A light from the past, sweetness of old. The *lempok* was stirring stuff, made from fresh durians thrown in a thick mass in a Trengganu brass pot, flesh and stone, and stirred and stirred with bonding and sweetening ingredients—and coconut milk, perhaps—to a beautiful crust. The resulting paste bore the thread of dreams, unlike the ersatz goo wrapped in cellophane now masquerading as 'durian cake'.

Mother had neither the patience nor the skill nor the manpower to make sweetmeat herself. She'd order her *lempok* from Batu Rakit, then the world centre for durian concoctions, and a sweet stick called *rökök Arab* from a lady living behind the walls of the Istana Maziah, this dream so perfect its maker had to be confined within a royal palace. The Istana Maziah was an old-fashioned *istana* with an imposing front. It stood at the foot of an old *bukit*, Bukit Putri (Hill of the Princess), among a colony of royals, servers and hangers on who lived in the back of the building.

15

It was—and still is, probably—a ceremonial palace, entered through an arch of old Malay design (the *pintu gerbang*) which, as word had it, had a little apparition straddling its legs from one side of the arch to the other, long after the sun had sunk in the horizon. Trengganu people had a predilection for apparitions like that.

Our *nasi dagang* came from only one woman, called Mök Song, who plied her trade at the crack of dawn and was already packing up to go by seven o'clock when her rivals were just about to break even.

I'm reminded now of Bukit Putri as it's Ramadan, a time when some Trengganuers would wax lyrical about its purpose—the hill I mean. Atop this hill is an old bell, cast by Trengganu makers from the sturdiest brass. It hangs on a bar in a small hut, not far from a shelter made from bricks, a mysterious place built perhaps by some old sultans as a spot to while away an afternoon while watching the *perahu besar*, the Trengganu junks sailing in laden with salt, Senggora tiles, rice and exotica from old Siam. Beneath this brickwork is a dark, deep cellar from which have emerged many legends. But back to the bell (the Trengganu *genta*) which was struck every day during Ramadan at *iftar* time, the breaking of fast. And then again and again just before dawn in a fit of boisterous chimes to mark the beginning of the day of fasting.

My father used to take me to the Masjid Abidin (White Mosque) after *iftar* to stand in the back row with other little boys for the *tarawih* prayer of many *raka'at*s performed only during Ramadan. The repetitive movements of the prayer were exhausting, but the atmosphere was filled with the sounds and feel of Ramadan.

One night, after prayers, I met the man who struck the *genta* in the *jama'ah* who insisted that my friends and I should see his place of work—an offer that was both cruel and kind. The footpath up the hill was unlit, and it cut through many wild bushes from which lurked many dark creatures of our imagination, and the quiet places of repose of people who had died in the distant past. When we finally reached the bell and the brickwork resting place where legends emerged from its darkest pit, Kuala Trengganu glowed brightly in the distance and there we stood, silently, apprehensively in the dark. The ringer shone his torch at the bell and then looked over to the other side. 'That's the old arch to the *istana*,' he said, 'and from beneath it hangs, every night ...'

'Oh do shut up!' we all said.

Far below at the foot of the hill, behind the *istana*, I saw a tiny light flickering from the window of a little house. And I was sure it was Mök Nöh making her famous *rökök Arab* and other scrumptious native cakes.

Diamonds From the Sky

ONE DAY, at the precise call for the noon prayer, there was a rain of *agar-agar* on our little community.

This was no ordinary *agar-agar* but of the finest variety. They were green, red, yellow and blue, crinkle-cut bite-sized diamonds. It sent Mother rushing out in her prayer shawl, punctuating her rapid movement with words that I still remember: 'My *beleda*! My *beleda*!'

This path to disaster began in the quiet hours when Mother was labouring over her hot stove, peering and stirring in a brass *kuali* that contained a transparent and bubbly goo. Trapped in the embers, like an elongated insect, was the long green leaf of the pandan tree. The scented, blessed pandan has a ubiquitous presence in Malay cookery.

When the mixture was to the desired viscosity, she poured the fluid in as many trays as she could pull from the kitchen cupboard (which wasn't many), and into any other tray-like things that'd serve her purpose. These being mainly old Huntley & Palmer biscuit tins, food-trays painted with a smiling Nyonya extolling the virtues of some local tea, or the lids of any old containers that could hold her gelatinous stuff in sufficient depth and quantity. Before pouring them out into the various trays, she'd mix in just the right amount of some magic drops to make the *agar-agar* glow in translucent gold, red, green or opal blue, filling the whole kitchen with the sweet scent of vanilla.

Early in the morning, just as the sun was rising, I watched her use a serrated cutter to slice the jelly into inch-long shapes which she arranged neatly in two large trays to put out in the sun to dry. For the children, the *agar-agar kering* were the colours of the Trengganu Hari Raya, the feast of Eid to end the fast, the *bulan puasa* of Ramadan.

A window in our house looked out onto one aspect of the local

17

community, especially the *surau* that stood cheek by jowl with our house in the huddled way that *kampung* houses stayed together. Ours was a tall house, much taller than most, that literally looked down onto the daily life of the community. In the moonsoon months there loomed in our window a menacing sky, and the *belinjau* trees swaying from side to side looked extremely supple. As a child I stood for hours looking out from here, listening to the roar of waves on the distant shore.

Mother looked out of the window too but with a purview of shorter remit. It was the corrugated iron rooftop of the *surau* that she was interested in, especially as it was sloping gently past our open window, and easily within her reach. When she looked to the sky, her mind was set: it was a right, bright day for putting the *agar-agar* out to dry. Out went the trays onto the sloping roof, held in place only by their tenuous hold onto the protruding heads of the roofing nails. The midday heat would crystallise the *agar-agar* pretty quickly.

But with noon also came the call to prayer, and in Trengganu then (as now) it would start with the beating of what we called the *geduk*, a massive drum of cow hide whose long barrel hung from stout ropes attached to the lower end of the sloping roof in the back of the *surau*. Beaten with growing intensity, it preceded the muezzin's call, the boom-boom-booming sound that shook the rafters, awoke the dozy, and sent the trays tumbling down from the rooftop, *agar-agar* and all.

I happened to be in the back of the *surau* just when this technicoloured rain began to fall, sitting by an old curmudgeon who was a distant uncle. He was a *surau* regular who was quick on the draw with acid retorts about the slightest thing that irked him so. When my mother's distressed call was heard between the booms of the *geduk*, he deigned to give the briefest look at the scene of devastation then, without batting even an eyelid, he walked silently back to the inside of the *surau* to pray.

It was not the sight and sound of my poor mother in her prayer shawl that became the defining moment for me in this comical episode but rather the unbemused expression of the old curmudgeon who bothered to even look at all. You need to have lived on this earth for quite awhile to be able to look at diamond-shaped jellies of many hues showering down from the sky on a clear day, and be able to dismiss it without so much as a sigh.

Ice on the Gunny

ROSE SYRUP, sweet since the 1930s. By late afternoon the pavement in front of the *pasar* was lined with blocks of ice, some covered in sawdust, others wrapped in gunny sacks. The rasping sound of the sharp teeth of the saw meeting the shimmering face of the ice, making deep cuts in parallel rows in the ice block, then another line cutting the rows in half again in a cross-cut. Then a sharp hack with the cleaver down the clefts would break those smaller blocks free, to the delight of street urchins and errand boys sent out to buy this essential balm for the dry rasping throats of adult fasters; and ice too for the milky, syrupy drink that'd quench the thirst from a long day's *puasa*.

Children fasted too, but most of them were given special dispensation to eat at noon. In our household this was considered infra dig, so we braved it out with a full day's whine, salivating fiercely as the afternoon drew on when the aroma of the *akök* or the *bubur lambuk* bubbling in Mother's kitchen became just too irresistible.

This was Kuala Trengganu before the fridge became the precious white good for the plebs. Selling ice blocks by the roadside was a source of extra income for the boys for Hari Raya clothes, or for a jaunt after Raya prayers to the Capitol or the Sultana, two local cinematic fleapits that incessantly rolled out old films from the Shaw Brothers and the Cathay Keris stables.

By those ice sellers in the Tanjong market, as the shadows were lengthening and the sun was turning a different shade of yellow, came the *kuih* sellers. These were womenfolk who worked over their hot stoves from the break of day, incessantly stoking the fire with coconut husks or firewood, brows dripping with sweat and eyes ever watchful that the products of their labour were not burnt to a cinder. By five o'clock in the afternoon they'd be ambling out of their domestic workshops, round woven baskets balanced precariously on their heads, filled to the brim with veritable delights and fancy cakes. There were stalls and stalls for these sellers, all arranged in a row.

This is the roll call of Trengganu comestibles: *nekbak, apang ssakör, berönök, perut ayam, wajik, lömpat tikam, asam gumpal* and, of course, the *putri mandi*, the princess in a bath of shaved coconut and palm sugar.

In this age of the fruitcake, who remembers them all now? Recently, while sampling the Turkish Imam Biyaldi, so good as to make the *imam* faint, I was reminded of the Trengganuesque Cik Abas Demam, a culinary product so good that the eponymous sampler (Cik Abas) ran hot and cold.

But not everything was sweet and sickly. There was *röjök betik*, a Trengganu salad of green papaya shaved into thin strips, covered with a sauce of fish, chilli and coconut sugar mixed in vinegar. Then there was, of course, the famous Trengganu *röjök kateh*, not strictly a salad, but a chilli-hot vinegary preparation of cows' trotters. Also the *ceranang*, a true salad of blanched vegetables (mainly *kangkong*), bean sprouts and tofu covered in a thick dollop of peanut sauce.

Just before sunset—before lilting cries of the muezzin came forth from various little prayer halls in the community, before the cannon roared from distant hills, before the Trengganu bell rang out its doleful chimes from Bukit Putri by the harbour to mark the time for *iftar*—the kids would roll up their gunny sacks for the day, stash the day's takings in a Milo tin and head for home to unravel a fierce weapon, the *bedil buloh* that fired volleys of carbide power, much to the consternation of elderly village women who'd be shocked by the booms into fits of uncontrollable verbal assault (mostly pertaining to the pudenda).

To *melatah* is a peculiarly Malay and Eskimo affliction, and is recognised as Eskimo hysteria. All that ice on the pavement couldn't have cooled down the distemper.

Noises on the Ether

EID DAY OR HARI RAYA would suddenly come with the pealing of the *genta*, followed by a sudden shift in tone in the Masjid 'Abidin from *tarawih* prayers to the *takbir,* then perhaps an announcement on the radio.

We had a radio with a lit-up dial that carried the names of many cities of the world. A long needle moved across its face to pick voices that came from distant parts: New Delhi, Ljubljana, Moscow, Warsaw, probably even Gdansk and Timbuctoo. From each stop came ghostly voices from afar, but mostly they were just high-pitched gurglings across the ether.

On Radio Malaya came the awaited report of a moon sighting in the sky skies above Teluk Kemang. It was the earliest glimpse of the Eid month of Shawwal. Teluk Kemang was the best place for moon sighting in all of Peninsular Malaysia.

As soon as the news settled in, Mother would hasten to the kitchen to boil a huge pot of rice which she'd put aside to cool awhile. Then, when all her other work was done, she'd dollop the rice out onto a mat of banana leaves, pull the edges of the leaves to the centre to bind the rice into a wrap, then cover this wrap with another wrap of *batik* material. Then it was time for her to call out to us to help her lift the *batu giling* to place atop the huge parcel. And there it'd stay till Eid morning, the rice snugly encased in sarong and banana leaves. Then, before our very eyes, she'd unravel a miracle. The rice under the weight of the *batu giling* had compacted into a massive cake of *nasi kapit*, to be diced and dipped in peanut sauce on the morning of Raya.

The *nasi kapit* is de rigueur for Hari Raya in Trengganu, as is the *ketupat pulut*, glutinous rice wrapped in *palas* leaf triangles, then fried in coconut oil. There was also another *ketupat* wrapped in little parcels woven from the long shoots of the coconut tree. Raw rice was poured into the woven containers, then boiled in a pot until the rice fluffed out and pressed itself into a cake under the pressure, just like the *nasi kapit*.

Uncertainty about when it would end because it depended on the moon sighting added to the excitement of Ramadan, but preparations for it were made well in advance. Cakes were ordered from the specialist makers: *putu kacang* or *apit-apit* that rolled into crisp cigar shapes from the hot griddle. We used them as edible straws for hot Milo. *Rökök Arab* was my favourite, ordered from Mök Nöh who lived behind the walls of the *istana*. *Rökök Arab* was *apit-apit* with a college education—rolled like *apit-apit* but solid as cigar. It was greased with Trengganu *ghee*, our *minyök sapi*, smothered in Mök Nöh's devotion and love then fried to the consistency that would transport you to another world.

Around the middle of Ramadan, Mother would assemble ingredients of pandan leaves, sugar and *agar-agar*, magic dyes in little bottles and the merest hint of the essence of vanilla. She'd stir them all together in a thick brass pot over a wood fire until they blended into the right consistency for her to pour into a tray. This was the beginning of the diamond-shaped *beleda* that was put out in the sun to dry into a myriad of colours: sugar-coated shapes of green and red and golden yellow, shining translucently like glass crystals.

On the Day of Raya

ON THE MORNING OF HARI RAYA we wore hats and folded our *samping* tight around our waists in case it dropped when we stood to pray. We took what little money we got from Father and hoped there'd be more along the way. This normally came in the shape of coins—normally ten sen, rarely twenty—wrapped in tubes of rolled up newspaper, broken open by men who stood before a pleading crowd as they either handed them out piece by piece to everyone or showered them all on the crowd. Coin showering was a favourite activity among our local benefactors during Hari Raya, but we never got more than a few coins to hold.

Me (right) standing with my siblings on Hari Raya.

On Hari Raya the *genta* clanged, the cannon roared and the sound of the *geduk* came booming down from the tower. Even *tèksi* pedallers wore their best clothes, but we hastened on foot through Kampung Dalam Bata, out on the long road through Paya Tok Bèr, then a right turn into Kampung Hangus, joining the throng already moving towards the mosque known as Semejid Putih in our lingo. The towers had voices coming down from them: '*Allahu Akbar! Allahu Akbar! Allahu Akbar!*' We knew them to be the voices of Bilal Said or Bilal Deraman, friends of Father and fathers of friends we had at school.

It was the smallness of the community in Kuala Trengganu that gave it the hi-you-there-how-are-you kind of atmosphere. But even then most of the people we found there on Hari Raya were complete strangers, albeit well dressed in Trengganu *söngkèt* when the *söngkèt* was still very affordable. There were all those men in flowing robes, and so many women in prayer shawls moving in a dazzle of white at the women's side of the mosque by which I entered on Fridays and normal days. There was Pök Ku Haji Ambak with his *serban besar bakul*—turban the size of a basket, as my late elder brother so succinctly put it—and there were Hajis who wore stiff, square *igal* on their heads to keep their headcloths from going astray.

Hari Raya was a special day, and woe betide anyone on that day who went to sea. Shops were closed but people milled about everywhere, and there was something merry in the air. This was the day after the night that taught me melancholy from watching the last drops of oil flickering their last dancing lights around the wicks of our home-made *pelita;* after all the children had gone home with the lights doused from their *tanglong*s, and the shops were all closed and quiet from row to row, with not a flicker left of the life that had given so much joy barely an hour before, except for the occasional movement of rats that slid below the shops to nibble on the merchandise while the shopkeepers were away.

Father had a brother living next door to the mosque in a large wooden house that's now been packed up and half rebuilt elsewhere due to the government's recent effort to 'clean up' Kuala Trengganu. This uncle was a much-travelled man who took us on our first ride in a luxury car. After the Raya prayers, we all gathered in his house and sat on the deep sofa as I looked up to his overhead bookshelves that housed a two-volume set of

Winstedt's *Unabridged Malay Dictionary*. I used to look through it as my finger travelled through words that became such delights by dint of their being defined by an outsider. From my uncle's window I could look out to reminders of mortality and of people basking in the joy of a holy day. Closest to the house was a burial ground that had many tall and quaintly shaped grave markers, and next door to it was a house called the *marja'* which, by name, meant the place for consultations (presumably with the *imam*), but which I knew was used by the mosque stalwarts for sleeping, dining and for appointments with the mosque barber. The *marja'* had a quaint smell: a combination of the sap of the papaya tree in its backyard, of trimmed hair and of the sleep of people after a heavy meal.

Hari Raya was one day that relieved us of the ennui of living in a town that sat on the edge of an open, rough sea. Everything looked different on that day for a child: the shops were closed but there were faces of joy, the adults were still tall but they stooped for you to hand out a nickel and there were food and cakes aplenty. The town was awash, it seemed, with *akök, buöh ulu, nasi kapit* and slices of fruitcake made by a foreign woman called Big Sister.

We slipped out when the adults were feeling dozy and looked for fresh avenues in an old town after it came alight on the morning of Hari Raya. This was after we'd visited all the *tok*s, cousins, uncles and aunties who lived in Seberang Takir. With nothing better to do, pockets jangling with a bit of silver, we normally headed for the Capitol to see Minggu, the doorkeeper, dressed in his Hari Raya *baju* made in the same pattern as his *kain pelikat* below. I think even Pök Mat of the lower, bug-ridden class wore a *söngkök* for this day. Next door, at the Sultana, Mat Ming put on his special self on this special day—but was still aloof to children and grumpy as grumpy could be. He was no relation of the then screen star Mat Aming but because of his prominence, this cinema was more Panggung Mak Ming to us than Panggung Sultana. This was before the word *pawagam* had been invented by P. Ramlee.

There was little chance of our getting tickets for any of the shows on that day. For one thing, the doorkeepers who were amenable to our approaches on other days became more reluctant on Hari Raya. For another, the cinema owners, for reasons of personal satisfaction, made the ticket booths accessible only through little holes cut out of a broad mash of steel. Queueing was an uncommon practice in the Kuala Trengganu of my day, so bidders for tickets piled themselves in one huge heap in front of the wire mesh, exposing themselves to the danger of losing an arm or a leg, or of having their glass eyes crushed and delicate parts mangled in the mêlée.

The sad thing about Hari Raya was that it came and went all in a day. And the sadder thing about it was the way it dropped us again with a plop into the middle of everyday reality. Father had a way with Hari Raya based on the state of his economy: he'd buy us only shoes that we could wear again daily to school, so our shoes were mostly white Bata, and the same too applied to the colour of our shirts so, in parts, we were in our Hari Raya outfit throughout the year.

Sounds From Afar

THE SOUNDS YOU GROW UP WITH always remain, no matter how far you've travelled, how changed your life may be.

I grew up in Kuala Trengganu to the sound of Singaporean beauties waddling duck-like in the afternoon sun, sultry women of light ebony that made heads turn, followed maybe by wolf-whistles. They came in a lyrical adulation, straight out of a blaring horn-shaped speaker that was placed in the upper-storey window of a coffee shop named Bhiku, the meeting place in our community of fishermen and market vendors, petty clerks from government offices and the occasional Hajis with their skullcaps wrapped in tailed turbans. Children were there too from the neighbouring houses, but my parents were of the strict type who'd never countenance this business of being at a loose end around the marble-topped table of the café Bhiku. My visits there were short and business-like, mostly early in the morning to do the family errand of buying the *roti canai* that were lifted piping hot from the griddle and rolled up in pages of yesterday's news, most likely the Jawi *Utusan Melayu*.

Some afternoons I'd walk past the Bhiku coffee shop to do other errands and would hear those songs again, sung by R. Azmi in his enormously popular, teasing tone.

'*Hitam manis, hitam manis, pandang tak jemu, pandang tak jemu*'
('That sweet dark lady, always a joy to behold')

And then the disc would turn again on the radio request programme:
it would be R. Azmi again, singing:

'*Macam itik, pulang petang, dia jalan melenggang*
itu dia Nona Singapura.'
('Duck-like she waddles in the afternoon,
this lady of Singapore that is mine'.)

I knew them all by heart because the requested songs were played
out loud, and our house was in the direct path of Bhiku's horn-shaped
megablaster.

Today I found a postcard that took me back to those sounds—a pre-
printed song-request postcard that a listener sent in to the Penang branch
of Radio Malaya, requesting a song called '*Senyum Dalam Tangisan*', ('A
Tearful Smile') by Mahani Rahmat. As I'm familiar with neither singer
nor song, no tune came lilting into my head as I read details of the request
with great fascination and looked at those stamps of the—please note
spelling—Trengganu that I knew and loved. The postcard came from

Song-request postcard sent to Radio Malaya.

26

Kuala Besut, a tiny town not ten miles from where Father was born.

Looking at the title of the requested song, I expect it was a little doolally doo-lah of a heart forlorn and a smile for all that, even when the object of your love's gone. How sweet and sad the sound of old.

This was—and still is to a large extent—the plight of Malays in song: pining always for some lost love, or for some unreachable one admired only from afar. But until very recently, love wasn't the only thing that afflicted them. They were underpaid for a start, and they did what they did for, well, a song; and R. Azmi was no exception. In song he sounded like an easy-going, playful lad, but life was hard for this itinerant singer. Soon after our family moved from Trengganu I was told that he'd died at a young age, not in the comforting presence of his family, but in the home of some kind soul who'd given him a room for the night. He was a man who lived in a suitcase which contained all he had, including a fresh shirt still wrapped in cellophane. How could a man whose voice came so liltingly sweet from the loudspeaker in the café Bhiku, who gave so much joy to my little town, have met such a tragic end to his life?

My heart was ripped when I heard that.

How the sounds came rolling back when I read that song-request postcard that's resurfaced on—of all places—the eBay website: the coffee shop, the little town where I grew up, the playful voice of R. Azmi and the many faces that still live in my mind. Kuala Trengganu was a hybrid place of many faces, of many sounds: Tamil music from the radios of the southern Indian spice vendors, Hindi music from open windows; the raucous banter of fishmongers, and the bustle of the Tanjung morning market that brought the *Orang Darat* with their firewood, handicrafts, vegetables and baskets of fruits from the forests of Trengganu.

There was a sound for each part of the day that regularly went like clockwork—and the most reliable at keeping time was the *azan* call to prayer that drifted in the wind at certain times of the day. At dawn, when the streets were empty but for some stray dogs, in the air so fresh and quiet, my father would be the first to rise in preparation for his early morning walk to the Zain al-Abidin Mosque. He'd go about his business to the early sound of the *tarhim*, the prelude to the morning *azan* call, and then, just at the start of the *azan,* he'd start his walk to reach the mosque in time to join the dawn prayer.

The *azan* of Bilal Sa'id was especially sonorous and melancholic in turn, and I remember occasionally walking with my father to the mosque as the wind carried it in the crisp start of the day. My mother once told me that a friend of hers would be reduced to tears by the weight of introspection every time she heard this sweet, mournful call of Lebai Sa'id urging the faithful to prayer at dawn. O God is great! Better to be in prayer than sleep!

Getting the Goat

THE DAH-DAH-DUM MAN peddled *apang balik* at the far end of the market, close to the smelly bay. *Apang balik* was a thick pancake heated over a coal fire in a roundish brass tray. The dah-dah-dum man sprinkled sugar, raisins and sweetcorn into the simmering goo as the sweet smell wafted over the heads of children passing by. By the dah-dah-dum man was a huge cauldron made of hefty metal, about knee-height. In it he'd pour his *apang balik* ingredients: flour maybe, some yellowing matter, an egg or two for sure. He'd stir it and beat it with a stiff brush specially made from lengths of thin rattan, eight or ten pieces together, folded midway in two. Just under the folded loop he'd wrap a length of twine to hold the bundle together, then he'd place his stirring hand there, and he'd stir and stir and sing his merry song of 'dah-dah-dum, dah-dah-dum, dah-dah-dum'. Mother came home one day and told us that, so he became, to us, the dah-dah-dum man of the Tanjong Pasar.

There was more to this jolly man in Mother's amusing story. One day, Mother said, as she was moving about the shops, the dah-dah-dum man was stirring and singing and stirring when a billy goat took an interest in his cauldron of liquid goo. But the dah-dah-dum man continued stirring as he fixed the billy goat in his sight. When the goat finally approached to sample the raw, sweet stuff, the dah-dah-dum man swung his hand aloft and beat it with a whack!—with his stirring bundle of sticks, of course, that dripped liquid *apang balik* onto the billy's hairy coat. Then back went the dah-dah-dum man, unperturbed, to his job of stirring, 'dah-dah-dum, dah-dah-dum', goat beater stirring the *apang balik* mix.

Mother had an eye for comedies like that whenever she'd go gadding about. She walked with her face covered in a long and broad headcloth, quite in the manner of the chador worn by Iranian women nowadays. She went to Makkah in her teens with her parents, whom we never met, but little details of Makkah life sprang up in our daily lives from her. Clumsiness in our household work? We became, to her, the *Orang Judöh*, the rough and ready labourers of Jeddah port who must've spilled may items in their labouring wake. Sometimes, when we grew careless with the sarong around our waist, we'd be like the dhow Arabs who were ever displaying their wares. Mother's Hajj visit must've been filled with traumas like that. She must've seen many troublesome sights, many things for her to remember.

But Mother never bought the dah-dah-dum man's *apang balik*, nor the comestibles sold by the stallholders who came out in the night. She cast no aspersions on anyone, but she wanted things to be right by her own rigorous marks. If unsure, she wouldn't patronise a food shop because she'd want to know if the shop owner was an observer of the *solat*, the obligatory daily prayers.

I'd sometimes slip out in the night to look at the rows of lights dancing around the wicks of oil lamps in the stalls that were heaving with their trays of Trengganu delights: cakes, fried noodles and specially prepared dishes of rice. There was *nasi ulam, nasi dagang, hati sökma, lompat tikam, berönök, Cik Abas demang, putri mandi, perut ayam,* piles of fried noodles thick and thin and *hasidöh;* savouries galore and sickening sweetmeats. They came piping hot on flowery trays after dusk. Then, as their quantities began to diminish with the night, the lights of the kerosene lamps—the *pelita ayang* as they were called—also began to fade, and slowly the vendors would pull away, back to the kampong, into the deep night.

Digging in the Soil

IN FRONT OF OUR HOUSE stood a flamboyant tree, also known as the flame-of-the-forest. It was a barren tree that never flamed for us, but goats loved to feast on its bipinnate leaves. One day men came with tools and spades and dug a deep, wide trench just a few feet from its roots, so we braced ourselves for the surprise of the day.

I looked down from our window to see men working hard, nailing together planks to line the sides inside the trench, and then another wall of planks within, with a gap of some six inches in between. When the cement mixer arrived, they laid a hard floor on the trench bed, then poured molten concrete into the gaps between wood and wood. When it was set all around, the planks were stripped and the trench was a wide, open tank, an impermeable layer of concrete in its bottom and sides. They came back and covered the top again in thick cement, leaving two square openings covered by two heavy slabs that could be lifted using two rings of stout metal.

The lorries arrived again and men laid underground pipes to another site four or five yards from the vault, just by the main road, and back to back with the fish market. There, a narrow concrete structure soon rose, some sixteen feet long. In it were cubicles hidden behind wooden doors. And behind these doors were holes in the ground, with footpads for the squatting position, and an overhead tank with a chain that pulled and flushed the detritus along the pipes that were now laid in the ground, to the innards of the concrete tank by the tree that never brought us any fire.

That was a good day for folks with loose bowels, but a very bad day for us. Our house now overlooked a septic tank, and the fish market had an additional whiff intermingling with the traffic noise. About a mile from us, towards the roundabout which later housed an ersatz greenback turtle, they'd already built another *jambang* of a more period build; mostly corrugated iron sheets, I think, standing there, squat by the roadside, and they painted it green. Folk soon began to call the locality by its *jambang*. They called the place Jambang Hijau, Place of the Green Convenience. We were slightly more fortunate—our place name remained intact, noise and nose notwithstanding.

So there it stood, our public *jambang*, mute, I'd rather not say, because oftentimes there came from within a loud report. And it became a public monument, a privy and private place, unkempt and uncared for by the fisherfolk, by all the passers by who were caught short and by users of the fish market. I shall not venture into its interior for fear you're still enjoying your meal.

That then was a stinking gesture by the town council for visitors to our parts. It wasn't for the folks of the neighbourhood, of course, for we had our own private places which I shall not talk about just now. But it is suffice to say that for most of us it was an outhouse, normally placed in the back of the house. Ours was a large house built on tall stilts, probably twenty of them, standing some ten feet, one from the other. We had to walk between them, with torch in hand if after dark, to the back of the house to answer nature's call. It was a terrifying walk for a small child, then a quick dash back again after that to the upstairs comfort of the house, relieved that there was no chance meeting with ghouls or ghosts that lurked behind pillar and post.

Ghosts, as you know, live in the depths of darkness, and have their own scents to counteract the stench of the outhouse. But better the latter than roses in the dark, was our uppermost thought as we ran and ran back to the house. But once upstairs, as the clock struck one, there came a swishing noise and an overwhelming aroma that made us giggle in the dark. It was the unmistakable hour of the night soil.

The night soil man wore a pith helmet and carried a little tank on the back of his bicycle into which he'd empty the slops. And the slops were collected in the bucket that lay beneath the hole in the floor of the outhouse. Poor little night soil man as he went swish, swish with his brush of coconut leaf spines, pouring water into the bucket to make it clean for users who would fill it up again in the morrow.

Memory of Water

ONE DAY, CAUGHT IN A MOOD OF MERRIMENT, I was thrown into a *kölöh* in our neighbourhood *surau*. A *surau* is a devotional place, much smaller than a mosque, and in the *kampung*s of Trengganu it served as more than a prayer hall. It was the centre of activity, the meeting place of young and old, and was, more often than not, built of wood, with a prayer chamber and a narrow antechamber in the rear where old folk would sit outside of prayer times to doze off, or to chat about the price of fish or to nod and gape at people passing by. The youth of the village would gather there too for a puff of the *rökök daung* taken and rolled from the pouches of the old. The *rökök daung*, if you must know, is a tough dry leaf rolled into a long thin smoke after it's been filled with a string of tobacco.

Like most Malay houses, our *surau* was built on stilts, raised some five feet above the ground, and in the antechamber the floor planks were nailed with gaps in between, half an inch maybe, so they could easily be spat through. Before going in for the prayer, all impurities had to be spat out from the mouth, hence those gaps in the floor. The betel nut chewers were the most accomplished in this job, for their spits were of the brightest hue.

I've mentioned the ablution, so I must turn now to the *kölöh* which every little *surau* had in those days. It was an open-topped water tank, normally quadrandgular in shape though it could also be square. The four sides, built up to the level of an adult's waist, were made of concrete, and from what I remember, the *kölöh* was always placed by the steps of the *surau*.

Our *kölöh* was medium-sized, about four feet deep, and had interesting mosses and lichens beneath the surface of the water. Worshippers would dip their hands and arms into it and wash their faces, then scoop the water into large tin cans to wash their feet before finally going up to the *surau*. My father always warned me about using the *kölöh* which, he said, contained the remnants of sleep from the eyes of early-morning worshippers. I never could make out if he was saying this in jest or for real but I always, always religiously avoided the *kölöh* outside a *surau*.

So it was for my thoughts, perhaps, that I was one day thrown in there with a big splash and a lot of joy from bystanders and passers-by. They were two big boys who threw me in, so there wasn't much I could do after that but walk home with my clothes thoroughly drenched, and little expectation of similar merriment from Mother or Father. But unbeknown to me, Father had watched the proceedings—and my humiliation—from a window which looked down on the *surau,* and he'd already prepared some encapsulated wisdom for his returning son from the water. 'Familiarity breeds contempt,' he said to me from on high. Well, I was a little lad then, and he was looking down at me and talking in a cryptic tongue about those lads who'd chucked me into the *kölöh* of our *surau.* I don't hear the expression much nowadays, but whenever

I see it or hear it uttered, I'm reminded of my dear, late father and the *surau*.

Our *surau* was a merry place and a lively centre. It had a large communal well where every day at dusk gathered the lads and lasses of the village and their mothers and fathers for the communal shower. In the *surau* was a grand *geduk* or *beduk,* a drum with an elongated barrel that was covered taut with cow hide at its business side and left open at the other. It was hung horizontally in the back chamber of the prayer hall, by the stairs, and at prayer time someone would hit the drum extremely hard in a prescribed rhythm to summon the faithful to prayer.

Pök Lèh was the *imam* of our *surau*, a pious man of quiet authority who passed on last year at an age that must've been close to ninety. Sometimes, from between the thunderous sounds of the old *geduk* and men hoicking and retching through the gaps in the floor, I can still hear the voice of Pök Lèh sending up to our house the lilt of that melancholic tune that he'd perhaps devised himself from inside that old *surau*. It was a reminder of fleeting time and our mortality, and it's playing in my head right now:

'*Ingat, ingat, serta fikir sehari hari*
Kamu duduk dalam kubur seorang diri;
Rumah besar, kampung luas, itu ia
Akan tinggal itu juga akan dia ...'

'Remember, remember and think this daily
That in your grave all alone you will be;
Your big house and land so vast to view
You'll leave them and cannot take them with you ...'

Nails, Ropes and Old Vinegar

IN HIS SHOP, Pök sat beneath coils of nylon ropes, twines of hemp and raffia, shrouding himself in vinegar wafting in the air. He kept the vinegar in a *ppayang* in the back of his shop, down two steps in the storage floor. He had corrugated zinc for roofing in his back yard, bits of wood for minor repairs, lengths of bamboo sticks, fish hooks, nails for both concrete and wood and some sharp enough to give the *pontianak* a funny tingling in the shoulder. But we didn't have too many *pontianak*s in Trengganu then, so the demand came mostly from local builders and DIY-ers, not *bomoh*s on the lookout for ghostly high jinks in the air. Pök sold the nails by weight, and judged them by the *hun,* which was a measure of the depth of nails for the houses of Trengganu.

Pök wore gold teeth and a soft skullcap called the *ppiöh lembèk,* and underneath it, a perpetual smile. He was a belt-and-brace man who wore the *sarung pelikat* over his work trousers. When he was sat behind his hardware display, pickling in the wafting aroma of vinegar in deep claypots, he'd roll up his *sarung* maybe a foot or two to signal that he was at work; then at five o'clock he'd lower it again to his ankles, then he'd roll the long Haji's wrap around his cap before closing the shop and cycling in the direction of the muezzin's call.

I could judge the time of day by Pök's routine in his hardware shop, or by the blaring voice of Radio Malaya that came out of a giant foghorn-shaped piece of hardware jutting out from the first-floor window of Bhiku's coffee shop. This was public information radio that made Bhiku's customers stir their cups with a tra-la-lee, and sit up with the constant tooting of the time signals. I can't remember any of the news items that followed, try as I may, but I remember still the lyrics of R. Azmi coming from there that opened up a young mind to the delights of a faraway place and the charms of a sassy lady. I knew she waddled like a duck, in the afternoon light, with waist so trim and fastened tight. *'Itu dia, Nona Singapura ... itu dia, Nona Singapura.'* Ah, the delightful lady of Singapore! That was the sound as Pök cycled past Bhiku's shop on his way to the house of prayer, when market traders were just letting down their hair over steaming cups of tea and trading insults or homilies while waiting for the man in the back to shout over the din, *'Roti kaya!'* Roti *kaya* was, and still is, a slice taken from the long white loaf called *roti bata* or pillow bread, then toasted over the charcoal fire, smeared with Planta margarine and topped with the shop's own speciality of *kaya,* a local spread made from egg yolk with pandan leaf for flavouring, then thickened and sweetened with sugar and flour.

Sometimes Pök would stop at a coffee shop if he chose to close early. He wouldn't go to Bhiku's but to another one next door with a more conducive clientele. Bhiku's was a diverse company of fish traders, wayfarers and strangers freshly arrived on shore. There was a man in a stiff cap who lived on the top floor of Bhiku's shop right behind the fog-horn-shaped radio speaker. He'd been there for years and years, and walked with an A3-sized flat display box that was always wrapped in thick material when he was out on his morning calls. I never knew what he had, but I guessed that it contained stones like *akik, zamrud* and *delima*. He was known to us as Orang Kabul, the man from a land far away.

As the light faded and the village ladies were out at the community well, vans and lorries arrived in the wide space between Bhiku's and the general market with vegetables and fruits, sugar canes tied up in tall bundles, bananas from the groves of smallholders and onions in baskets called *jök*, from China, perhaps, or maybe India. Occasional traders from the *ulu* sometimes arrived on trishaws hailed at the jetty, with forest fruits like *ngekke, salök, pulasang, peröh*, and sometimes that mini, yellow, soft-skinned fruit called simply *buöh ssakkör*. Bhiku's busy waiters would then take in another pile of cups to wash, or unwrap another loaf of *roti* for these hungry deliverers of goods for the market of the morrow. They came just in time for the procession of ladies with young helpers, carrying smaller-sized baskets or tall kerosene lamps called *pelita ayam* already lit to guide the way of deep basins of house-cooked food carried by lady traders for their evening food stalls that traded long after Pök had done his last *solat* of the day and hung out his clothes that still bore just a little whiff of vinegar.

Breath of Mettle

AYÖH WANG WAS SLIGHT AND WHEEZY, a fragile, stooped man in his white T-shirt made in China by the Pagoda people. He wore his *batik sarung* as a matter of faith. On normal days he'd make *kerepok;* on other days he was a man of brass.

I often saw him, huffing and puffing in the compound of his house. Then, when his asthma subsided, he'd walk the paces to his work house.

35

It was a shed, smaller than a badminton court, of four stout trunks supporting a roof of thatch; on one end of the hut, behind a screen, was a pole that stood in a wooden tube sunk into the ground. The pole curved again a few feet below the ground to run parallel with the topsoil. It ended in an opening at the base of a fiery furnace. Just outside this shed, another pole leant on a fulcrum before it jutted out into the air. It had enough give to snap back like a lash when pulled downwards. This was the stick that powered the pole that had rags and old jute bags wrapped around its end below ground as it stood in the wooden cylinder. As the pole was pushed down, by Ayöh Wang's son, it whooshed air to the furnace, breathing life into the embers. Then it was pulled out again by the reclining stick to which it was attached, then pushed down again by the son with a whoosh, then it sprang back again only to be whooshed down again, then up then down, and so it went until the embers were glowing hot. Ayöh Wang, scratching his head, was set to go.

This was the morning of the *mengembus,* from *hembus,* a word that means, evocatively, to blow with a whoosh—the rod pushing down the cylinder pushing the rush of air that kept the coals aglow. It was another activity in our little corner, past the *surau* and the community well, through the weather-beaten grey timber that held the gap in Ayöh Wang's fencing of woven bamboo that stood twice the height of a little child.

This was hot work that made your shirt cling to your body in a glue of sweat, but when the temperature reached that height, Ayöh Wang would pull off his white top and issue directions dressed only in his *batik*. He'd have slung on his shoulder, by then, a long strip of east coast regulatory wear, the *batik lepas,* of hand-painted local cloth that made a head gear or body wrap on a rainy day, or simply just a handy bit of all-purpose material. They were mostly orangey with patterns of local flowers or off yellow, but like many things of the recent past, you don't see them hanging around much anymore.

The *mengembus* was preparatory to the *menuang* which would have kept Ayöh Wang busy the whole of the month before. He'd have started with the *menarik,* which was another activity born of fire. Wooden moulds shaped like trays, pans and pots were dipped into a brass pot placed over a wood fire, a witch's cauldron of bubbling wax that stuck tenaciously to the wooden moulds, taking their shapes and their contours. Then Ayöh

Wang set them all aside to dry them out another day.

Then, when he wasn't too pressured by his *kerepok* work and his asthma safely at bay, he'd trim the coated wax on his moulds one by one on a foot spindle. As it spun, he'd expertly move his trimming blade into the wax to shave out thin slivers of excess wax. This he'd do with increasing precision until a heap of wax shavings lay around his feet, and in his hand, the unmistakable, hard-edged shape of a tray or a candlestick or a dish that'd gleam out at someone's nuptials.

Then Ayöh Wang would retire for an early night, to rest his hands for the following day when he'd be dipping them again, this time in clay. The exposed surface of the wax, say of a tray, he'd coat in clay; and when that was done, he'd carefully peel it off the wooden mould, to coat the other, unexposed side. Then he'd shape a little spout that'd make a little funnel to the wax, before putting it aside to dry for another week or two.

Now this little funnel was the basis of the *menuang* that gave shape to Ayöh Wang's craftwork in metal. With the coals glowing and his son diligently pumping the fire, Ayöh Wang would produce little crucibles; he'd fill them up with scraps of brass and bullet casings that came by the sackful from scrap dealers. He'd place the crucibles gently with a caliper into the furnace until the scraps melted and glowed like liquid fire.

Menuang is the carrying out of the word *tuang,* that is, 'to pour'. It gave the name to this work of pouring out red-hot metal into clay spouts to cast into pre-moulded shapes. This was dangerous work for steady hands, with the *batik lepas* coiled tightly around the head to absorb rivulets of sweat. When the glowing stream of brass poured out of Ayöh Wang's crucible into the spout, it rolled down and hit the first bit of wax and consumed it instantly. So Ayöh Wang kept his hand steady and muttered another *bismillah* till the fiery contents went down the spout and replaced the waxen shape completely within its casing of clay. This was wax replacement much like *batik* art, but on a far more dangerous scale.

And what Ayöh Wang got for all that work was the coarse beginning of his brassware: a tray, a dish, a spitoon maybe. And there followed again from there days of work on the foot-worked spindle to trim the rough object into shape, to polish the surface to a glitter.

Ayöh Wang's art had a long history, and I often wonder if it's still done now. It was from this heart of our community that was born the

37

genta, the great bell that clanged from Bukit Putri overlooking the harbour to mark the beginning of the month of Ramadan, or the festival of Eid or Hari Raya. In olden days, the brass bell clanged too when an *amok* was on the rampage, and people would all rush back indoors.

The present *genta* on Bukit Putri was made by these people but not, I think, by Ayöh Wang's forefathers. It was not cast in Tanjong, the brass-crafting base of Kuala Trengganu, but in the grounds of the palace itself, at the foot of the hill.

Leaves in the Skylight

OUR NEIGHBOUR PÖK ANJANG was a lanky man in a *sarung pelikat* held in place by a wide belt. For his top he wore what my parents called a *kanciperat* shirt made of silky material, round-necked and buttoned halfway down the front. He smoked a cigar and made sauces hot and mild for his *röjök*. At the gloaming of each day he lit up his carbide lamps, put them in the corners of his specially constructed pedicab, then he plied his trade along the streets of Kuala Trengganu.

Pök Anjang had glass cases that he placed on either side of his mobile kitchen-cum-vehicle. In them he had heaps of noodles, assorted greens, hard-boiled eggs in a pyramidal heap and the fried lungs of buffaloes and tofu and things magical. In the middle of his carriage he had a stout frame on which he placed a huge pot that was kept bubbling by a glowing coal fire. In the front he had a wok, sitting ready to fry his *mee*. He must've tasted his sauces too many times before making his daily trips on the road—probably the hot one more than the other, as for all those times that I saw him pedal past on our roads, Pök Anjang never smiled.

He had many assistants, young boys on whom he constantly spat his bile, or ladies who appeared suddenly one day and were not seen again on another. They all, when they were there, helped him to chop leaves, stir pots or simply sat as targets of his bad temper. I used to watch all these goings-on from the back of our house, through the leaves of a henna tree. But we were never, at any time, tempted by the culinary products of Pök Anjang as by then our mother had already divided this world into two types of people: the *mmayik* and the *tak mmayik* (the 'yes' and the 'no's) and Pök Anjang fell smack into the latter.

'So-and-so's not *mmayik*,' Mother would say, so we avoided a particular make of *nasi lemak* or *apam balik* or *tepung pelita*. Mother categorised strictly and was a woman from whom there was no appeal, and everything moved on her every say-so, so we shopped for our food selectively. But as for Pök Anjang, we were all in the know as he was a close neighbour at the back of our house, and I'd seen too many goings-on there from behind that henna tree. A person who didn't have Mother's certificate of *mmayik* was allegedly unable to distinguish between clean and dirty. It was a very complicated word for Mother to know and use in those days for, in later years, I discovered that it had come to Trengganu via the Arabic *mumaiyyiz* which means, in fact, puberty. The idea was that a person who'd come of age would've been able to distinguish between hygienic acceptability and the no-no.

Pök Anjang, when we knew him, must've been close to fifty, a man who kept himself much to himself and never spoke to anybody other than his kitchen people. He left the house as soon as the sun had set and came back late at night, spreading brightness in the *kampung* with the carbide-powered lamps on his *röjök* vehicle. He spat a bit and grumbled a little, then all went quiet as Pök Anjang dozed off to sleep, dreaming dreams about his *röjök*-eating customers.

One day Father pointed out to us Pök Anjang's new interest in horticulture which he practised in a very strange way. For all that wide expanse of ground he had in front of his house, Pök Anjang had literally gone through the roof with his potted plants. So from our house, looking at Pök Anjang's roof, I could see strange leaves sticking out here and there. It was not until the local police arrived and took Pök Anjang and his plants away in a car that Father told me the truth: that Pök Anjang had been smoking his home-grown leaves, or he'd probably been scattering bits of them in those sauces hot and mild for his *röjök*-eating people.

Our House People

WE HAD PEOPLE COME TO OUR HOUSE each day to chat away the hours, or to do little errands in the daily kitchen of our family. There was a frail lady called Tok Mèk who appeared early every morning, just as the fresh vegetables were being laid out in the market and when the fishmongers had just finished hosing down their fish displays in the *pasar*. By then the *Orang Daging* (lit. 'meat people') were just beginning to hone their broad butcher's blades, pulled from short scabbards tucked in the back of their *sarung* of many colours. Tok Mèk would walk her unsteady steps, with lips trembling. I couldn't be sure if she was quietly chanting the *zikr* or if it was a tic that came with her growing years. She'd leave with the shopping list twirling in her head, then come back about an hour later with the list items in her basket, minus one or two that had evaded her. It then fell on Pök Su, another itinerant who stopped almost daily at our house, to follow up with the shopping chores—that missed out *kati* bag of Indian shallots, or sugar wrapped up in newspaper.

Pök Su came back and sat himself at the top of the steep stairs that led into the kitchen section of our house. He had a *batik sarung,* worn as a sash across his chest and anchored to one of his shoulders. This was the old *selèpang* of *kampung* Malays, a stand-by material that served as a pouch for carrying fruit, as a head wrap on sunny or rainy days, or as an emergency bandage in street battles. On top he wore the Malay *baju* that had two lower pockets for his dried-leaf cigarette skins and his pouch of dark thin strands of tobacco; and beneath it, a *batik sarung* which he replaced with the *pelikat* one day a week, as a concession to Friday.

Both Tok Mèk and Pök Su made regular daily stops at our house, sometimes simultaneously, pausing for a glass of sweet coffee. Tok Mèk was the quieter of the two, thinking much and saying little. I remember her stopping to talk to me once on her way to the shops, to lament the number of wicked people who were taken each day to the blazing furnace down below. Then she held a faraway look with rheumy eyes. Pök Su had more worldly stories: he told us of his walk to Pahang on some urgent business and how he had to perch overnight on a tall tree when the water level rose very suddenly around him somewhere near the Kemaman border. He once said that in his youth he used to play the game of *buöh gömök* on Hari Raya somewhere in Indochina. He didn't tell us where specifically, but it must've been among the Cham Muslims in Cambodia. The *buöh gömök* was a flat seed with a tough, ebony-coloured outer shell. They were washed ashore from some distant place (probably Cambodia) in the monsoon tides, and were much prized as a *kör*.

Another man who also regularly visited us had the warrior's gait, his legs opening wide as he walked with slightly bent knees. Whether this was due to his earlier life in martial arts or owed more to his arthritic knees, I couldn't be sure, but for some reason, we called him Pök Mang Bödöh. He was a simpleton, a touchy man who once told us off for talking too loudly near him as it interfered with his concentration while cleaning a brass pot with *asam jawa*. The word he used was *gamang* which, in Trengganuspeak, means uncertainty or nervousness when something is distracting you from an activity.

However, when the mood took him he used to tell us his life story. One story stands out to me now as it gave a glimpse into the oddities of life on the east coast that carried on until his youth, at the beginning of the last century. He told us how he and a group of other men used to travel to Kuantan to play what was known as *mmaing karut*, a game of nonsensical horseplay and you'll see why. It involved masses of grown-up men dressed in fancy dress charging at one another in an open field as if at war.

Mmaing karut could have been a celebration, or the culmination of a reception party, or a way for the hosts and guests to show how pleased they were to be together. Some, no doubt, got hurt and others, driven to frenzy. It could have been on one of these excursions that Megat Panji Alam got a glimpse of his fair lady Tun Teja, to whom he was later betrothed. He then lost his love and life in a real fight with weaponry with a group sent by Sultan Mahmud of Melaka. Now there was no *mmaing karut* there, I can tell you.

A Community of Shadows

AS NIGHT FELL and the light turned ever deeper into the colour of our *songkök*, it was never completely still. The drone of lorries coming in at irregular intervals, the occasional patter by the well of the *surau* as women scrubbed pots and cleared ashes and half burnt wood from the cooking place, and the *kerepok lekör* were all coiled up in the deep baskets of woven bamboo. Lights flickered from distant houses, the last drop of kerosene burning in the chamber of the *pelita ayam* fading into the wee hours.

The *kampung* was a cluster of houses with light stealing through the cracks, and the air dark enough to show the gleaming stars high above. Female stallholders with children as helpmates, or husbands reappearing just in time from the coffee shops to help carry home the leftover foods in baskets or trays, in a procession that melted into the dark along little lanes between houses now lit by the feeble lights of homecoming people. Street urchins and barrow boys were settling in for the night, in boxes that were stored and reached by crawling under the chicken-wire fence around the sheltered market. By first light the following day they'd be up again, bantering and stretching under the yellow light of the street as the *bilal*'s voice carried across the morning chill in melancholic lilts of the *tarhim* before the *azan* call to dawn prayer.

But it was not time yet for that. As the sound of traffic faded, lazily came the goats, preparing for sleep on the warm tarmac, only to scamper again when awoken by the bright glare of lights from cars that had no business to be in a town when there was nothing else to do but sleep, in this bewitching, bearded billy-goat hour.

Things that went bump in the night were magnified may times for the young tossing in bed. It could have been spirits, or spirited folk gadding about in the dark. Indian shopkeepers were already asleep in front of their shops, surrounded by drapes sewn together from flour bags. Sometimes chickens squawked, rats scuttled beneath shops, then all was quiet again in the dark. Woe betide a young child caught short in his bed, a young child who made the journey down the stairs in the pitch black to the little outhouse at the back, guided by a dim Eveready torch, fraught with wild imaginings and everything that came to life from inside his head. Then as he sat, well past midnight, in the little chamber in the back of the house, a hand belonging to a pith-helmeted man would reach out to the chamber pot that he'd empty into a bigger one on his bicycle. The night-soil man went as unobtrusively as he came, walking in the light of the miner's lamp attached to his hat, moving from house to house, then cycling away with the laden tank securely tied to the back of his night-soil bicycle, avoiding goats half awake in the streets, to a secret place where the town council kept the night soil.

Night was a long time if you were awake, staring into the melancholic light of the weak night-time bulb that accentuated shadows but actually showed very little. You would prick up your ears under the blanket for the slightest sound, for Pak C**** who groped beneath houses to pull chickens from their coops to take away in his bag of swag, rooster, mother, eggs and all. He had a way of doing this, as we learnt at playtime in the schoolyard, a silencing way with shallots and magic and away he went with bag and chick incapacitated allegedly by mumbo jumbo.

Then from afar came a murmur, some barely recognisable words breaking into a chorus that gained strength behind the houses in the wide berth between the bamboo fencing, ours and theirs. You would jump out of bed to peer from the back window, to see the moving light, men and boys in their *baju* and skullcaps, and the *kain pelikat* worn for a serious purpose. It was the band that gave cohesion to the community, that pulled us together in this and that. Father would rise from his *tahajjud* on the mat to go back there again after he'd given them a cursory look.

This was a feature of our Tanjong community in times of hardship and hours of need. The group moved from house to house, into shadows and past lamps still tied to verandah posts, in their last flicker of light. The sound of the *ratib awör* chilled the uninitiated and gave comfort to those who knew. *Ratib* is an Arabic word, meaning incantation of the name of God and *awör,* the shortened local version of the standardspeak *hawar* meaning epidemic, of veterinary disease or worse. It was the sound of my childhood, that gay intensity from murmurings afar. It could have been the sounds of the *ratib haddad* or some other blessed words, but it gave strength to us and spirituality and an awareness that we were never alone in the dark.

Carrying the Picul

ON DAYS WHEN OUR GRANARY BECAME LEAN, I stood with trepidation at the bottom of our wooden kitchen stairs and stared at those legs wound taut by varicose veins as they placed weight on the treads. It was the billhook man, with his apron of *batik* wrapped around his khaki shorts, a cape fashioned from a *batik* print around his back and on it, in a bundle of back-breaking weight, a picul of rice in a sack of burlap.

A picul must've been a word derived from the act, *pikul,* the carrying of a heavy load on one's shoulders or back. In Trengganu in those days—as was in the other states—a picul was a lot of weight, almost sixty-one kilograms in present day measure, or a hundred and thirty-three and a third pounds if you're still in avoirdupois.

Avoirdupois was a word that was imprinted on the *dacing* of our rice merchant Wang Deramang, and it has stuck in my head ever since. There were sixteen ounces to the pound, and there were nine treads to our kitchen stairs that stood inclined at an angle, with treads worn out by years of rain and sun, and by folk who sat and threw their gaze from there to the teeming market beyond our front gate.

The billhook man trod very carefully as the *cengal* wood groaned and sagged. One false move and he'd be reeling backwards with the load, but if his luck held he'd land with the bag of rice as his bed. But if the old stair wood gave way, he'd be diving through the window with the picul bag on his head.

We had uncles, aunties and friends who came to our house on most days who, as a mark of their familiarity with us, would sit on top of the stairs to chat and sip tea or coffee while we got on with our daily chores in the house. Bai, the breadman, parked his round bread basket on an apron between the stairs and the house, then he perched himself on the seventh or eight tread from a pot that stood below, a pot from which he'd probably scooped water to clean his feet before making the ascent to the kitchen part of our house. There he'd sit, enjoying the blessing of the shade, his coil of rag still on his head, and his hands reaching out into the basket for our orders from the top of the stairs. From where I sat I could see all that he had in the basket: the *kaya* in the Cow & Gate tin, the round *paung* and the *bata* crusty loaf, and the crunchy finger biscuits that we dipped into our hot Ovaltine and transferred to mouth very quickly before they fell into our laps in one moist heap.

Once a week, or twice maybe, a father and son would come into our shade, each carrying a shoulder stick loaded at both ends with firewood cut and bound into bundles of eight or ten, each the length of the ruler in my schoolbag. The son would usually park his shoulder stick and load near our well, just three paces from the stairs, while the father would rest his load and squat under another part of the patch of shade. Each wore shorts, covered with a *batik sarung* that went down to his feet, but was pulled up again in half midway down its length and tucked into a short curtain around the waist. Around each of their heads was a wrap from a cloth that is no longer seen, longer than it is wide, and hand decorated with flowers or tendrils of an unknown shrub. They spoke with a strange lilt, and came downtown in a boat that would've drifted down the muddy water of the Trengganu at first light. From their conversations I gathered that they came from a place called Telemong in the *ulu*, which was a dark place in those days as it was way upstream and surrounded, perhaps, by thick trees, and hobgoblins and spirits of the wood.

The father and son were, in fact, forest workers, going into dense thicket to fell trees while the stronger among them hacked the fallen lumber into short pieces of wood to light the fire beneath our cooking pots. For bundling the wood they used the skin of the bamboo, as it was sharp at the edge and strong for holding together the load. We bought ten or twenty of those bundles to stack beneath our house for kitchen use but sometimes, for special dishes or cakes, Mother would burn dried husks of the coconut that burnt with a fierce smoke.

Che Kör was the father's name. He was a mustachioed man who drank coffee as he spoke about the wood that was, even then, becoming scarce from where he worked. His son, Che Muda, I remember to be a handsome lad, who wiped sweat from his face with his headcloth as he spoke, and who told us many stories about the dark forest. They'd drink their drinks and replenish our reserve of firewood, then they'd go with their shoulder sticks and a lighter load.

One day Che Muda arrived without his dad and put our order in its place. Then he sat on the stairs, sipped tea, wiped his face and told us the sad news. He was felling trees as usual in the forest, he said, when a big one fell, then he heard his dad cry 'Allah!' from where the mighty wood had crashed down. That was how his dad went, he said, crushed by the tree that had given him life.

After that Che Muda became an irregular visitor to town, then he too faded completely from our days.

End of the Day

ON THE MOUND AT THE RIVER MOUTH the lady lit her lamp and sat on the sand, eyes peering out to sea. *Payang* boats were bobbing in the waves, *penambangs* plying the waters and *töngkangs* pulled close to shore. There were skeletal remains of boats that were once afloat but now long dead, sticking out curved ribs of decaying wood in the mud among scurrying little crabs and the mud skippers of Pantai Teluk. *Ikang ddukang* existed beneath the ripples and we'd step on them too many times and hollered home with their sting burning through our soles. With just their masts now standing proud, the *perahu besar* of Wang Kamang stood in their own mists of memory. Memories of Senggora visits for terracotta tiles, visits to other coastal towns for bags of salt, *gunis* of fragrant Thai rice, some seaweeds we called the *kerabu sereh* that looked like tangled sandy coloured hair from the tangled heads of some terrible ghouls. We did not know how Wang Kamang returned the favours of these Thais—with bags of dried *kerepok* pieces perhaps, varieties of Trengganu bananas (I got twenty at the last count) or maybe just *karongs* of flat fish dried out in Trengganu heat.

View of Pantai Teluk looking towards Bukit Putri.

As the light began to turn grey and the breeze blew gently into *ggarék*, a light appeared on the distant line where the waves lapped into the sky and the clouds came down to drink the sea, then another shone brightly from a mast. I can't remember now if it was the Hong Ho or the Rawang, but the lady knew that it was her sailor man coming home. She took her lamp and waved it and waved it and waved. 'I'll just place it there for now,' she said, as she hooked the lamp to a tall pole and looked out to sea to the lights that were gleaming from the boat. It was then time for us to go, for the *geduk* drums were belting out from the *surau* and Imam Pök Leh was just re-tying the knot in his Haji's turban before leading the *ggarék* prayer. We walked home past the house of Alias Söngkök, past the stalls now all deserted, into the fluorescent lights of the Tamil shops and their array of Zam Zam hair pomade and sticky green Gul Bahar in tall bottles that held the gleaming pompadours of our ever hopeful belles and beaux.

We walked past the *wakaf* where folk were still hearty-voiced in the shadows, making the last moves in the game of *dam*, aiming for the quick finale of the *buöh ggarek*. *Wakaf*s always smelt of goats at this time of day, the sweaty *hamis* of the *kambing neruk*, the long-bearded, thick-horned billy goat that sometimes peered into the mixing cauldrons of market vendors of the *apam balik*. Billy goats always had something to say at this time of day, something that sounded like the muffled sound of suppressed laughter. Sometimes we fed them leaves from the *pohong bbaru* that gave the *wakaf* its noontime shade. *Pohong bbaru* was God's gift to our over-fed goats whose day had hardly ended, of course, for they—both billy and nanny—were just coming to their penultimate stop at the *wakaf*, to sit and eat the *bbaru* leaves from proferring strangers. They were just waiting for their final move later in the night, to lie in the oozing warmth of our Kuala Trengganu roads in front of the *kedai kopi* of Pök Löh and Wang Wook.

Tanjong never ended abruptly. The market was locked shut behind its *mata punai* wire-mesh, but vendors soon came out as it grew dark: processions of lads and lasses bearing trays of *mee goreng* and various concoctions of *lauk*; the *putri mandi* princess basking its sweetness in a bath of shredded coconut; and all the *belebak* and the *akök* and something I don't see much of these days, *perut ayam*.

I liked the *mee halus* of Mök Söng, that stood in a tall mound in a tray, under the flickering lights of her *pelita ayang*. Walking further down towards the bay, along the multi-coloured rows of cooked food under the flickering lights of the kerosene *pelita*, you walked out from the smell of cut chilli, home-made condiments and a head of steam from the hot juices of creamed coconut, into the sour smell of long bamboos stewing in the still water and the deep dwellings of mud skippers in the *teluk*. Here they stored bamboos tied in rafts, waiting to be split and woven into tall fencing that kept secure the compounds of many Trengganu houses. This was the work of Wang Kamang. When he was not plying the coastal waters or sailing the shores, he mended fences for us all.

On the coast the houses were mostly fenceless because our Tanjong was mostly like that. You walked to the well of the *surau* and entered the gates of Wang Mamat, then walked out again through the open border on the other side. Fencing was a fanciful thought in a community where everything was shared by all. Ours was a fenced house but the market vendors from the *ulu* walked in every day to use the well.

You could walk in and out of people's compounds and talk to them as they sat on their verandahs or their stairs. But sometimes there was picket fencing of waist-length stakes to keep stray children from stepping on the *kerepok* that were drying out in the sun. Thin goats still squeezed through the stakes to tread on things, eat the leaves and munch on paper for dessert. Which brings us to the question outsiders are wont to ask about urban Trengganu goats: why do they wear a horizontal stick around their necks?

Why, to keep them from squeezing through the pickets, that's why.

Walking on Water

THERE WERE PUDDLES beneath the houses and running water in the *surau*. In more remote parts, *surau*s were known as *bala söh* meaning hall of something or other. *Söh* could have been a corruption of the Arabic *sahih*, for legitimacy or validity, or the Trengganuspeak compaction of the Arabic *saf*, for the lines in prayer. Arabic played a great part in the daily lives of Trengganu people, visiting them in their vocabulary, their food and, of course, their apparel. A grand man, known to us as Ku Haji Ambök, went to the mosque on special days with robes flowing and children in tow. They were like the sheikhs of Araby; and Father once made an Arabic pun from a Trengganu place name, Atas Tol, pronouncing it as *ala tol*, importing into it Arabic instruction as well as ambiguity. *Ala tol* could have meant 'over the tol' (i.e. the Trengganu *atas tol*), or the Arabic for 'walk straight ahead'. I am not aware, I'm afraid, of the meaning of *tol* that we were supposed to be going over.

If for some reason you find yourself underneath a house, you do not walk in the water. These puddles were known as *air cör*, and *cör* is another puzzling word, though Winstedt seems to hint that it may have come from the standardspeak *cucur*, which is a long and thin trickle, or the drip, drip, drip of rainwater from the edge of the roof woven from leaves of the palm tree. *Air cör* was harsh water that dripped and splashed from the kitchen into the soil, mixing with the dark earth beneath Trengganu houses to form puddles that looked and smelt like *budu*. This was in the days before public irrigation that came very late to Kuala Trengganu.

Water also flowed from the *surau* and *bala söh*, from the *kölöh* where men cleansed themselves before prayers, from the *cerak* that flowed via a culvert from the *kölöh* into a long-box water catcher that stood chest-high above the ground, and also from the community well. The *surau* was the centre of our community that stretched as far as the eye could see, but from the window at the back of our house we couldn't stretch our sights far enough to Surau Besar because of the imposing height of two *mminja* trees. There were at least five *surau*s in our midst that were the hub of our community: there was Surau Pasir close to the shore, Surau Haji Mat Kerinci by the bus stop, Surau Sheikh Kadir near our house, there was a *surau* under deep shade with a large fish in its *kölöh,* and one with the name of Surau Telaga Besör (Big Well). Early in the morning and when the light dimmed out at dusk, most of the village, men and women, converged to the wells of the *surau*. It was there one day, in a fit of high jinks, that I was thrown into the well (well, not quite, it was our local *kölöh* actually).

At other times of the day water flowed from the *surau*, from the unplugged funnels of the *cerak*, or was scooped out from the well with a heavy bucket that, in our case, was moulded from brass by the hands of our Wang Mamat who, when not tending to the well of our community, helped his wife, Mök Song, to roll long sticks from boluses of fish that he threw into the cauldron to boil. This was our *kerepok getel* or *kerepok dekör* that is now known to the world as *kerepok lekör*.

The smell of fish, the long drip of the *air cerak* onto the arms of the faithful and splashings of dish-water into the *cör*. The clanking of the brass bucket hitting the sides of the well, the soothing sound of water on hard concrete, wind rustling through the leaves of *mminja* trees, punctuated by the asthmatic wheezings from the balcony of Pök Wè: these were the sights and sounds of our Tanjong, that now, because of changes in the *kuala*, is close to falling off the edge of Trengganu.

Snaps and Studios

FOR A TIME, Sulong set up shop above Kedai Pök Che Amat, the man with vinegar reeking from his backroom and enough strings and ropes to stretch from Tanjong to Batu Rakit; and if on some bedevilled nights, high-pitched *ngilla* laughter issued in the moonlit air, Pök had enough nails in the front of his shop to rein in the whole cacophony of *pontianak*s back to civilian life. We lived in the comfort of Kedai Pök our hardware store.

But in Sulong's above the shop the high-pitched *ngilla* was out of place so you merely smiled and kept perfectly still. Sulong was our photographer who poked out from beneath his blanket the bellow and his magic eye, and then, a week later—never less than that—he'd have your image ready on a square negative with your teeth all black and your hair prematurely grey. Accompanying that, of course, were the crisp photographs, printed on matte, of you and accompanying adults, smiling beneath his flat moon, standing as more likely than not, by his fluted pillar that stood on a brick base that was made from fibre board.

Sulong took the colour from our lives and gave us only black and white, but in our family we wore mostly white as Father believed that white was apt for Hari Raya in Sulong's studio. The white Raya clothes then served as our daily schoolwear. One day not long after our pose,

Sulong rolled down his canvas backdrop, took his hollow column and his bellowed camera down the stairs and spent the rest of his career as an itinerant photographer. I think I saw him again once, stretching his black but now moonless backdrop between two sticks in the open air, doing a brisk trade in passport and identity card photography.

In the Lay Sing Studio across the road from the Masjid Abidin we hired the Rolleiflex twin-lensed camera with a viewer set in a deep hole in its top. Lay Sing was more of a photo-processing and cameras-for-hire shop than a photo studio, with its moon in motionless clouds. Lay Sing, if that was he, was a lantern-jawed man who seldom smiled when he emerged occasionally to grab a bite or to shout orders at his young lads. It must have been the fumes of those chemicals in his darkened room—plus, I think, some light-omitting ingredients added as our photographs turned out mostly very dark, even if taken in broad daylight. His eldest son, Ah Leng, spoke fluent Trengganuspeak and spent many futile hours instructing us how to get our snaps right. 'It's the f— stop!' he'd say. 'It's the f— stop!' and that was the nearest he got to swearing at us.

Photographs were Ah Leng's life, whether it was the good ones that he printed from his day on the beach or the bad ones that we took in the unperceived darkness of our Trengganu light. He let us loiter in his shop to ponder his exhibits of Trengganuspeakers frozen, passport-sized, in black and white; and most of the time when we saw him he was never wearing a shirt. One day a man walked into the shop and, for some reason we never knew, plunged a knife into his shirtless top. The light was taken from Ah Leng's life just when I was losing interest in the f— stops of photography.

Without Ah Leng to visit we ventured further out after our dusk prayer at the mosque to while away the time before the next one was due. There was the Redi Photo Studio in Kedai Payang, twenty steps and more from the bookshop of Pök Löh Yunang, where loitering was discouraged by the fortress-like front of the shop. There was a glass case of films and disposable flashbulbs that kept customers on the outside. There were photographs in the display windows that were viewed from the outside colonnaded walk, of people with smiles that seemed a world away from our Ah Leng or Sulong's moving photo studio. There were large-sized portraits of men with epauletted shirts at Redi's, and they wore *söngköks* with rich trimmings. There were sons and daughters of Trengganu *towkay*s smiling out their happiness, and schoolteachers and civil servants in passport-sized formats or in colour.

Redi's workers worked from behind the glass-case counter and we knew none of them by name. But on Saturdays they had underaged girls helping out with the trade, one of whom I knew quite well as her desk was right beside mine at school. There was a narrow entrance at the right of the case, taking you spiralling up the staircase to a full moon rising above in a studio of fame amid hand-painted clouds. I saw them all, I think, with all those happy people in those photographs of varying sizes amid the baubles and the Agfa publicity boards and the instant cameras made by the Ködök (Kodak) company.

Fluorescent Rays

ABOVE THE LITTLE SHOP, diagonally across from the occasional whoops in the Kelab Pantai and the mellow sound of billiard balls constantly clashing with each other, was a hand-painted signboard with the letters IBRAHIM standing bold over the eponymous man's other lower-case designations as electrical contractor and wizard of the domestic wire. This was well before neon, when the weather-worn paean to Ibrahim stood the nights under a glow of chilli-shaped bulbs, hand-painted in garish blue, green and red, lighting up and going out in unison on a garland of electrical flex, coupled and sheathed by their makers in China.

Ibrahim's was strictly a business shop with little for children's pleasure even if, on occasions like Hari Raya, his chilli-shaped lights flashed on and off till late, throwing tinges of primary colours on passers-by and wayward members of the Kelab Pantai, adjourning late after a long day around the table. On the shelves behind the counter of his dark shop were boxes of bits and parts, electrical wires coiled in their spindles, and sockets, plugs and things we called *ba* or *bo* of varying wattage trapped in clear- or pearl-tinted bulb-shaped bottles. There were long glowing tubes of *lampu panjang* under whose glow we read books at night, or sat to eat or read the Qur'an in turn under the instruction of our genial teacher named Che Yi.

Everyone was Che in those days, men and women, and so it was to Che Ibrahim that I was sent for a little magic tube called the starter on occasions when our flourescent long *lampu* flickered or refused to light up at all. On another occasion Father himself went there to buy something in a flat box that he pulled out as a long, stringy green tendril that grew on it the tiniest of tiny bulbs of bright colours, encased in plastic sepals. Leaning out of a window at the front part of our house that we called the *surung* (a use I've not found in any dictionary), he hung it across the breadth of an old frame that once draped our front windows with the flowering branches of the *tikang seladang*. This was *tujuh likur*, the joyous night of the twenty-seventh Ramadan when house compounds were brightened by the flickering lights of kerosene lamps and children emerged from dark corners of our village with their candle-powered lanterns to make merry or watch the faces of other well-off children glowing in the bursting stars of magic sparklers.

When night fell Father flicked the switch and we knew from the bulbs that burnt their intermittent lights into the darkness—of red and green and blue—that it would soon be Hari Raya.

We had a tall house overlooking the *pasar* and the sundry shops of Tamil merchants, who put on their pristine best for Hari Raya: sarongs of white Indian cotton and white Indian shirts that glowed in the morning sun. In the Masjid Abidin they tied white handkerchiefs around their heads to keep their hair in check before they knelt down in prayer. They were stalwart men with sad eyes, their heads in business and their hearts in Mappalaikuppam in the district of Tanjore. In Tanjong they had their feet on hard earth and frequently in the high tides that sank their shops in sea water.

Behind our house, from the little window that looked down to the roof of the *surau* Tok Sheikh Kadir, we saw bright Malay shirts coming out from the houses, ladies in floral *baju*s and Trengganu *batik* and men and boys with new *söngkök* hats shaped from the finest velvet, probably by the hands of Che Awang, the village hat maker. We had, if we were lucky, Malay *baju*s tailored by the inestimable Ku Su, the tailor who worked from within the *kota*, the grounds of the palace. I say luck had a part in it because the business of Ku Su was such that even in the first week of Ramadan, he was already turning away customers.

By the time our great bell pealed forlornly from atop the *bukit* and the chorus of *takbir* began to rise to the rafters of the great mosque, the quiet Jalan Pantai that cut through our community was already beginning to fill with people—from Ladang at the far end, from the bowels of the many Tanjongs on the coast and from Kampung Nisan Empat on the other side, a sandy place that I remember for its creaking bamboos. This was Kuala Trengganu unlike any other day: men and women in their finery, Trengganu *söngkèt* catching the glint of early light, rushing trishaws, cycling Hajis and fresh-faced boys in bright colours brushing past men and womenfolk stealing glances at the varieties of holiday apparel on this bright day of Hari Raya.

As Ramadan was a month of fasting, it was the food that made our Hari Raya: our Trengganu *nasi dagang* with tuna fish, glutinous *pulut* rice in many shapes and flavours and *agar-agar* jelly, cut and dried in the sun throughout Ramadan until it was encased in crystallised sugar. There was *buöh ulu* or *baulu* which I think came from the Portuguese *bolos* and, my favourite, *akök* of duck eggs, made from flour and sugar, baked in the glowing heat of coconut husks in a special brass mould made by our Tanjong people. I have my other favourites too, like *buöh gömök* and the quaintly named *perut ayam* which is neither chicken nor entrails but which is probably extinct now.

The bright lights burned on even after Raya. Even on the night itself, after all the eats and visits had been done and we were all home again to wind down in our private corner, it filled our hearts with melancholy to be looking out to our Ibrahim lights, bursting with colour over the abandoned street and the *pasar* below. The *genta* on Bukit Putri was quiet again for another year. We could see by its flashing beacon that warned ships at sea that here, beneath this descending hush, was our little town of Kuala Trengganu.

Man in Mufti

SOMETIMES, LATE AFTERNOON, we'd walk to the *ujong tanjong* and watch the dots on the horizon or the *payang*s coming to shore with their catch. There were barges bobbing up and down in the busy waters, the river mouth that put the *kuala* in Kuala Trengganu. And Cik Jusoh, the beachcomber, walked past us with twigs and sticks in his hands, picked up as they were washed ashore.

Cik Soh, as we called him, was in mufti, clothes which were unlike those that he wore to the mosque. When wearing the former he had a rag coil around his head and a tattered sarong around his waist, a sarong known as the *kaing ssahang* that Trengganu males hung on a nail sticking out of the wall, or on a wire stretched taut across the verandah as an all-purpose clothes hanger. The *ssahang* was casual wear for days when we couldn't be bothered with a sarong, shirt and a *söngkök* at a jaunty angle. It was a single item of apparel that covered your parts from the navel to just below the knee. The head piece was another rag of faded batik, rolled like a snake that coiled placidly over the brow.

In his foraging work, Cik Soh struck an interesting pose, his trunk bent slightly forward, and his hands crossed at the wrists behind his back. In this manner he held two or three pieces of driftwood in his hands. Cik Soh kept the wood away from his body or clothes because, in his eccentricity, had a clinical dread of the unclean parts of his body, like his feet, or the dust of common people. He kept himself to himself and parts of himself from himself, and rarely spoke to other people for fear of being touched. Standing now against the setting sun, with his hands pulled behind his back, he had the silhouette of a praying mantis.

The day's end pushed our Tanjong people to the water to earn their keep from the incoming *payang* boats or to sit and enjoy the buzz of work. Driftwood provided fuel for domestic fires, and children threw sticks, dug holes and chased crabs that waved then bolted to their tiny holes when the waves came back. This sent the kids back to the sandy mounds, zigzagging between adults on their haunches, their sarongs loosened at the waist then pulled to the top. '*Jjalang mmölek bila gi ppata*' ('Tread carefully when you're on the beach') they used to warn the freewheeling novitiates, for those burqaed squatting men (and sometimes women) were using the beach as one big toilet in the open air.

When the light began to fade, we'd find a safe place to sit and sometimes we spoke to a woman who waved a hurricane lamp towards a dot of light out at sea. As if by magic the beam of light would twinkle back, and she'd wave again with a contented chuckle. Her husband was the pilot on a ship that was coming into the *kuala* with trade from the godowns of Singapore. We had many men in Trengganu who wore their job descriptions with their names, one such that I can still remember is Pak Ali Pailét, but in this instance I'm not sure if it was he.

The beach was a blessing to us and a fear. On some nights, when the moon pulled in the tides, our Tamil shopkeepers pulled their sarongs up to a decent level for them to wade in and rescue merchandise from the water. In his youth, Father said, he used to squeeze lime juice on his freshly shorn head to get the extra head-chilling oomph from the sea breeze blowing ashore. When the sea was rough, heaps of twigs and *buöh rengas* were washed up as the waves lapped in with a mighty roar. There were dead cows, lengths of rope and *gömök* seeds that we used for *kör* in children's games, and long tendrils called *rumput jjulok* that had a pulpy core that we dipped in ink before shaping them into pretty flowers. A crowd gathered one day in the back corner of the market to leer at a dead body that had been washed into the *teluk*.

Then a boat was washed up one day, blown by the monsoon winds from the distant shores of Sulawesi. With it came a mighty man we called Bachök, who liked us and stayed on to father a son called Mat who went to school with my brother. When, in his old age, Bachök expressed a wish to go back to the shore from where he'd blown into our midst, the hold of Kampung Tanjong was already so firm on him that he stayed on, to be laid finally to rest in the earth of Kuala Trengganu.

The shore which Bachök was washed up on is no more, washed out in dribs and drabs into the sea by the changing flow and pull of the water. Ujung Tanjong, as we knew it, is now submerged like some lost kingdom under the sea, and sometimes I even wonder if people still squat on the sandy dunes of our *pantai*.

Eggs in a Net

COMING INTO TOWN along Jalan Batu Buruk, looking right at the roundabout that once had the *penyu*, you'll see to your right a little wooden house in the middle of a sprawling cemetery. I am told that the turtle is no more now, that it has been replaced by a replica of the Batu Bersurat

(Trengganu Stone) as the standard-bearer for Kuala Trengganu. But the Kubur Tok Pelam (Tok Pelam Cemetery) is still there, still drawing in family members of the deceased, and its ground is still being dug up for dead people.

I've been intrigued by Tok Pelam ever since I started going to Sekolah Ladang which, I'm told, still stands nearby. The cemetery bears the name of a man with a strange title, Tok Pelam. More than that, among my school friends it was whispered that in the quaint wooden house built over the cemetery was an egg from an exotic bird called the *buraq*, a speedy traveller that covers miles and dimensions in a tick. It was one of life's mysteries to me, when I was at the Sekolah Melayu Ladang, that such an exotic bird had chosen to lay an egg in a wooden shack in a cemetery on the fringe of a quiet town called Kuala Trengganu.

After we left Kuala Trengganu many years ago, my memory of the cosmic egg faded with the years until very recently that is, when I went back to the the town and the Tok Pelam via a blog. Then I remembered the egg, which may or may not have existed, as I retrieved an old picture that I've kept in that dark attic under my thatch, covered as it is in a patina of dust from passing years.

The egg of the *buraq* described from memories of a distant past, can I say any more than that? A flashback to an urban tale of childhood years, maybe? I wish I'd ventured into that wooden house the last time I was in Kuala Trengganu (fifteen years ago?) to say a prayer for the dead within, then to cast a glance around the house for a shred of evidence to substantiate my childhood story.

Last week I was looking at a beautiful book of words and etchings by Ilse Noor, published fourteen years ago. In the section on 'Terengganu' I read these chilling words:

'The strange coincidence at the end of my journey, of coming upon a small wooden house and coming to know of two huge eggs hanging in nets in two corners of the empty attic, puzzles and troubles me.'

This was the mausoleum to Tok Pelam that the artist Ilse Noor was describing, and the eggs of the *buraq*, they were there! Except that the guardians of the tomb told her that these were the eggs of the *cenderawasih*, a mythical bird of paradise of Malay folklore. But how could a mythical bird have laid those eggs that dangled in a net in a mausoleum in Kuala Trengganu? I began to hear an old Malay song:

> '*Cenderawasih burung kayangan,*
> *Terbangnya tinggi, tinggi di awan ...*'

> ('*Cenderawasih*, bird of paradise,
> Flying high among the clouds ...')

But I'm grateful to Ilse Noor, not just for confirmation of the existence of those eggs ('*The eggs ... look like ostrich eggs, hanging there unchanged from time immemorial ...*') but also for information about the mysterious Tok Pelam.

According to what Ilse was told, Tok Pelam, whose real name was Abdullah bin Abdul Aziz, was born in the year 1819 (1235 AH) in Hadramaut, Yemen. He was one of three preachers—the other two were Tok Pulau Manis and Sheikh Ibrahim—who travelled east, landed in the Malay state of Patani (now in southern Thailand) then travelled further to Trengganu. The Kubur Sheikh Ibrahim, another well-known cemetery

Mausoleum of Tok Pelam.

58

in Kuala Trengganu, is just a couple of hundred yards from Tok Pelam.

According to Noor, Tok Pelam lived in Kampung Ladang (where he was buried) and directed the building of the mausoleum in the last year(s) of his life. The house remains a curiosity in the town of Kuala Trengganu, with its two carved wooden doors (secured by a string). It also has another feature that is unusual in Trengganu house building: its walls are painted with 'flowering plants growing out of vases' and its ceiling decorated with geometrical flower motifs. The inscription on the doors says that Tok Pelam died in 1319 AH, at the age of eighty-four.

The only thing that troubles me about this bit of history (as told to Noor) is Tok Pulau Manis, the distinguished Trengganu saint and scholar whom I've mentioned a few times in my earlier Trengganu notes. If this was the same Tok Pulau Manis who gave religious instruction to Sultan Zainal Abidin I, he could not have been a contemporary of Tok Pelam as he died in 1736, nearly a hundred years before Tok Pelam himself was born. Furthermore, Tok Pulau Manis (whose real name was Sheikh Abdul Malik) was descended not from Yemeni stock, but was a scion of one Sharif Muhammad of Baghdad. He himself, though, was born in Kampung Pauh in Hulu Trengganu in 1650.

So more puzzles then from those eggs.

Saints and Singing Birds

I HAVE SCANT MEMORIES of birds, and the twitterings in my head are either misplaced or misheard. In *Conference of Birds* (page 296), I said that Grandfather in Kampung Raja, Besut, kept pigeons in elaborate cages, only to draw a swift and knuckle-rapping email from my brother, who wrote:

Error. They weren't merpati *but* ketitir, merbok *or Zebra Doves. To enhance the voices of the* ketitirs, *Tok Wan [Grandfather] would feed them a whole pickled* cili padi. *In fact not 'feed', but shove down the throats of the birds. Done so, he would then tease them with 'arkkk, arkkk' ... Then he would bathe them* dengan menyembur air dari mulut dia.

So there you are, vivid imagery in your mind's eye and the distant playback of the songbird, so haunting and so sweet, it is said, and so plaintive a cry as to make grown men weep. Celestial sounds coaxed from the angelic voice boxes of little birds by bird's-eye chilli, its heat drowned in vinegar and doused by a soothing spray from the pouting lips of Grandfather—'*dengan menyembur air dari mulut dia*'. 'Arkkk' and the bird said, 'Kooo!'

I was just recovering from this alarming thought, actually, when my mind was diverted by a comment made by Atok about the exotic bird the *cenderawasih*. Mighty pleased I was to wonder about an even more distant land of shamans, and long-tailed birds dangling from clouds by the strength of colourful plumes.

I have never seen a *cenderawasih* in my life though, I spoke and sang about them when I wrote about some intriguing eggs in *Eggs in a Net* (page 56). They were *burak* eggs, we children whispered in each other's ears whenever anyone carried word of their alleged presence in the tomb of our local saint, Tok Pelam. The funny thing is that we never bothered to go and take a peek into the tomb ourselves, even though it wasn't far from our Sekolah Melayu in Ladang.

It was only recently, while looking through a beautiful book of notes and etchings by Ilse Noor, that I found that those eggs really do sit in the tomb house, cradled in net hammocks. It 'puzzled and troubled me', said Ilse Noor. I was completely astounded. She was told by the custodian of the tomb that they were eggs from the *cenderawasih*, a bird of paradise that still flies nowadays in East Malaysia, so high in clouds of myths and facts as to strain the necks and minds of both shamans and fanciers.

I have actually been meaning to go back to Tok Pelam (real name Abdullah bin Abdul Aziz), so now that I've got the opportunity I shall take you there, not directly to him but to another saint named Sheikh Ibrahim, a fellow Hadhrami (i.e. from Hadhramaut in Yemen) who, like Tok Pelam, arrived in Trengganu via Patani in the nineteenth century. Sheikh Ibrahim is a name that is as well known in Kuala Trengganu as Tok Pelam as they both have cemeteries named after them—in proximity in death as in life, the two neighbouring *kubur*s of Tok Pelam and Sheikh Ibrahim.

Tok Sheikh Ibrahim is remembered in folk history as the man who single-handedly drove away ships that were shelling Kuala Trengganu by simply walking up and down the coast uttering prayers and supplications to the Almighty. The story goes that the enemies saw not him but hundreds and indeed thousands of men waiting to defend the shore, so they just pulled from the coastline.

William Skeat, who visited Kuala Trengganu in October 1899, said that the shelling was done by men of the Maharajah of Johor. But not so says historian J.M. Gullick in a short footnote to an extract from Skeat's report in his traveller's anthology, *They Came to Malaya*; it was the British that day who sent most Kuala Trengganu folk scrambling for the hills.

I have been to the Sheikh Ibrahim Cemetery many times but was never made aware that the Tok Sheikh himself had been laid to rest in this sprawling burial site, so I shall have to rely on Skeat to give us a description of his grave:

'*The grave had five posts* (batu nesan) *at each end, making ten in all, instead of the usual single post; the superfluous ones had been added out of the funds provided by the saint's many devotees. To them also, presumably, was due the fact that it was protected by a triple mosquito curtain, and an* atap *roof shelter was built over it.*'

Pays au Chocolat

IN THE HOUSE WHERE I first learnt to read the Qur'an, they rolled a sticky brown paste, still hot from the pan, into a thick long string, then cut out inch-long sections that were individually wrapped in square bits of newspaper.

Some days they changed the recipe and turned sugar into thick caramel, then buried a peanut in each blob and moulded the glassy outer layer into the shape and size of a bullet and sold it wrapped in transparent coloured paper. We paid five cents for three of those, and placed one in our cheek to add some sweetness to the time we spent from one errand to another, those sugary bullet-shaped *buöh guling* wrapped in transparent colours of green, red and blue. For the richer taste of palm nectar we had to stop to peel off the newsprint wrapper that finally came loose with a word or two still sticking to the brown sugar. But you popped it into your mouth nevertheless, knowing that you had the skill honed by your many years as a muncher to spit the papery words out through your teeth as the sugar melted in your saliva. This was *cokelat nnisang,* born of the fluid tapped from the spathe of the coconut then boiled in a heavy pot until it was reduced to a brown nectar.

Nnisang—a word that came from the standardspeak *manisan,* meaning 'sweetener'—was sugar of the *kampung,* sold as flat round discs with a surrounding rind of tough, sinewy leaf that cut deeply into an unwary finger. It was this *nnisang* that lent sweetness and colour to our *cokelat,* a word that in Trengganuspeak described a variety of sins from the gobstopper to the luxury of its cocoa-born father. When we tired of *kampung*-made sweets, we took our five cents to the grocery shop to swap for two bits of clear glass called *cokelat ra.* The 'ah' sound in *ra* was a nasal sound that described the effect of the mint as it burnt a hole in our palate and rotted our teeth to the core.

On the bridge on the road to the town's *masjid* was a shop called the *kedai bbunga* that probably had flowers in its wallpaper (hence the name) but it had more delightful things than that in its jars. They were sweets from many lands: dried fruits wrapped in Chinese paper, Cadbury's Fruit & Nut bars and fruit pastilles that turned your teeth a bright colour. Needless to say we visited the shop only rarely because of our limited means, but sometimes—budget permitting—Father brought home biscuits from there which came from an exotic place called Reading, or a bunch of grapes that brought an enticing aroma into our childhood, or cans of fruit cocktail from Tasmania. In a cylinder made from heavy paper came thin, red, dried discs of *gambir China, buöh kerecut* that are now known as Chinese dates and *buöh kana* that looked and tasted like rugby balls. There was *buöh ssemak* that was actually the Japanese *kaki* fruit, dried, flattened and exported in a layer of white mycelium or fruit sugar (tick whichever is applicable). It was a veritable cornucopia-on-the-bridge shop opposite the fire station and diagonally across from the corner prayer house that was the fishmongers' *surau.*

Father had a little debt book kept in his name in the *kedai bbunga* which the Bbunga brothers pulled out of a one-kilo Planta margarine tin that hung from the ceiling by a long string that rolled on a pulley. They could not have been brothers at all, but we assumed that they were: one man was round with his head completely shorn, wore a button-necked T-shirt and the blue Chinese precursor to boxer shorts (Mother called him Awang, the name she gave all Chinese shopkeepers); the other was a man fully hirsute in his top half but not as merry as his bald friend (so Mother didn't give him a name at all).

We were sweet-toothed in Trengganu and loved our *nekbat* and *dodol,* which was white and came wrapped in the dried spathe of the palmyra and wrapped again on the inside in a delightful crust of white sugar. As our house was cheek by jowl with our *surau*, we were treated at least twice a year to some chanting by our local South Indian shopkeepers during the Mawlid of our Prophet and of a famous saint from Nagore. After finishing the prayer at dusk our *imam,* Pök Lèh, moved over to one side for our spice vendors and textile traders to hold sway, first in a gentle murmur that set the tone, then to a crescendo that led to the *salawat* and the finale of the *Qasida Burda.*

We were not often allowed to venture into the night but heard it all in full shout as we sat around our dinner table. We knew we were missing out on a lot when the pleading noises started to roll as the food parcels were being handed out; but the following morning, as we were preparing to go to school, we were seldom disappointed by Yusuf, our Tamil contact in the spice trade, who would bring to us parcels of *nasi minyök* from the night before and something else that always made me smile: thanks to him I became acquainted with the goodness and the sweetness of *ladoo.*

Wind Over Troubled Water

DURING THE MONSOON MONTHS the sea was a demented beast, lashing with a mighty roar, eating into sandy ramparts and piling up tangled heaps of debris: sodden branches and dead animals, seaweed ploughed up in knotted balls and tree trunks fallen far away. Once, there was a dead body that drifted to our side of the shore. Fishermen came home and snuggled under extra sarongs draped over shoulders then pulled tight to the front into a fold. On verandahs they sat and munched boiled tapioca dipped in white sugar, teeth blackened by residues of strong coffee sweet as the village damsel.

During normal months the waves merely dissipated at the water's edge, fizzling out in a sigh, scattering surf and sending crabs scurrying sideways to their bolt-holes. In the monsoon months the sea was a cauldron of grey pulled to shore by a hazy curtain of sky that wore a coat of matching colour. The water lashed, chopped and growled, eating into our beaches and pulling sand into the turmoil. When the rain let up, we walked to the coast and picked up whatever it had thrown on the shore: the flat-shelled *buöh gömök*, tough and dark as ebony, or the slender *rumput jjulok* with its spongy core that we pushed out like spaghetti. The *buöh rengas* was the size of a fist and would lay in wait, but was avoided by those who knew. It made you itch and God knows what else besides, and ditto too for the jellyfish that lay in a daze after being tossed and rolled in the water. We took *buöh gömök* home, bored holes in them and kept them in an ant's colony. Once the ants had had their feast and left the *gömök* shell light and hollow, those skilled in '*gömök* craft' took them home to fill them with molten lead, to love and spit on their shells, to love and polish them with kiwi before they were bandied about as objects of desire. Weighted *gömök* were used as hurling objects in our games, or smashed against rival *gömök*s as children do with conkers in other parts of the world. While waiting for the *buöh gömök* to fill with lead we gave vent to our artistic side and soaked the long pulp of the *rumput jjulok* in ink or the red dye of the *kesumba,* then shaped them into pretty flowers.

The monsoon was the wind that blew in the chill, not the rain that clung to its coat-tail. Starting life as a Siberian draught, it turned a corner on Chinese shores and became the north-easterlies that blew from November to March through Trengganu. There it turned the hanging-down mops of our coconut trees into straight hair blown to the backs of their ears. It lifted thatch from our rooftops and lifted the sarongs of the unwary; it brought changes and material upheavals, blew umbrellas into a 'V' shape. The tail wind steered the ship of *Ibn Battuta*, and brought Hadhrami men to our shores—sailors and preachers of Yemen, chanting the *hizb* of the *bahr.*

In the market of Tanjong the fruits were covered in glinting beads of fallen rain as women vendors snuggled under plastic awnings, and pea-green umbrellas; fish was scarce and roots, the tapioca and varieties of *ubi* and *keladi,* were thrown into the fire and eaten with sugar or scraped coconut mixed with salt while watching buyers and errand boys, middlemen and *kuih* vendors scurry by, celebrating the numbered days of the *samir*. The *samir* were dried palm leaves sewn into a hood-shaped top with a cape that flowed down your back to reach down to your heels.

It rained so heavily in these *tengkojoh* months that we also called it *musim gelora*, the unsettled season, and when it rained for days on end, Kuala Trengganu became one big puddle. Nature spoke to us then, in the rustling of the trees and the saturation of the tall *meninjau* that stood outside our east-facing window. Rain prattled on the corrugated roofs of coffee shops and tyres splashed constantly over puddles. The sea was a mix of sounds: of distant wails and a tiger's roar, trapped under a broody sky.

Talking to Animals

SOMETIMES ON SUNNY DAYS, when the plants were bright green and our front gate was ajar, a call would come from the kitchen of our house to the corner of our front yard beyond the well. It came in a threatening note, and probably a few scales below the speaker's normal register. 'Bok! Bok!' it went, sometimes accompanied by a drumming on the kitchen door.

We had plants in our front yard: *sukun, pohong jarök*, a flowering plant called the *tikang seladang* that sat on a pergola and a common plant called the *ubi gajah*, of straight stem and broad canopy that looked and behaved very much like your common or garden *ubi kayu* except that its roots were poisonous to the human palate. However when chopped into fine bits, it slid down the gullets of hens and ducks without giving them even the bloat. We had no poultry in our front yard but we grew the *ubi gajah* in any case as any old stick would sprout leaves in those days if you poked it in the right soil.

The goats that squeezed through our front gate cared little for all these plants but went straight for our banana tree. Each goat clambered on its stem using its forelegs, then tugged the tip of one frond with its bare teeth to break it at the base so it drooped limply enough for the goat to tug and chew it while standing firmly on all four legs. It was for them that the *bok* sound was made, for in the lore of Trengganuspeak, *bok* was for goats a dreaded sound that came from the human primate.

The goats spoke back to us, of course, in sounds that we called *ddembèk* because the language that goats spoke consisted mainly of *bèk, bèk,* or something like that.

To call the goats, their owners made a sound that went *bah bah* as they proferred them leaves from the *bbaru* tree.

So goats had an ear for sounds that came up from the throat, but cats had an ear for more sibilant sounds. As they approached a plate of fish waiting to be thrown into the fryer, they'd be warned with a *shhh* but if they proved to be persistent animals, the second admonitory word took a harder edge that went *cis cis* and a wise cat would be good enough to pull back now.

Stray chickens pecking and treading on the *kerepok* laid out to dry were warned off with a *siok* that leapt out from the human mouth, then maybe another one for good measure.

At times when the animals had to be called—in the morning when Wang Döllöh fed his ducks with *ampas sagu,* the fibrous waste from the sago stem once it had been pressed dry—he'd cry out: *'Diii-di-di-di-di!'* in a voice that rose to a higher note as he sprinkled the feed out to the ducks.

Cats came when they smelt fish but early mornings, when they were still curled up by the stove, they answered to the sound made by the meeting of the tip of the tongue with the roof of the mouth, the *ch ch ch* sound that was reminiscent of the gecko *cicök.*

Bigger cats were best avoided, especially if they had stripes on them, but if you had reason to visit their lair to forage for goods, the general consensus was not to mention them by name or wake them up from their slumber, but to offer a general salutation like the *salam,* and then claim kinship for your right of way. Something like *'Assalamu alaikum! Anök cucu nök tumpang lalu!'** would probably work for you (but please try it first on your domestic pets).

***

* 'Peace be on you. Your kith and kin asks for permission to pass.'

A Corner of Country

Man of Metal

LAST SATURDAY another link to my past was severed when news came that my cousin Wan Salleh had died. He was a cousin but more of an uncle to us as he was much older and already working when we were too young to tie two pieces of string together, let alone the shoelaces on our Bata shoes. The last time we met must've been ten years ago, maybe more.

When news came that he'd died, all I could think of was the dark tunnel, the heat and people walking about in a colony on a hill so far removed from the mainstream that it took hours to reach by the only railway track in Trengganu. We were all standing there at Sura Gate in Dungun, a little town described then, as now, as a sleepy place in many pages that I've read. But Dungun then was the outlet for all the iron ore of Bukit Besi, a town on the hills that pulled iron from the earth; and my cousin worked there in the employ of a company named—if my memory serves—EMMCO, the Eastern Mining and Metal Company.

Our journey would start from Sura Gate in Dungun which only had two rows of shops. The heat was intense, and the trains were a long time coming. The journey upwards, to the hill, was even longer, with the train going *chug-a-lug, chug-a-lug* around the next bend, then upwards into the green forest of the next incline. And it stopped at every station that appeared along its journey in this wild, isolated terrain. At midday in Trengganu the heat was intense. I heard someone say once that it was the heat from all that iron in the hills.

Sometimes it would stop between stations for no apparent purpose, standing there on the tracks in the eerie silence of the jungle, then bringing additional anxiety with the occasional hissing of the engine. And then it'd move again into the deep, dark tunnel, *chug-a-lug, chug-a-lug* with anxiety overload. My auntie cautioned my mum once in a hushed conspiratorial tone to hold on tightly to her handbag. 'Hold on to that, hold on to that, this is the tunnel of the roving hands,' she said before it all turned dark.

When Bukit Besi finally came into sight, it was a great relief. It was a strange artificial town built to serve the company, with workers living in lines and lines of company houses, uniform wooden structures on the terraces of the hill. It must've been a great place for the workers in this community of camaraderie, fun, even, for the children who lived and grew up in this unique tin town unlike any other in Trengganu. It was because of this, perhaps, or the long tedious journey to get out there or the mists of isolation that hung over Bukit Besi that it never won a special place in my heart.

But that isn't to say that there wasn't fascination enough there. Anyone journeying to Bukit Besi would return with a sample of ore to use as a paperweight or to show to disbelieving friends, and from that they'd talk about this community on the hill that was so different to the rest of us. My late cousin, as I could see it, enjoyed his work, took an active interest in the welfare of his fellow workers (he was a union officer) and still had time to pursue his hobby of photography.

I was—and have always been—fascinated by trains, but cannot remember much else about the journey to the *bukit* and back, except that it was arduous and tiresome, and I was always glad when it ended. But having a train made Bukit Besi unique among Trengganu towns, as no train line ran anywhere else in the state by the royal order of Sultan Zainal Abidin (also known as Marhum Haji), a devout man and one of the great Trengganu sultans of modern time. He saw it only as a means of transport for the intrusion of all that would corrupt religion and the way of life in the state. And as for the social upheaval that it would bring? No thanks, he wouldn't have any of that. And so it is that, until today, Trengganu is the only state in Peninsular Malaysia that's not linked to the railway track.

I remember Bukit Besi now, and my cousin, with great sadness. Tin mining has ended in Trengganu, and Bukit Besi is no longer there to re-visit. And as for my cousin, I'm grateful to him for the memories he gave us of this unique place. God rest you, dear cousin, may you be among the righteous and your life's works be rewarded.

Kitabs and the Pahang Mail

MY FATHER, GOD REST HIS SOUL, was a widely read man who made straight for the Abdullah Al-Yunani from the Masjid Abidin as soon as he'd finished the *Isha* prayer. The Abdullah Al-Yunani was the sole distributor of newspapers when family businesses still held sway, and the Yunanis were a prominent Chinese-Muslim family in Kuala Trengganu. It stood in a street of textile merchants and photo studios, and next door to it was a shop that my mother always referred to as Kedai Yamada (Yamada's shop) even though the man in it was as far removed from Yamada-*san* as the mangosteen is from the pineapple. He was, in fact, of Indian origin and went by the name of Mr Fernandez. Mr Fernandez kept clocks and watches in his shop that was out of bounds to little boys who couldn't tell the time of day.

Father would wait patiently every evening outside the Abdullah Al-Yunani for the arrival of Pahang Mail, the lorry service that brought goods to Kuala Trengganu from Kuantan in Pahang, or Kuala Lumpur on the

A wedding photo of the Al-Yunani family.

73

other side of the world. That was how newspapers were delivered to us in those days, at dusk, after the *Isha* prayers, when folks on the other side had already discarded their daily rag and were settling down to their evening meal. Outside the Abdullah al-Yunani people would be chatting and waiting for their first glimpse of the day's headlines, while the types were being set and the presses rolled in Kuala Lumpur for the next day's page, another day's paper.

Sometimes when I followed Father to the mosque I'd end up standing there too with him, in my *kain pelikat* and *baju* Melayu sometimes in windy, monsoonal weather, waiting for the day's delivery. While waiting for the lorry to arrive, I'd creep into the shop to look at the stock of books and comics and the old *kitab*s that the Abdullah al-Yunani was famous for. *Kitab*s, as I knew them, were Muslim books written in the Arabic language and script, or sometimes they were Malay books written in Jawi-Arabic characters. I remember some, like *Taj-ul-Mulk,* which contained invocations and recipes for poultices, and the book of *Tibb* which was the materia medica of our local herbal *bomoh*s.

In daylight, when Father was at work, I'd walk further up the road to Kampung China, the Chinatown of Kuala Trengganu. I had a friend there right by the Chinese butcher, and a schoolteacher who lived across the road; but my constant delight was the Chee Seek store. The Chee Seek was as precious as the Abdullah al-Yunani, but represented a different shade of reading matter. It stocked Chinese books, of course, and comics, and the US version of *Reader's Digest* which was heftier and jazzier than the British edition, and Chee Seek had a little surprise in the back of the store.

Cramped behind the stacks and shelves and magazines that dangled from overhead wires was a little business run by a middle-aged Chinese lady called Mök Mèk. She could've been Chee Seek's mum, or his only daughter, or an aunt or mother-in-law, but she was the quintessential Chinese earth mother dressed in *batik sarung* and *baju kebaya,* whose deft hands manufactured the *ceranang* and the *kerepok lekör* that were different in texture and looks from the ones made by Malays on the shore. The *kerepok lekör* was the speciality of Trengganu, but only Chinese *kerepok* makers made them from shark meat or *ikan yu.* Mok Mèk's husband, Pök Awang, was seldom there as she tended to her customers in this tiny store that stayed open because of a secret arrangement with local officers at the town hall. Pök Awang was a roving ambassador, a dealer of stuff, a Taoist man in Chinese trousers who roamed the streets on some errands or urgent matter. He was a medicine man and a soothsayer, perhaps even a necromancer. I saw him once at the house of a neighbour, exchanging homilies with the man of the house while his wife and sons were busily crushing fish for the day's *kerepok lèkör*. He spoke fluent Trengganuspeak, which is as foreign to out-of-state persons as Swedish is to a Swahili speaker. He tailored his advice according to his customer: once I heard him say to our neighbourhood *kerepok lèkör* man that for a house to receive a maximum number of blessings it must be facing the Ka'abah in Makkah.

The Chinese have a long history in Trengganu, dating back to the time of Zheng He (Cheng Ho), the eunuch Muslim admiral who visited Trengganu in the fifteenth century, or even earlier. In the nineteenth century prominent members of Trengganu Chinese families were given special dispensations to issue coins in return for services to the sultan, but this was abolished by the British when they took control of the state's coffers.

* * *

After this piece appeared in my blog notes, fellow Trengganuer Pök Ku wrote in to correct me on the exact position of the Kedai Yamada. It was not the one I mentioned as Keda Fernandez, he said, but the one a few doors away. I stand corrected and thank him for his memory.

Beluda Hands, Singing Head

IN HIS HEAD HE CARRIED SONGS from a very long time ago. From his hands came the fruits of recipes long forgotten. In the morning he baked *roti paung* and *beluda*, which is probably best described as the Trengganu muffin. There are people everywhere who bake sweetish buns as golden and as brown, but I have not seen a *beluda* since my childhood days.

Pök Mat's *beluda*s were baked in cigarette tins, if you remember what cigarette tins were like. The tin was roundish, about three inches in diameter and stood as tall as the cigarette was long. It had a lid with a catch that had to be prised open to keep its contents fresh. Once emptied of cigarettes, Pök Mat filled the tin—many tins—with his secret recipe, each brimming with the dough that had risen in the night. He pushed the cigarette tins well into the back of his wood-fired oven.

I sometimes wonder about the fate of those Trengganu men and women who smoked those nefarious cigarettes that gave Pök Mat all those empty tins to fill with his *beluda*.

The *beluda,* when pulled piping hot from the oven, had a spongy consistency and a mien that delighted a child's fancy. I ate many *beluda*s on my way to school and, if I was lucky, there'd be some left when I returned home at the end of the day. I stood many hours, before school started, waiting to be served while Pök Mat sweated in his baking shed, pulling this tray out, shoving another in, and all the while giving orders to his kith and kin to wrap this up or take the money from someone who'd had his or her turn already.

The *beluda* in a cigarette tin was the stuff of childhood dreams, and the art was not just in the baking, but also in the ability to make it pop out of the can, still steaming and unbroken. Even when cold, the *beluda* was still the bolster of dreams.

Maybe, in my recollection, I've '*beluda*d' Pök Mat for too long, and made light his other talents. Pök Mat baked two varieties of bread, maybe seven, it was a long time ago, you understand. Then he also stirred a huge pot of a Trengganu *gulai* with bits of meat bobbing up and down in a thin, darkish sauce which was also his other feat of renown. The sauce was poured over his *nasi minyak,* rice cooked in a quantity of grease, gleaming and steaming in the cauldron, then made merry with grains that were coloured red, green and yellow.

Some mornings Pök Mat would rise at the crack of dawn and to the occasion, and baked *beluda*s and buns. Then, at other times when the mood took him, he would stir the *gulai* in his pot, douse a little of the sauce onto portions of steaming rice sectioned out on papers lined with banana leaves, waiting to be adorned with chunks of meat and chillied condiments, then wrap and take hurriedly to the famished at the breakfast tables of many a home in our littoral town.

Then one fine day someone found an old gamelan set in the recesses of the Palace of Kuala Trengganu, but there was no one to beat out the tunes from these ancient instruments. So Pök Mat pushed aside his boiling cauldron and his oven that was wafting with the smell of burning wood and the aroma of the *beluda* and the *paung,* and made merry music for a while on these instruments with tunes that he must've learnt when he was young. Pök Mat, I haven't told you, was also known far and wide as Pök Mat Nobat, a royal player in the *nobat* ensemble of old Trengganu.

Nobat, you see, is royal music, played only on special occasions by men who beat a drum, blew on a Malay trumpet and played a few other instruments that I've now forgotten. Only a few states in Peninsular Malaysia had the *nobat,* and Trengganu was one of them. *Nobat* music gave out some quaint lamentations that have been attributed by some to mysterious sounds heard by men far out at sea. The *nobat* music was not written but kept in the memories of a select few.

So you can imagine our Pök Mat pulling out the *beluda* and the bun while, in his head, ran the wailing and the bleating of the *nobat* winds and the wild beat of ancient drums.

* * *

Soon after I finished writing this piece my brother wrote in to point out that I'd mixed two Pök Mats into one character. The Pök Mat who made *beluda* and the *nasi minyak* was, in fact, nearer to our house, and he was called Pök Mat Senani. The other Pök Mat, the royal *nobat* and gamelan man, was Pök Mat Nobat and he, as my brother correctly pointed out, knew no *beluda.* I have, however, decided to keep this piece intact and let the man I've written about remain a composite character, as a tribute to them both.)

Chiaroscuro Morning

I TOOK THE PICTURE ON THE NEXT PAGE in Sabak Bernam, Selangor, Malaysia at about quarter past ten in the morning. We were waiting for a boat to take us to a *kelong* about six miles out at sea. The river—Sungai Besar I think—was quiet, there was a solitary bird perched on a branch, and the opposite bank looked unfriendly and inaccessible. It wasn't too early, but the morning was gentle, still: the sun wasn't yet too bright, there were scaly clouds in the sky and shafts of light were coming through in a most wonderful way. If you look closely at the sky you'll probably see some of that in the picture.

When I was a child I had a recurring dream of waking up early in the morning in a house by the sea in Kuala Trengganu. It was always very early, as the weak grey light was just coming into the house through the open front door which I couldn't see as there was a screen between it and me. But I could see the light coming in from the sides of the screen into the room, slowly lifting the remaining darkness of the previous night. It filled me with extreme melancholy, sitting in that semi-darkness, looking at a burgeoning day.

Looking at this picture now I feel a bit of that old melancholy creeping out from the crevasses of my memory. Funny how the past can suddenly appear in a picture taken years later.

A view of Sabak Bernam, Selangor, Malaysia.

A *kelong,* by the way, is an off-shore structure built by fishermen to house fish traps, and was built from tree stems or bamboo. I was half-expecting to see this kind of structure when the boat came to take us out to sea, but as we approached it I realised that it was not made of wood but concrete, and was poised out there like an oil rig standing proud in a rough sea. This *kelong* actually called itself a resort, with dorms and suites for people who fancied a few days listening to the ocean waves. The people I saw there were mostly fishing enthusiasts, with rods and things, and they looked very happy.

Whispering Wanderers

IT'S BEEN A TOPSY-TURVY WEEK. I saw a *pontianak,* but only on celluloid, and she turned out to be a real banshee. I wonder why *pontianak*s don't fly properly. The one I saw came down vertically and went for the jugular; but I'm happy that this Malaysian film's raked in three awards in Estapona, Spain, and another in Tokyo. Respect, as they say in hip-hop circles. Since seeing this banshee I've not wronged ladies nor trod on their painted toes. I can't bear to think what they'd come back as if wronged by me.

There weren't many *pontianak*s in Trengganu, but *pelesit*s seemed to roam quite freely. *Pelesit*s were creatures apart, and were kept mostly by some crones of the community. I remember my mother telling me one day that so-and-so had a *pelesit* handy. Only a few days ago I met a captain with the Malaysian Airlines who said that when he was growing up in Trengganu he'd lived in a house in Hiliran with his parents, brothers and a few other things that did the bump thing in the nocturnal hour.

'Oh,' I said, 'I know the house because my cousin lived there when it was still painted yellow. There was a lady there who never looked you in the eye and who used to do the chores for the wife that my cousin had just wed.' This was before the captain grew up in the house, of course, and what's interesting about elderly ladies who didn't look you in the eye was that, in Trengganu, they were believed to be harbouring little companions beside themselves to do the chores. One of the many things I heard when I too was little was that this lady kept a *pelesit* which she was anxious to be rid of. *Pelesit*s came to you in many ways, but I shall not bore you with that right now.

'Do you think that was the same thing that was bothering us?' The captain asked.

'Funny your asking me that,' I said, 'but I'm not sure.'

I've not seen ghouls but many fools on my way to where I'm now. All the ghouls I've seen are celluloid-made and the fools, of course, they go where wise men fear. There weren't many ghosts in the Trengganu that I grew up in and the ones I knew I never saw. This *pelesit* belonging to the little lady was the whispering type that kept whispering this and that into her ear. That's what my cousin told my mother one day. My cousin was a religious man who spent many a year in the Al-Azhar Mosque in Cairo, so he must've exorcised the little lady of her trouble. Funny that the little fellow chose to stay on to visit the man who'd one day fly our national carrier.

There was another ghost that we vaguely heard of but never got to know as we were never allowed out in the bewitching hour. That was the *hantu kangkang* of the gateway to the Istana Maziah in the Kuala Trengganu harbour. The Istana Maziah was a ceremonial palace that sat in the back of a sloping span of green that was known to us as Padang Malaya, but it was only later that someone thought to name it Padang Maziah. It had a couple of flaming trees of the forest—the Delonix regia as I remember—and a row of tall palm-like trees that we called *pinang gatal*. The *pinang gatal* was a handy tree for pranksters who were so enamoured of the fruits it bore. They were small pellet-like seeds covered in soft reddish skins that made your friend itch badly if you rubbed one hard enough on his exposed parts. Well, you wouldn't do it on your enemy, would you? Or on a total stranger. So there we were, returning from a day in Padang Malaya, cheering and jeering while a friend scratched and scratched the back of his neck, which was the favourite spot for an attack with the *pinang gatal*.

But back to the ghost of the palace gateway, the *hantu kangkang* of the late hour. To do the *kangkang* on the palace gate was a feat even for ghosts as it involved the parking of one foot on a foothold on one side of the gate and another on the other, a span of at least four or five yards, I dare say. It was said too that the *hantu kangkang* came out at midnight and bestrode the gate in this curious and rude way, but for no reasons that I know of.

Istana Maziah, Kuala Trengganu.

Fish on a Bicycle

OUR COUSIN DAH was one day knocked sideways by a *tok peraih* travelling at speed from Kedai Payang to another fish market in Ladang.

Kedai Payang, if you know Trengganu, is almost in the town centre, and Ladang is some fifteen minutes away, maybe less depending how the *tok peraih* flew. *Tok peraih*s were sinewy men often found under a conical *terendak* hat. They rode sturdy bikes with a rack at the back on which was placed a rectangular cane basket filled with the latest fruits of the sea. We'd all skated or slipped in the fish markets of Kuala Trengganu, but cousin Dah was the only family member I know who'd had the fish market come crashing down on her.

*Peraih*s were middlemen who waited all day in coffee shops, then sprang to life late in the afternoon when the *payang* boats came back to shore. They were tough cookies and hard bargainers. Each wore baggy khaki shorts draped over with a *batik sarung*, rolled up to the knee with its hem pulled up and tucked into the waistband. On cooler days they'd discard the *terendak* and wrap their heads in a band of long material, quite in the way of the Kelantanese *semutar*. By five o'clock, at *peraih* speed, the fish—*kembong, selar kuning, ikang keras ekor, ikan jebong* and the occasional *ttuke,* probably cousin to the skate or *pari*—would be in the Ladang market opposite my old Malay school, the sea smell wafting to the roundabout later made famous by the Trengganu turtle.

As it happened, cousin Dah was crossing the road when the *tok peraih* came at breakneck speed on his way to an important customer. She fell to the road in shock but was otherwise unhurt, and her pride smelt of fish that day. The *tok peraih* merely shook his head in disbelief and continued on his urgent journey, while his one free hand pressed even more agitatedly on the rubber bulb of his handlebar horn that went *phat-phat* all the way.

Late afternoon was *peraih* time in the streets of coastal Kuala Trengganu, when these fish couriers pedalled fast and furious to their customer retailers in Ladang, Pasir Panjang or Chabang Tiga, that bustling market at the intersection of roads that took us to deeper parts of Trengganu.

This incident of cousin Dah and the middleman was one that I savoured with much hilarity—only after discovering that she was physically unscathed, of course—because the *peraih*s were busy and sturdy men who were only visible at speed, and there wasn't one that I knew personally. You only saw them when they were dismounted among the market stallholders, and that was after their business was done as they walked about with their sarong skirts lifted like stage curtains half-drawn when the show was nearly over. And then they'd disperse and disappear till the butt end of the following business day, with their bicycle horns going *phat-phat, phat-phat,* warning people like cousin Dah of their pace of travel.

I remember Ladang not only because Dah came to grief with a basket of fish near there on that fateful day. At *peraih* speed, it was a good few minutes still from Ladang that she met the flying wheel: a place near the bend known to us as Tanjong Mengabang, in a landscape of coastal shacks, smart houses and coconut trees all the way to the sea. Tanjong

Mengabang had a peculiar hum about it, and a funny breeze that blew in a certain chill.

When Mother told me stories of Trengganu past, she often spoke of Pök Mat Ngammok who, one day, went berserk after some matrimonial crisis and went on a killing spree. Pök Mat was buried there, she said, among the coconut trees of Tanjung Mengabang, and funnily enough it was near the house of another Pök Mat, a telecoms linesman during the day, who was often at our house at weekends for some carpentry work. In those days my father was a telephone operator at the Kuala Trengganu exchange and Pök Mat was the man who put those copper lines on poles that stretched as far as you could see; so they shared a certain camaraderie.

It was near Pök Mat's house that cousin Dah had her piscatorial day, but it wasn't something that he remembered clearly. Just over three years ago, when I saw my father for the last time, we were chatting in front of the house in Kuala Lumpur when a car drove into the driveway and out from the passenger side came a rheumy-eyed man so full of smile. This was the same Pök Mat of years ago who perched on poles among copper wires, but now he was walking very slowly.

My father and he had a lot to talk about as they'd not seen each other for many years. Then Pök Mat asked about a certain person, my father's friend, who used to be Pök Mat's boss at the telephone exchange in Kuala Trengganu. He'd come to Kuala Lumpur with a purpose, Pök Mat said, because many years ago the boss gave him fifteen ringgit too many in his pay packet, and now he wanted to hand it back before he went to his Maker.

Ferry Across the Water

TO MOVE ONWARD TO BESUT after the bustle of Kuala Trengganu the bus had to go down a slope and struggle up a ramp onto the ferry at Bukit Datu. It was a hairy experience, but too late to turn back now as there were scores of other vehicles, big and small, in the tailback waiting to pour into the dip for a ride across the swell.

The ferry was a raft of blocks of wood that took the weight of four or six vehicles, assorted pedestrians and people cycling into the yonder. In one of its most menacing parts, a tugboat pulled it across the Trengganu River to the bank where the journey continued through isolated villages and deep jungle.

Ferries crossed many rivers in Trengganu then. In Dungun there was a ferry point, and in Kemaman there was one at a place called Geliga. An express bus once slipped its brakes on the deep incline to the ferry and dove into the swell. I remember that early evening in Kuala Trengganu when our poor cousin from Seberang Takir came back quite dead and sodden with other unfortunate souls, all laid out in the back of a lorry.

The road to Besut was heat and dust over a long stretch that wound and dipped along the road that ran on forever. In the monsoon months, seen through the condensation on the window, the view became a smudgy watercolour, leaves smeared green against a brooding sky and the continual swish, swish, swish of windscreen wipers. Kampung Raja in Besut wasn't sixty miles from Kuala Trengganu, but it seemed a very long way.

We were taken there during school holidays to meet cousins, uncles, aunties and more cousins twice removed, and *tok*s galore. *Tok*s were older people—grandfathers, grandmothers, grand uncles and anyone else dressed in *sarung pelikat* and Malay *baju* with the walking stick of senior years. Kampung Raja was dark during the night and long during the day but always, always there was a gaggle of people.

My grandfather had a sprawling house in Kampung Raja, meaning Village of the Ruler, opposite a Malay school. It was as big a house as a child could imagine, with capacity to accommodate a few coachloads of people if the occasion called for it. But sometimes occasion didn't, and it'd be quieter then with ladies rustling up things in the back and my grandfather at his table by the window, poring over some dog-eared *kitab*s. He kept spotted doves and puffed on cigarettes made from sun-dried leaves filled with tobacco strands, then rolled into a thin needle-shaped cigarella. Kampung Raja was quiet—unsettlingly so—even in the daytime. There'd be the occasional rumble of a motorcar in the distance, or some murmur of conversation from passers-by; then the birds, bored by their life in captivity, would lament it so: *kur-kur, kur-kur* came their woeful tales. The Malays call them the *tekukur*.

In the daytime when my cousins were distracted by their own things, I'd walk the ground and stuff myself on *jambu,* or water apple, or star fruit that hung from scrawny trees. Or sometimes I'd walk barefoot across the soft sand in front of the house to the spreading cashew trees—known here as *pokok ketereh*—by the roadside. The cashew tree is useless to a growing child, its funny fruit inedible, but adults pluck its shoots and serve it at the dining table as *ulam* to be dipped in *budu,* the dark fish sauce of Trengganu.

At night, when the *lampu pam* came out, we sat under its bright light to dine on white sheets spread out on the floor. Then the pressure lanterns would hiss the night away, their light fading steadily come the midnight hour. The *lampu pam* lit many homes and many roadside stalls in Trengganu, their fabric mantles glowing brightly under pressure and kerosene power.

Late into the night, when the pressure dropped and the light turned yellow, we'd gather around Ayöh Ngöh (Father's brother) and urge him to tell us a story. No, he'd say, he had to go, then he'd relent and tell us a wonderful tale spun out there on the fly—the epic journey of Pök Wè. Pök Wé was an unlikely sarong-wearing, *baju*-clad man, the *ketayap* topped hero of Trengganu. Ayöh Ngöh's Pök Wè was a plucky man with terrible indiscretions, who thought nothing of repelling the odd adversary by breaking wind. His speaciality, said Ayöh Ngöh, was the *kentut singgang,* his wind power basted in terrible concoctions and served like *singgang*, that special dish of Trengganu.

When even Pök Wè became tired and the lamp mantle grew even dimmer, Ayöh Ngöh would rise and put out the diminishing mantle. Semi-darkness would descend on the room and we knew it was time for sleep and for Pök Wè to go.

Raja of Besut

THE SMALL TOWN OF KAMPUNG RAJA slept at the end of a road; going further still you'd have fallen into the river. It was the Besut River, probably, with coconut-lined banks, bushes on the other side, broad expanses canopied in leaves with little kids picking up pebbles and throwing them back into the water. My grandmother's cousin twice removed—or perhaps closer than that—lived on the side on the incline that ended the road, in a row of wooden shophouses that never had any shops, but he struck his trade mostly in gold, making rings and burnishing the metal. He worked too in silver, polished stones into shape and placed them on pendants and rings for nuptials. He knew the occult qualities of rubies, amethysts and emeralds. He beat metal and spun yarns as he worked, polishing stones until they glowed. Once, he pared off the solid part from the beak of a big bird we knew only as the *nilling* and shaped the *paruh* of the *nilling* to sit atop a ring as a stone of dull yellow.

I never found out what or who the *nilling* was but that, for me, was part of the mystery of our grandmother's twice removed Tok Cik Li, the jolly goldsmith of Kampung Raja.

The Kampung Raja that I remember was a quiet corner of Trengganu, with two shops in its town centre that was just around the corner from the

Grandfather in full regalia.

workshop of Tok Cik Li. One shop was run by a man we knew as Cik Bbakar, and the other by the family of a man called Wang Semail. In front of the shop was a market that had raised slabs on which the sellers placed their wares: fish, herbs, fruit and meat. By noon the market dissipated into the murmurs of just a few people who were still there to exchange homilies of the day; goats moved in quickly and sat between the slabs, looking as disgruntled as they ever were, before the market people came back again after *asar*.

Our grandparents lived in Besut, as well as cousins, aunties and Tok Nyang who lived in a house under the *tar* tree. The *tar* was actually the *lontar*, a straight-stemmed, tall tree with leaves that spread out like fans and fruit that settled in a dish and looked very much like jelly. Tok Nyang was frail and old from having seen too many monsoons blow, but I knew even then that she made the best jackfruit preserve in this whole world.

Kampung Raja was a long way away from us, even if it was only sixty miles. We rode the bus that took nearly half a day, past the tumult of Chabang Tiga, then down a straight road through padi fields, down an incline and then finally onto the ferry of Bukit Datu. The ferry was pulled by a tug to the other side where the road wended into deep forests, wide spaces of grass and clusters of trees; and then a solitary woman would cross the road to return to her house behind the hills. Then as the bus whirred round the bend in Sungai Tong or Chalok, we craned our necks to the right as Mother pointed out our cousin's house that perched on the slope on the roadside that also served as the local grocery.

The Kampung Raja that we went to had beach-like sand that gave growth to the cashew. We walked the footpaths that were beaten in the grass, and there were clusters of *kemunting* along the way. The sky was vast and it was quiet all around us, even in the middle of the day. And then we heard Besutspeak, its sing-song lilt more Kelantan than Trengganu and made the Wang in the shopkeeper's name into something of a Wèh. We even heard that Besut was once a province of Kelantan that was lost to Trengganu in a cockfight, but I have not been able to trace or confirm this with certainty.

Our grandfather stood in an embroidered hat with that stern look of office, in his crisp, white, starched dress uniform like some functionary in the photographs hanging on the wall. When we knew him he was already retired, and wore his regular mufti of the *kain pelikat* and Malay *baju*, his head wrapped in the white *serban* of the Haji. Once or twice he pointed out to us the imposing house down the road, past Tok Nyang's rambling shack, past the tall, broad-leaved *tar* trees. He said it was the *istana* of Tengku Indera. We walked past the house many a time and looked to see if Tengku Indera was looking out at us because grandfather made it sound as if he was there still.

But I've since found out that Tengku Indera (who also went by the name of Tengku Long) in fact died years before, in 1936, and he was the last Raja of Besut in the palace that was built for him in 1879 by Besut craftsman Long Yusoff and his band of local carpenters. That gave rise to the origin of Kampung Raja as it is still called today. The palace, built entirely of wood with carved panels on its doors, walls and many windows, contained not a single nail. It was completed in 1881 and still stands today, but in another place, in Kuala Trengganu, as a showpiece of the skills of our forefathers. It saddens me that it no longer stands where it's meant to be.

Besut came to the attention of Sultan Mansur Shah (1726–1793) when pirates arrived to turn this sleepy fishing village into a riotous assembly. The sultan sent his son Tengku Kadir to drive them out (they fled to Pulau Perhentian, we are told) and as soon as the coast was clear, the sultan felt that his son deserved some reward so he made him head of the locality, and that was the first act in the naming of Kampung Raja.

Wind-lashed Waters

IT'S NOT SURPRISING how Trengganu is peopled by folk with water-drenched souls. Trengganu was as wet as wet could be—there was rain, floods and ferries across rivers of milky tea. Then there was the river mouth of the Trengganu, the river itself and the *kuala* that gave the capital its name, a long snake's body that stretched from the *ulu* where dark and deep primaeval dreams lurked to haunt the polity.

The Chinese Turcoman traveller Zheng He came to Trengganu of the Ulu in days when sea travel held sway. He must've created quite an impression in his finery, walking on the earth that was soon to be revered by Trengganu's own Chinese community, to the spirit of Ong Sam Po. He was a Muslim who later travelled to Makkah by ship but died at sea before reaching Arabian shores. His graves are many, in various places, consecrated not for his body's repose but in memory of his spirit and soul. Admiral Zheng He was buried as he had lived: at sea.

In Trengganu during the monsoon months, when the rain paused awhile but the wind still came with gusto, we used to walk along the beach of Pantai Tanjung to see the debris swept up by the waves—piles and piles of twigs, branches and driftwood aplenty. Sometimes there were dead animals, and once there was the bloated body of a poor soul. That created a buzz. But mostly we went looking for a flat seed with a very tough shell the colour of ebony called *buöh gömök*. This was a flat piece that could be thrown and was used in games that children played, or as a keepsake to spit on, polish and show to friends at school.

Sometimes there came ashore long thin weeds called *rumput jjulok* which we took home. We pushed out their spongy spaghetti-like cores that we soaked in dye and shaped into pretty flowers. They were sent to occupy us on rainy days.

Further inland were padi fields (the *sawöh*) and *paya* marshlands, nearer the hills that we saw as distant shapes from our windswept shore area. The rice fields gave a different kind of shape to the people living there. During the monsoon season this flat land became waterlogged, and fish and leeches came out in its overspill. It must have been a source of joy to the young and the young at heart, but we were too far removed from there. Also inland, water opened new avenues for joy, like the concrete *jerömböng* tunnels that were meant to drain the water on soggy days and wash the kids away, in play of course.

Near my school, the Sultan Sulaiman Primary, there was a *sawöh* on one side of the road and a marshy *paya* on the other. For some reason we ignored the padi but jumped heartily into the pond for its magic-carpet quality. On the surface of this long stretch of still water were lotus leaves and varieties of exquisitely shaped water lilies; but mostly we were intrigued by the long-tendrilled water plants that knitted into each other's arms to form a spread of carpet over the surface of the water, with green, red, blue and yellow—leaves, shoots and flowers. There were bees abuzzing overhead and in between the myriad colours, and dragonflies' humming wings, sometimes punctuated by the lowing of the distant water buffalo. Our water mat was of the most magical quality, strong enough to take even an adult's weight as it bobbed up and down gently over the mysterious depth that lay hidden down below. I knew there were leeches lurking there as sometimes we saw them stick steadfastly to the legs of cows, and sometimes we even scooped them out of the water only to have them slip through our fingers and go their slippery way, looking for cows that weren't bothered by their bloodsucking ways.

Closer to the school, in the school grounds itself at the far end of the playing field, was a vast mound of shrubbery and creepers that had many hidden passages and tunnels that we crept into when it was sunny and mischief was the order of the day.

Those were long days and fine days, and days when we didn't have a care in the world.

Rainy-day People

IN THE MONSOON MONTHS of extended bleakness, the sea gave a constant roar. Most days were too wet to venture out, or too dreary in the in-between periods when the sky momentarily held back the seasonal downpour. Chilly wind and maids a-scrambling when the sky burst open again; market vendors unfurling green waxed-paper umbrellas. They sat still on their mats of pandan leaves or on plastic sheets, soon to be surrounded by the puddles.

Rain of many types fell on Kuala Trengganu, some drizzly wizzly, some in the middle of a sunny day, and occasionally what we called the *hujang hambat Orang Tua,* the playful rain that sent elderly folk scrambling only to pull back instantly to that place behind the clouds where rain normally hid once the old folks had found shelter. The monsoons brought serious rain, not *hujang* for the *Orang Tua*. It rained and rained for days on end, the sky a dirty grey colour. Melancholy gripped us by the jugular.

I used to stand at the window at the back of our house on days like that, looking out towards the open sea hardly a mile away. I could not see the sea though for the houses and the trees, but the noise was hauntingly near, of waves lashing and beating ashore like distant tigers caught in watery snares. Early mornings were made cheerier by the masses of traders who came down to the market with fruits and vegetables, fish and household wares. South Indian shopkeepers in the spice alley pulled plastic covers over their sacks of coriander, dried chillies and shallots heaped out in front boxes. Then they stretched out the tarpaulins from the front edge of their roof to attach to the front roof of their opposite neighbour. Spice alley was safe from the daily downpour.

I'd watch all this from our front window which looked out onto the market corner. I saw people waiting under shop awnings for some let-up, traders hurrying wearing their conical *terendak* hats, or under the *samir,* made from dried palm fronds spread over a rattan frame that men wore over their heads and their backs like the stiff wing of an exotic fly. The rain roused moods with different rhythms, as coffee shops filled up with people detained by the weather, brooding over hot cups of tea.

In the kitchen Mother would make rainy-day food, like tapioca boiled with a hint of salt and to be eaten with sugar, a dab at a time, as we watched the people hurrying by. Sometimes she'd throw sweet potatoes into the wood fire, or some bananas the likes of which I don't see now. When all was quiet in the afternoon except for the distant roar of the sea, and when the rain had let up awhile, I'd be sent out, umbrella in hand, to Mök Nöh who sold *putu piring* from a gap in her fence of woven bamboo. *Putu piring* was tapioca flour, filled into a dipped dish then sprinkled in the centre with brown coconut sugar. After that it was covered again with tapioca flour, and compacted with another dish to take the shape of a flying saucer. These pieces of art were wrapped in white linen and placed in groups of three or four in a steamer, to emerge again minutes later in a head of steam that put the heat in the Trengganu winter. Mök Nöh also made a *de luxe* version called *putu halba,* with fenugreek, coconut sugar and rice flour.

The monsoon rains stopped many things: fishermen came home to sulk on the shore, newspapers from the west coast were kept out by floods that sank the roads, and Kuala Trengganu became what it really was, a marooned island by a roaring sea.

The Trengganu River flowed more fiercely now, slowed down only momentarily at the *kuala* where pure-white surf mixed with the gushing colour of milky tea. *'Air hulu turun döh,'* ('The *ulu* water has come down,') Mother would say when this happened, giving the signal that we were in for a long period of uncertain weather.

It's the wind that I remember most, wind that came down in a gusty chill as I waited for that *putu* in that gap in Mök Nöh's curtain of bamboo.

A Word in the Head

MY LIFE IN TRENGGANU was very brief, having left it when I was still in shorts; but memories etched there have been the most lasting and, if anything, have enriched my life. Many years ago, sitting one night on the deck of a rickety passenger boat on Lake Nasser in Egypt, we were looking up at the starry sky, a group of us—assorted wanderers from many parts of the globe: Egyptian fellahin, young backpackers, an Egyptian lad and his travelling mate who looked at me and said, 'You're a Muslim, I love you very much,' then offered me bread to dip in molasses. Then a New York doctor named R. Binder pointed to the sky and said, 'Look, the Big Dipper, it always points to The North Star.' And there it was, the Plough (or Big Dipper, as Americans call it), with its bucket edge pointing to Polaris, The North Star, bright as a jewel.

I had just travelled across North Africa then, and was proceeding towards Wadi Halfa in Sudan to catch a train to the little village of Atbara. I was still very green, and the world, especially then, seemed a very strange place. I was longing for my own northern star; a strange sensation to have in the head (or heart) especially as I'd already left Trengganu many years before; but travelling takes you back to strange places.

And as I sat there on the boat that rolled gently in the calm night, I was thinking of Pasar Tanjong, Kedai Payang, Cherong Lanjut and Kuala Ibai of my schooldays, of *putri mandi* and *nekbat,* and Mök Nöh's *rökök Arab.* Trengganu was calling me again, so I went home, went back to the town and saw it still intact. Soon after that my mother died and was buried under a tree in an old cemetery in Ladang, not far from the roundabout of the turtle.

Trengganu has a strange hold on people. Even those not Trengganu-born but who stay there only briefly get bitten by a strange bug. I had a very good schoolfriend in Trengganu who was born in Perak but spoke Trengganuspeak with great gusto.

Blown in by the Wind

THE BIG BOATS ARRIVED FROM THAILAND with bags of salt or Senggora tiles. These were the *perahu besar* of Trengganu, or the *perahu bedar* often seen moored in the *teluk* inlet just by the shore near our home. We had a friend named Wang Kalèh—whose real name I believe was Wan Sallèh—whose father sailed these coastal waters. His name was Wang Mang—again, perhaps Wan Osman in his identity card—so he was widely known as Wang Mang Perahu Besar.

Nearer the *pantai* lived a boy who was my junior at school and who had funny eyes, what the Malays called *mata sabun*. Using the word *sabun* meaning soap didn't indicate that his eyes were soapy but vaguely blue in colour. He was rumoured to be of European descent, probably

The Perahu Besar, *a typical Trengganu sailing boat.*

93

a French man who'd landed, baguette and baggage, on our shore a long time ago. It seemed an unlikely story but an interesting one nevertheless, so I sometimes called him Cher Perancis, which gave him a little smile.

Quite recently, after I'd made some serendipitous discovery about the *pinas* boats of Trengganu, Cher came back to me in a different way. The word *pinas,* as I discovered, came to Trengganu from the French and German word *pinasse,* which means a medium-sized sailing boat. In the 1840s a certain Frenchman by the name of Martin Perrot came ashore in Kuala Trengganu and married a local girl. When his name reached the sultan of that time, Sultan Baginda Omar (1839–1876), he was summoned to the palace and ordered to design a royal schooner to match any Western ·vessel. And so began the journey of the *pinasse* or *pinas* in Trengganu waters.

The big boat of Wang Mang, I'd venture to say, must've been a descendant of the *pinasse* that sent Trengganu men far and wide into the archipelago. Wang Mang brought goods home, mostly from Thailand: bags of rice or crystallised salt in bulging bags woven from pandan leaves, and maybe even the ghost hair seaweed, *kerabu sereh* that we soaked overnight in water and ate in a sauce of chilli, sugar and vinegar. The weed came entangled in a mesh, felt like cat gut and looked like it came from the head of an unkempt ghost with blonde hair. I never found out what he took with him on his outward journey, though I sometimes wished that he'd take his son Wang Kalèh away from us, if only for a while.

Kuala Trengganu was as isolated as any town could be on the peninsular shore, but as the sea was wide open to us, we were never short of seafaring people. The ship *Hong Ho* came bobbing up and down in the distant waves and dropped anchor within sight of where we were. The *tongkang* barges rowed out to it and came back with bales and bags for local traders. A gunboat once came ashore and filled the streets with Pakistani sailors; and long before that, when those sailors were still kids at school, a lone sailor was washed ashore and felt the same tingling that Monsieur Perrot must've felt years before. He too stayed to marry a local girl.

For some reason we gave him the name Bachök, though he wasn't of Kelantan stock but from Sulawesi across a wide stretch of water. From the stories I heard, Bachök was blown in by the north-east monsoon when he went sailing one Sulawesi day, and the next coast he saw was Kuala Trengganu. I remember Bachök, who was attired in the way of the workmen of Kuala Trengganu: khaki shorts that reached to his knees, with a *batik sarung* wrapped over the top, its hem pulled up and tucked and ruched around his centre. When the ships came in, men who could carry a *pikul* bag of rice on their backs would walk back and forth along the waterfront, cigarettes stuck to lips and billhooks at the ready. But Bachök wasn't like that at all: he walked with a sharp *gölök* or machete and earned his keep by clambering to the top of coconut trees and chopping the trunks into little logs as he journeyed back to earth. Bachök was a coconut-tree cutter extraordinaire.

One day I watched in awe as he cleared three coconut trees from the corner of the market that was in front of our house. The first rule of Bachök climbing was never to follow the local custom of hacking footholds into the trunk; he simply moved up, gripping the tree with hands and feet until he reached the very top. Once there he'd throw down the coconuts one by one, then the leaves would come shooting down, then the part we'd be waiting for, the heart of palm which was a rare treat for us. After that he'd slide down a yard and chop down the first log of trunk that he'd throw down with a big thud after a suitable warning to passers-by. He'd go down another yard and do the same, and then the same again until he was back on firm ground with the once-tall tree just a stump below his knee. Bachök was one of the two Sulawesi people who made me eager to reach manhood; the other was the film star Maria Menado.

Like many people who grew up by the sea, I never learnt to swim at all. But we were acutely aware of the sea, its powers and dangers, and our vocabulary and ways of seeing were influenced accordingly. When we made too much noise in the house, Mother would say that we sounded like the noise of *wakang pecöh,* the noise of shipwrecked sailors. For a long time I thought that the *wakang* of Trengganuspeak was a corruption of *wangkang,* a Chinese ship, perhaps like the one that Admiral Zheng He (Cheng Ho) sailed to Ulu Teresat in the early history of Trengganu. But recently I discovered how wrong I was when the word *padewakang* came my way. It's a Sulawesi word for a seafaring vessel. My mother's *wakang* must have originated from there.

It could've also been the vessel that Bachök came in on when the monsoon winds blew him ashore all those years ago.

Light by the Window

MY GRANDFATHER, AS I REMEMBER HIM, was a lactose-intolerant man who did not suffer fools gladly. He lived in a very large house in Kampung Raja in a street named after Haji Omar, a famous religious scholar of Besut, a place about sixty miles form Kuala Trengganu. His was a long road, untarred and unpeopled; not that Kampung Raja was underpopulated but its people always seemed to be engaged elsewhere for the most part of the day. It was one of those rural roads, furrowed by straight bare lines close to the edge on either side, then it had a long straight row in the middle that grew tufts of grass and small, resilient weeds or wild plants with bright flowers.

The edges of the track were shorn down to the bare earth by car tyres, the occasional heavyweight lorries or minibuses that rolled along there by night or day. Cyclists appeared and disappeared again into

A group photograph of a Malay School, Kampung Raja, Besut. This school was next door to Grandfather's house.

96

nowhere, and sometimes drones of conversation reached my ears from the mouths of passers-by when I was somewhere in the *jambu* tree. The house was shielded from the road by a long hedge and a couple of cashew trees which had pear-shaped leaves with fish-bone veins that stood out very prominently. There were straight trees with silvery bark that peeled off in a papery consistency, trees that rose straight up on the side of the compound that rolled only very slightly. I think my grandfather referred to that as the *beris* side, even though the *beris* land was commonly found by the sea, with sandy soil of the whitest purity. On a normal day, with the butterflies flitting about and my grandfather's pet birds cooing occasionally, and the soft morning light glinting off the green of the trees, the countryside had the most wonderful sight and feel. Then a motorbike would rip past from the other end of the road, sending everything into brief cacophony.

There was a fair-sized school opposite the house on the other side of our hedge, but I never saw any life there except in Father's photo album (an old class group photo) as our visits to Kampung Raja were made during term breaks. I only saw groups of people outside Grandfather's house at the end of a short walk to the *pasar* via the rolling road that sloped down to the river. And even then, past noon, the market would have been deserted except for maybe a few people who were popping in and out of shops, of which there were two when I was there: one run by a man called Encik Bakar, and another by a family whose daughter went to Sultan Sulaiman Secondary School in Kuala Trengganu.

The journey to the shops via the *kampung* short cut was better for tasting the delights along the way. There were *kemunting* berries to pick and eat, and a weed that we called *pohon malu,* a shy prickly plant that closed its leaves when you touched it and wouldn't open up again until it knew you were safely away. There was *temucut* everywhere, a long culmed love grass that stood like bottle brush with seeds that pierced deeply into trouser legs, even to the hems of your shorts, for it rose to those heights, but back then we were not very tall. Sometimes we'd walk with our grandfather, a sage with his tuft of grey beard, his shorn head under a white Haji's turban that had a tail which went over his neck. He limped slightly with age, this venerable man in his Malay *baju* and freshly starched sarong that came from Pulicat of India. And there we were, like Pied Piper's children, following in tow, listening to our grandfather's memories of things here and there. Once, mid-sentence, he saw a shallow hole dug in his path, probably by children as an act of mischief for the day. At once Grandfather switched channels, launching into a long tirade against kids and what he'd do with them if ever they came his way.

Grandfather was the patriarch of the family around whom spun our daily life. A host of uncles and aunties in the kitchen and grand uncles and cousins once or twice removed, converged on the house daily. We laid out a huge spread on the floor at lunch and dinner time, and ate *kampung*-reared chicken, and herbs plucked from the hedgerow; and durian fruit mixed into *budu* sauce that was kicked into life with crushed chillies. The shoots of the cashew were cooked with freshly grilled fish, and then there was a funny-tasting fruit that was called something or other, yellow in colour, pickled and tasted oh so foul. *Binjai* it was probably called by the elders.

On quiet days, tired of exploring the *beris* area or the *jambu* trees, we'd walk the quiet road past the *tar* trees. These palmyra palms were mighty and tall, spreading leaves out wider than the coconut tree but with smaller fruits to delight the cognoscenti. (*Tar,* I suspect, is the Besut compression of *lontar,* whose leaves gave writing material to generations of Malay scribes, and whose *nira* fuelled their reverie). We'd stop by the house of Tok Nyang and hear her moan awhile. At her age and with her skinny body bent almost double, she'd every right to do so. But when Tok Nyang made her jackfruit jam and gave it to us in a jar, it was as if the world, the people and the quiet streets of Besut were all united in one happy choir.

I knew little of Besut except for the long straight road of Haji Omar, the shrubs, hedges and the *tar* trees. And the massive house of our grandfather that was always busy with kith and kin and other people. At the break of dawn they'd all rise to pray together, with Grandfather as the *imam*, and Father and Mother, and aunties and uncles all standing to prayer in straight parallel rows in the *surung* of the front of the house that overlooked the *beris* area. As children we were sometimes allowed to sleep on as the prayers took place; and when I woke up on these days to see the grey light already creeping into the corners of the room, I'd hear a comforting murmur of chants coming from different areas.

At sunrise Grandfather would roll his first cigarette and sit by the window, avoiding the bright ray of light. He'd look up to hear the cooing of his pet birds, then he'd open his loose-leaf *kitab* to ponder some theological principles; or he'd make rustling noises as he put on his reading glasses to read the day's *Utusan Melayu*.

Ah Chin and Father

AH CHIN THE TAILOR had a pact with Father: to benchmark all his work to an acceptable style. He carried his measuring tape like a doctor carries his stethoscope, his eyes peering over the lenses of his nose-tip reading glasses, the thickness of the base of a bottle. He stood maybe five feet tall with a few inches more to spare, and he was probably the thinnest man in Kuala Trengganu. He smiled broadly as he wrote into his order book, notes all jotted down in cipher, and into the box for each customer he placed a snip of the desired material. And he had this one-liner—'*Tak boleh yankee-la!*'—that he whispered through his toothy smile. And that was the pact he'd made with Father.

My first trip to Kuala Lumpur and the Merdeka Stadium, 1960s. I followed Father for his job-promotion interview during the middle of my school term.

Our school trousers were all cut on Ah Chin's table, perhaps because, of all the tailors in Trengganu, he was the most compliant to Father's sartorial style. The Ah Chin easy-payment plan must've been another thing that persuaded Father to take us to the bespoke house of this beanpole. Father had his own ideas about how long our shorts should be and the accepted width of flares that Ah Chin executed with alacrity and a smile. No *yankee-lah* just about summed it all up.

Yankee was the Trengganu term for the figure-hugging style, the drainpipe girth of shorts that exposed half your thighs and hugged your bum so the wallet bulged from your back pocket like a table, mountain high. A *yankee* inclination showed a person to be of frivolous mien and with a tendency to whistle at passing gals. The antithesis of this was the dress code of the *mata-mata*, if you remember the policemen of old: skirt-like shorts with double pleats, shorts dropping from a line just above the waist, reaching down to the knees and well below.

Father in his Ah Chin trousers, with me and our KL kinsman En. Nordin.

I have a photo of Father standing proudly in his Ah Chin-tailored twills, hands in pockets that bulged out to show the width of the material. I was standing to his left, in my school uniform whites, shirt perhaps from Globe Silk Store and shorts in full spread to the cut of Ah Chin, our toothful tailor. To our right, in sartorial contrast, was a relative I never knew we had, who was a veritable townie, in a contented pose and standing smart like a true man-about-town fellow.

This was in the KL of old, with dredging companies dragging up the earth in mining pools and rubber estates spanning the edge of town in orderly rows of canopied pillars. There was the Islamic Restaurant in Batu Road and the Stadiums Negara and Merdeka. In fact, it was in the Stadium Meredeka that we were standing on a day when I was playing truant from school to be with Father at his job-promotion interview. The stadium made me gasp in awe, having seen nothing so cavernous in Kuala Trengganu, and as the Petronas Towers are to present-day gawpers, the Stadium Merdeka was then to me.

Father was set in his views on trouser width and how far shorts should hang below the knees, but he was a mischievous man in many ways. On mornings when he'd run me to school, as soon as he'd returned from the mosque he'd jibe and make silly remarks about things he'd seen along the way as I sat sideways on his tall gentleman's Raleigh bicycle, perched on a *kaing ssahang* wrapped around the horizontal bar between him and the bike's handlebars. I knew then that it was against the law to be travelling thus—because Father told me so—but he told me he'd made a pact with the *mata-mata*. He made many pacts like that within the confines of Kuala Trengganu, including one that enabled him to send me to the Sekolah Ladang some two years before my schooling years. As soon as I got off the bike at the primary school (run by a man called Mr Wee Biau Leng, whose headmasterly white shorts were of a width that would have made Father wax lyrical) he'd make a parting joke as I reached into the rear bag of his bike for a *roti paung* or two that he'd bought on his way home from dawn prayers. One day a classmate who caught us in our shared glee gave me a puzzled look. 'Who's that man who dropped you here?' he asked. When I told him that that was my father, he came back in astonishment: 'Why were you both so gleeful?'

One night Father told us of Ah Chin's weakness for the smoke. He told us that Ah Chin had been visited earlier in the day as he was sitting in his darkened room at the top of his stairs—the *loteng* as we called it in Trengganu—puffing on his exotic pipe, and floating with the smoke that made him drowsy and wafting into a higher fantasia. There were things thrown out of the window, Father said, the sound of shattering glass and the rush of enforcement officers—he'd heard it all as he passed by on his way to prayers. We held our breaths for our beanpole of a smiling man. During the Ramadan that came after that, Father took us back to Kampung Daik to be kitted up again for Hari Raya; and I was happy to see that our tailor was still there to measure us and renew his pact with Father, looking as he always did, like he'd just emerged from a crack in the door. As he pulled out his tape measure and jotted notes into his book, he gave Father a knowing smile.

Just a pip's throw from Ah Chin, over the bridge opposite the red fire engines of Kampung Daik, was a shop known as the *kedai bbunga*, a name which was Trengganuspeak for 'the flowered shop'. It could have been its wallpaper that gave the shop its name, but I can't say that for sure. In it was a man who seldom wore a shirt, but stood in a pair of what was the precursor to boxer shorts. With thin dark stripes running vertically, the shorts were held around his waist by a string that ran through a waistband and knotted in a bow just above the button of his belly.

Father had a little book there which the man—who was known to Mother as Awang—kept in a fair-sized tin that he hung from his ceiling and which he pulled down when needed by the device of a little pulley. On the cover of the notebook were the figures '555', a standard type of notebook kept by many shops to keep track of the credit records of their customers.

The *kedai bbunga* smelt of apples, bananas and the *buöh lai,* which was the Japanese pear. There were biscuits made by the Thye Hong company, and little balls of crunchy biscuits topped with little twirls of coloured sugar. There were preserves from the land of Awang's ancestors, Chinese dates we in Trengganu called *buöh kerecut* and rugby-ball-shaped Chinese olives, or *buöh kana.* In sacks came preserves of an unknown fruit, with seeds that you spat out once you'd eaten its fleshy parts, sweet and red, with flies scrambling away from it as Awang scooped out your ten cents' worth onto the page of a newspaper. There was *buöh ssemök* in a clear glass jar, flat, dried and coated with a layer of white fungus or maybe sugar. It was many years before I saw the fruit in its fresh, uncompressed shape, going by the name of the Japanese *kaki*.

Awang also kept many things that were invented to make a child's mouth water: Cadbury's Fruit & Nut chocolate bars, Smarties to throw in the air and swallow and biscuits called Reading and Marie. Assorted Huntley & Palmer biscuits came in tins, though we'd be lucky to take one home in a year. And there were grapes, canned lychees and *buöh ddara* the size of a large marble; its dried brown skin thin and brittle. Rattling inside as you shook it was the once succulent flesh of the fruit, now dark; shrivelled and clinging tightly to its dark shiny stone, the size of a small glass marble. I pushed one up my nose one day for reasons that are now obscure to me and was immediately taken to the hospital.

Choc au Lait

AS THE SUN BEAT DOWN TOWARDS MIDDAY, when the sums failed to add up and the alphabets were no longer willing to spell, a van pulling a large cylindrical chamber at its rear arrived just in time by the gate of our school. It had large letters written on its green body, a word that we pronounced 'Mee-lo'. We queued up with the teachers, licked our lips and waited and waited for the long, cool sip that came in a conical paper cup as we pondered the correct pronunciation of Nestlé.

And then, if we were lucky, we'd be walking home with a tablespoonful of the chocolaty powder packed in a plastic sachet.

We were not really Milo fans and rarely used the Milo can in our household. We were Ovaltinees, yes we were, even if that wasn't what we were called in our part of the world. Ovaltine had an orangey image, against the deep green of Milo. But wasn't there then a little logo of a man on the Milo can, all dressed up in animal skin with a dead animal slung over his shoulder?

Much of the marvel of Ovaltine came from its producer, a company I remember as A. Wander, which made me think of Goosey Gander, as in the song sung by us—and our teacher—at school. She also sang to us about the little doggie in the window as she played the piano, but spoilt it all by taking the love-struck girl to a place called Kota Baru where, for me, she remains to this day:

'I must take a trip to Kota Baru
And leave my poor sweetheart alone ...'

At home we scooped Ovaltine into a glass, mixed in dollops of condensed milk, then poured in hot water from a flask. Sometimes we had finger bread, sold by the *bai roti* in a round basket the size of the tyre of the Pahang Mail lorry, perhaps bigger. It was a foot deep and rested on a coil of cloth that sat on the *bai's* head to take the weight of it all. There were rolls baked to a brown crust, soft white bread stuck together like terraced shophouses that we called *roti bata*, crispy biscuits like mini toasts and *suji* that crumbled between your teeth, covering the front of your shirt in fine powder. In a little flat-topped can that the *bai* prised open with his spreading knife was a home-made spread, the gunky, flour-based paste in which eggs were beaten to give it a yellow colour. There was sugar in it too, of course, and coconut milk and maybe even sunset yellow. *Kaya* was creamy, sweet and cooled your gullet on a hot day. But most of all when we had Ovaltine bubbling hot in a glass, we waited for *bai* to come in the noon heat with his round basket of comestibles.

Bai was an Uttar Pradesh man with a twinkle in his eye; I think his name was Abdul Kadir. He had a thick moustache that wagged even as he spoke. His rotund body he squeezed through the frame of our front gate as he bent his knees slightly to avoid toppling his head-basket on the overhanging bar. Then he'd walk up to the kitchen side of our house, wooden stairs creaking under the weight of body and bread. Then, placing himself at the top of the stairs, he'd lower his basket slowly onto the short apron that lay between the stair top and our kitchen threshold. He sat, profused in sweat, muttering homilies about the heat of the day. We'd buy from him the finger-shaped bread, *roti keras* and *kaya* that he'd scoop into a glass, then off he'd go into the light, casting a wide, round shadow.

I'd think of *bai roti* as Akbar the Mughal from my school books but he'd spoil it by leaving on his head as he rested on the stairs not the splendid headdress of the Emperor, but the coiled up rag that dampened the weight of the basket that had been on his head all day.

We bit off the two ends of the *roti keras* and used the open-ended stick to suck up the Ovaltine from the glass, then we'd chew on the moist stick that was already beginning to crumble.

Some days when we couldn't wait for the *bai* we'd spread a thick layer of condensed milk on a slice of bread, then sprinkle Ovaltine powder on it. It was a chocolatey, sweet, doughy treat that revived you after a day at school.

Even now when I see it done by little kids I'm reminded of sunny days.

Pellets of Sweeteners

A MAN IN WHITE lived in a row of shophouses in a dusty street in Kampung Dalam Bata. He was probably tall, as every adult was when you were of a young age, and he wore baggy trousers that narrowed into tight bands at the ankles, and a shirt with front and back flaps that dropped almost to his knees. He smiled as he said, 'How are you?' and chatted a little with Father about this and that before he stooped to look you in the eye.

Dr Qureshi was a reassuring figure and a homoeopathic practitioner long before anyone could spell the word in Trengganu. He gave not jabs into your arm or bum but produced medicine that looked and tasted very much like little pellets of sugar; and they couldn't be touched by your little fingers nor gulped down with steaming tea. I don't know if they did me much good then, but even now I still think of Dr Qureshi whenever I take the occasional dose of *nux vom* or the high potency *pulsatilla*. And then later came another man on the homoeopathic path to our little town of Kuala Trengganu. His name was Dr Burhanuddin al-Helmy. Though he stuck to the principle of fighting like with like, he chose not to do it from a little shop in a quiet street, but through fiery speeches as he peddled his politics from a rostrum in the middle of Padang Malaya.

There were also men in white at the General Hospital who gave you tablets marked M&B, but they were probably not doctors at all but people on a different pedestal whom we called our *dressa* in Trengganuspeak, a loan word from the English 'dresser'. The *dressa* was a useful man to know in those days because he kept you in good supply of M&B, which served as an alternative when homoeopathy was a little slow at treating things like ulcers that wept and had a good following of the bluebottle fly. I remember Mother once pounding the tablets in her stone mortar and pestle and sprinkling the powder into an open sore. We were M&Bers long before we became aficionados of the pink Vinac and white Aspro.

There was a private practice too that catered to the sick in Kuala Trengganu, run by a man called Dr Sunder Raj who lived in a big house on the beach and had a thriving clinic in Kampung China. I probably met the man once or twice when he prodded my chest with his stethoscope, but mostly we saw those anonymous doctors or our competent *dressa* who sat in the local hospital and prodded our tongues for free.

Besides homoeopathy we had other alternative ways too when we ailed. Pak Haji Ali was a handsome elderly man with a grey moustache and a dignified manner, who kept a cool head under his turban wrap and a little cloth bag of roots and herbs. He also had a thick stick that he rubbed and rubbed on a stone slab that held a little water in its dipped centre. When the water turned brown from the stain of the wood, he'd pour it into a cup and held it close to his mumbling lips while he invoked the names of the Almighty. Not surprisingly, Pak Ali also taught the Qur'an from the verandah of his tall house that had a huge *kölöh,* or open water tank, at the bottom of his stairs. He was a teacher and a consummate practitioner, and was the kindest man that I knew.

There were bone setters and itinerant medicine sellers, with snakes, magic and loud megaphones to attract the daily punter. There was a man who came and went then came back again when the weather was right to bellow his name into a megaphone on the sideline as the market was in full sway. 'Come, come, come to Abdul Rahman Siam,' he would say, so he was probably a Thai national. He pulled out teeth by the slightest tug of his thumb and index finger. Any man with the slightest wobble, or a sturdy but aching molar, or who was probably tired of the old gnasher would make a beeline for him as a circle of spectators around him grew. Abdul Rahman took a wad of cotton wool, and dabbed it in his magic fluid that was deep and dark in the bottle. 'Cough!' he'd say as he gripped your ailing tooth, then out it came, root and all, and you wouldn't even flinch. Another tooth thrown into the pile that he'd placed before him on a mat, molars of many edentates from here to the Thai border. There was Tabib Ahmad Turki and Wak Malaya, and a man who did rude things with a short stick he kept waving at the punters. There were Indian men too with their performing children in tow, patent medicine and magic tricks, joining this roll call of street theatre.

But even in its strait-laced ways, orthodox medicine had its adventurers too. My grandmother in Besut had her regular doctor in Kota Baru, but for a while she was looked after by a Dr Alija, who came to her from a distant shore. For the first time, perhaps, we had a medical doctor from Sarajevo when it was still in Yugoslavia, and he became a native of Trengganu.

One morning some years ago, as I stood looking at the sunlight radiating from the backs of people going to work on the Lateiner bridge, I was thinking of Dr Alija. This was the famous bridge on the River Nilgacka on which a car sped one morning in 1914 with the mortally wounded Archduke Ferdinand and his wife, Sophie. I had come to see Sarajevo, the home city of my grandmother's doctor, but he was not there in his native soil. He'd been laid to rest for many years in the Sheikh Ibrahim Cemetery in the earth of Trengganu.

One day in the 1970s in Kuala Brang, Dr Alija caught a bus that was headed for the Kuala, not knowing that his journey was already nearing its end. Somewhere along the way he went to sleep and was taken to another place. He was a good man who practised his skills in exile and breathed his last as the traveller that he was, on a bus in Trengganu.

Ramadan With Father

FATHER NEVER FUSSED about Ramadan; he ate what we had but made the only concession to this special month with iced water. It came in a jug with *selasih* seeds floating like frog's spawn in a pond of pink. Mother made *air sirap* with pandan leaf, red food dye, drops of vanilla essence and oodles of white sugar that she stirred and stirred till all the sugary crust melted into the water. Then, when the kitchen air was filled with an aroma of sweet vanilla and the perfume of pandan, she left the concoction to cool down in an enamel pot before pouring it out in clear glass bottles.

We sat on the floor around a low table. Ramadan made our bellies cold from a surfeit of ice, and we'd make silent promises that we'd not take another drop of that cold tummy-bloating, sweet, coloured water with tadpole spawn floating in it that slid merrily down our gullets at each *iftar*. And the next day we sat again around the low table and broke the promise again and then again the day after.

Father rose early from the *iftar* table to do the dusk prayer. Then he'd hem and haw, put on his crisp sarong and his top of Malay *baju*, and he'd walk or cycle to the Masjid Abidin in Kuala Trengganu for the long Ramadan night prayer.

Kuala Trengganu Ramadan days were a din of sounds: the clanging of the brass bell on Bukit Putri, the cannon blasts from Bukit Besar, the throbbing drums from the *surau*. The murmur of sounds from the

Father on a cycling trip, 29 January 1955, probably on the road to Besut.

community well never ceased from sunset until the time of *sahur,* our first and last meal in the morning when Mother woke us up with her persistent calls as she fussed in the kitchen to heat up the leftovers from our Ramadan dinner.

Father would've already been up then, easily beating us by a solid hour. He prayed extra prayers during Ramadan, and read the Qur'an while waiting for the time for *sahur.*

This year, as Ramadan came, I saw Father again and when I was home, I felt him even closer. We were no longer in Kuala Trengganu but Kuala Lumpur. I opened the wardrobe and saw the *sarung pelikat* that Father had folded and stacked up in neat piles from his days of yesteryear. I took one that had deep blue and off-green stripes, and never felt closer to Father. His smell, the familiarity of how he looked, this reminder that he'd left us, that we once had Father dear.

I put it on but didn't have the heart to try one of his many *baju*s. Bravely I walked his walk to our local mosque to do the first Ramadan prayer.

Father had been dead four years, but he did so without a fuss. He went to pray on a Friday when I was away in London not knowing that he was out on his last leg, that earlier he had complained of being very tired—but he was never tired of his prayer. So he walked out on his last day with a grandchild (my niece) in tow who was fussing over him with an umbrella. It was Friday noon like any other, when the mosque was full. Father walked in the noon-day heat, and in the mosque he started to pace the carpeted floor. A friend who saw him that day said he saw him walk down to the ablution area then, unusually for Father, he came back and took his place in the back row.

God called him home as he was bowing to Him in prayer.

This was the Ramadan when I so poignantly remembered Father as I had only his clothes and his sarong to wear to prayer while I was here. He had kept them neatly folded in his wardrobe where he also kept his many *kopiah* that bore the signs of having been on his head in all weather, and worn out by years of prostration and prayer. I wore one to the mosque that day after I had put on his sarong but I did not have the heart to wear also one of his *baju*; and as this was the start of Ramadan, I remembered Ramadans, and I remembered especially Father dear.

Dee dee dee dit—dah, dah

THE LIGHT OF THE PRESENT has limited reach when you open the door slightly to the dark back room of your past. I can remember Sekolah Ladang, but only a few of my school friends' names remain intact. There must've been at least thirty pupils in that class when one day the teacher, Cik Gu Wan Chik, asked if *kucing* was 'cat' or 'cup' in the English language. He was an enquirer in that instance, not in his role as my teacher. And for reasons best known to him he thought that out of his many pupils, I was tutored in English at home and he spoke to me in camaraderie as he was himself a learner. I think I told him it was 'cup' for cat on that day, and he left it at that and never said anything more.

In the few times that I returned to Kuala Trengganu after we'd left our Tanjong home, I remember seeing Cik Gu Wan Chik emerging from his beach house on his Norton motorbike. I remember him smiling at me, and I hoped to God that he'd forgiven me for having misled him into leaving his cups out to catch the mice. I don't remember what he taught us at school, or the things he wrote on the board, or any stories that he could've told to keep us still.

One day a man with his clean white shirt stiff with starch turned up at school to stick bits of sticky plaster to our chest. I had to place

Father hard at work at the telegraph office.

half a coconut shell over it that night as I bathed at the well, to keep it dry and intact. Then the next day the plasters were lifted off our chests, and we were sorted out into two groups. The lucky ones—there weren't many—were asked to move away, then the rest of us were called out in alphabetical order. My name was near the bottom so I had time to tremble and look at the goings on that produced cries of 'Ouch!' and tears. Shielded behind an empty tin of Huntley & Palmers turned on its side, a nurse was sterilising a needle in an open flame. Then, when this was quite ready (when it cooled down, I supposed and hoped) the syringe was filled with some demon-killing fluid and the needle jabbed into our puny shoulders on the left hand side. I remember being close to tears as the sharp pain lingered even as I walked away from the starched man, his accompanying nurse, her needle and the upturned Huntley & Palmers tin. There were boys sniffing quietly at the side, and other boys jeering at the 'softies' now found among us. I still have a little bump on the left side of my arm from that BCG jab. BCG was for TB, said Cik Gu Wan Chik. And I'm pleased to say that I've not caught TB since that day.

The Sekolah Ladang then had an atap roof and stood on low stilts over sandy earth. In the sand lived little creatures named *cik ru* that had no discernible role in life that I knew. On those days when my heart was laden with *ru*, I'd crawl beneath the schoolhouse to fish one out and tether it to a strand of hair. This was a delicate job helped by my state of youth and my lack of role in life's roll call. The *cik ru* would be kept in a matchbox until I grew tired of its antics, or lack of. And then I'd let it go. At home on some warm nights I'd catch an earth-coloured beetle that tapped continuously on a matchbox with its sturdy little head. Tap, tap, tap it sent out its message into the night on a little Chilli Brand matchbox made in the Kelantan Match Factory.

The only person I remember from Ladang, though I can't remember if he was from our school, was a lad named Pök Ang. How a boy just slightly older than us became a 'Pök' I never knew, but he was bigger than most of us and was, in the prejudiced eyes of us kids, a human *rèmpéyék* because he was fishy, nutty and something of a cracker too. I feared him for what I thought he could do, but I never saw him beat or bully anyone. It was just his intimidating presence that kept us in a state of fear.

Father sent me, at a very early age, to Sekolah Ladang because he was a friend of Cik Gu Mat Jeng (Zain), and he thought I was better off at school than at home. Being a passenger rather than a fully enrolled member of the class, I enjoyed many privileges, like being able to turn up at school long after the early-morning line-up, long after the other pupils had done the obligatory horticultural work in the infertile Sekolah Ladang soil. I remember walking to school one fresh bright morning after Mother had combed my hair and given me my pocket money (fifteen cents, I think). Then I walked towards Tanjung Jamban Hijau in the most beautiful morning light, then took the short cut to school through the *kampung,* past the house of P. Jalil, over a tree trunk laid across a brook that had a cluster of bamboo creaking nearby. The noise of the rustling trees and the birds chirping merrily in the soft light invigorates me even now.

We had a variety of people in Kuala Trengganu to distract us from the banality of our daily life: there was Cik Bagus (Mr Good) who did odd jobs in the pasar but declined to work too hard because, he said, it would damage his *urat kentut,* or fart channel. There was Cik Mat Lembèk, the market man who wielded a stout staff to prop himself up because his legs were weakened from childhood polio—but a man whom God, in His mercy, kept in full voice. And then there was Pök Wè Kengkèng who walked like a man who'd just been lifted off a horse, legs kept permanently apart, hence his name. He had a roll of cloth coiled on his head like a petrified snake when he came to our house to grind spices on a stone slab. By self-acclaim, he had travelled widely in his youth. One day, in distemper, he interrogated my brother in Strangespeak. '*Hang nak pi mana*?' ('Where are you going to?') he barked, saying it was the tongue of the state of Kedah. I couldn't tell what got him into that mood or why he was haranguing my brother with the inquisitiveness of our north-westerly neighbour.

We lived in a tall house with rooms of space, built in the 1920s by workmen brought down from Besut by our grandpa. Next door to us was a *surau* named after a luminary called Tok Sheikh Kadir, who came, I believe, from Patani from whence came many other luminaries that gave much to our life and lore. A daily stream of people dropped by our house: friends and relatives, traders and wayfarers, itinerant scholars and *kitab* peddlers. They sometimes stayed the night and gave us a fascinating glimpse of life on the outside: a Tok Guru from Besut, distant relatives from Patani, a clairvoyant *bomoh* from Kota Baru named Pak Acu and two Pathan friends of Father's who brought bales of parachute material in their car that was then, in Trengganu, a novelty cloth that we called *kaing bèlong*. They sold this brightly coloured material the next day in the market, and most ended up as shirts or blouses that put the glow into our Trengganu character.

One day, instead of the tap-tap-tapping of the beetled matchbox in the front *surung* of our house there came a *dee-dee-dit, dah-dah* that went on into the night. Father was a telegraph operator at the post office, and telegraphy in those days was conveyed by the Morse code. That night a friend of Father's named Lockman was preparing to sit for his radio ham examination, and he needed Father to brush up his dots and dashes. *Dee-dee-dit, dah-dah, dee-dit.*

Even after Father retired and returned briefly to Kuala Trengganu, he never stopped being hospitable to friends in need. Before he left for Kuala Lumpur, Retnam worked as an odd-job man at the Kuala Trengganu Telegraph Office (which was opposite the then CEB and the Bangunan Pejabat Ugama), but when Retnam retired at the same time as Father he had nowhere to go, so he came and lived in the confines of our house. I

Father with his office mates outside the telegraph office, early 1960s.

113

remember Retnam having long chats about his working life on telegraph poles with a former colleague named Mohammad, our Pök Mat, who was also a regular at our house. Retnam was a reserved man, skinny, with lanky South Indian legs. He pottered around silently in our little compound, waiting for his mood to come, and when the mood finally came, he made lime pickle that was sheer joy.

Man at the Foothill

AT THE FOOTHILL FACING THE RIVER MOUTH was a cluster of houses and not far from that, a coffee shop that begot Kuala Trengganu's best player of chess. Next door to that, a quaint little place that was a news vendor and a bookshop, run by an interesting man with thick glasses and a Hitlerian patch of hair on his upper lip. He was one of Kuala Trengganu's perpetual *söngkök* wearers. His was one of those old-fashioned *söngkök*s that stood tall on the head and became the target for turbulent *ustaz*s at our local school of Arabic, the Madrasah (later Kolej) Sultan Zainal Abidin. It was a school that produced many local stalwarts: Dato' Wan Abdul Kadir, Trengganu's first minister in the federal government, scholars like Dr Wan Hussein Azmi and the Mufti Dato' Wan Manan from Duyung across the river, and our own Menteri Besar and later ambassador to the Arabs, Dato' Haji Wan Mukhtar.

At Sultan Zainal Abidin, everyone wore long-sleeved shirts and long trousers in spotless white and, of course, the regulation *söngkök*. Every morning before class there were columns of white marching on the stony earth, as if on parade. Once a week there was public speaking and classes on *tajwid*, where persistent mistakes would be rewarded by the clenched fist of the beturbaned and sunglassed *ustaz*, falling hard on the *söngkök*, pushing its rim down to the line just below your brows. Trengganu had a word for this: your *söngkök* was said to be *kerlök*. There'd be much merriment when this happened—gaggles of laughter from the class as the victim muttered softly beneath his breath, 'Oh drats, I thought he was fast asleep behind his shades!'

The bespecled man at the foothill who spotted that interesting moustache was known to us as Che Mat Dök Dèk; to others who knew him well he was just Mat Dèk. He was a very private man who probably concealed much aspiration and hope; to young passers-by he was just a strange man who squinted at you from behind thick bottle-base specs as he sat behind his dangling rows of *Mastika, Qalam* and the *Suara Jabatan Ugama Johor* that were his array of *majallahs*. He also stocked the *utusans Zaman* and *Melayu* and maybe even the *Kanak-Kanak*, but as business was slow in this neck of the woods, you could buy from him Monday's issue of the aforesaid even if you called in a week later. Quite a bit later in this shop's progress, Cik Mat would sometimes padlock his door and go for an hour's drive in his car with a stranger sitting nervously in the driving seat. He became, I think, one of the early driving instructors when cars began to multiply on our roads.

There's disagreement among locals as to the beginning of the sobriquet in Cik Mat's name: some say it came from the first words he learnt in his English class, the 'this' and 'that' and so *dök-dèk*; others say he was a fluent Tamil speaker and, to Trengganu ears, Tamil sounded very much like that. Our uncle who crossed over from Seberang Takir each morning used to hold discourses in his shop on this and that. To him the man's name was contracted to Mat Dèk and I never asked him why this was so—another one of my life's missed opportunities.

Madrasah Sultan Zainal Abidin, the Arabic school next door to my Sekolah Melayu Ladang.

From behind the shop, in the cluster of houses by the hill, came another character named Ustaz Ali whose son it was who became very adept at chess in that coffee shop next door to the driving school-cum-newsagent. Ustaz Ali had connections with the Datuk Amar family who lived in the shadow of Bukit Putri, in a cluster eponymously known as Kampung Datuk. I never found out in which establishment it was that this Encik Ali was *ustaz,* but as we often rolled down on our side on the slope of Padang Malaya on days when political rallies were held, I think I saw him a few times in the company of Dato' Onn Jaafar of the Parti Negara when he used our town as his political base.

From the hill also came another man whom I met often when Father took me to the Masjid, but I knew him better than that as he also worked in a little grocery shop that opened its doors beneath our house on the edge of the Tanjong market. The man was known variously as Che Awang or Che Mat, a talented elder of the Masjid who always looked as if he was suppressing an amusing memory that was just lurking in his head. On most days he'd be in his Malay *baju* top and his *kain pelikat*, and on his head sat a well-worn *söngkök* that grew a brownish band around its bottom edge. Che Awang/Che Mat was also known as Che Awang King George for his resemblance to the English monarch George V that Father once showed me on an old note; and he was a good doppelganger indeed. Che Awang was the only Trengganu person I knew who could do magic tricks, and sometimes he'd speak in a strange tongue that he said was Thai, but I couldn't say if it was real or made up. Sometimes when the mood took him he'd rattle out a string of words in a sing-song tone that sounded very much like an exotic tongue, but one day he told me that it was just a string of Chinese shop names in town that had got stuck in his head. He had a weird sense of humour and great talent, and he walked very briskly, stopping sometimes at a place you'd least expect to give it a long, curious look. Once, he told me of a job opening as a minder of the royal graves in the Masjid. The job required being there at night, in a compartment of the Masjid.

'Why don't you apply for it?' I innocently asked.

'*Nök mitök takut boleh,*' ('I'd like to but if I did I might get the job,') he replied.

There were old houses in Kampung Datuk, even brick ones, and the remains of what looked like an old fort. Datuk Amar was said to have been part of the entourage that came over from Johor to join our Royal House. He was a scholar in his own right, and sometimes he'd sit on the *wakah* near the *surau* that faced the river in Kampung Datuk to catch Yemeni sailors who'd just landed so he could practise his Arabic.

Glistening Cupolas

CUPOLAS CAUGHT THE MORNING LIGHT, glistening as they came out of the oven, six to a row, then six times again, shoulder to shoulder in the tray. Pök Mat pulled the *roti paung* then dabbed *ghee* on them, the gleaming domed tops baked to a light brown. This was Trengganu *ghee*, the *minyök sapi* from the milk of cows of the *Orang Darat* poured into clear glass bottles then bunged with a rolled-up banana leaf. On rainy days the liquid curdled into a corally yellowish-white cloud, or *tidur.* As Mother used to say, it'd gone to sleep. In the heat of Pök Mat's kitchen the *minyök* was now wide awake, spreading easily on the bun tops, the *roti paung*, lending them its rich, salty taste, and the aroma of *ghee* on a hot surface that was a gourmet's absolute joy.

Pök Mat went by many names: he was Che Mat Che Senani, or Pök Mat Nasi Minyök, but to most he was just their Pök Mat. He was a bulky man, tallish if I remember him well as he stood there with his baker's paunch, dressed in a white T-shirt that buttoned halfway down his chest. And his sarong—for he was always in his sarong, except on formal occasions—was held loosely around his waist, but I can assure you that it stayed there all day long.

There was a crowd already at Pök Mat's gate a couple of feet from his baking shed, and it was not yet seven o'clock. The sunlight was soft this time of day, and the bicycling crowd of schoolkids and the rickshaw drivers were breezing back and forth in the morning traffic of Jalan Pantai that used to cut the coast from the hinterland of our Tanjong. The *paung* kept coming out from the oven, catching the early light in their sheen, as Pök Mat stood and looked the look of fulfilment. Then he looked again as he pulled the sarong up around his waist and twirled the coil of cloth on his head.

His young assistants wrapped up the *paung* in newspaper sheets—two, maybe, for a boy to munch to class, or six for a family man to take home where spouse and offspring were waiting to break the dome and set free the head of steam from within, to dunk the bread into their hot cups of milky tea or Milo brought home from the stalls in cans that once contained condensed milk.

Roti paung was the art of Pök Mat but to me he was always the *beluda* man. The *beluda* was baked in a cigarette tin and stood taller than the *paung,* with its shallow dome top that rose above the open rim of the tin. You don't see or hear much of the *beluda* these days, but those who remember will remember it as a spongy bread, sweet and *lemök* to the taste, halfway between bread and a teacake. *Lemök*—which in standardspeak is *lemak*—is a problem word as its meaning stands between a little sweetness and richness and a little fat. It is sometimes used to describe a pleasing voice. I can feel the *lemök*-ness of Pök Mat's *beluda* and its soft texture in the mouth, and I hear birds singing in soft rays of light as Pök Mat's coil of rag cloth rises like a halo above his head.

Sometimes Pök Mat abandoned his baking altogether and sold only the *nasi minyök* for which he was also famous. He cooked the rice in a huge brass pot lined with a layer of fat (*ghee* perhaps) and when the time was right, he'd mix in green rice and red from smaller pots. So this was the nature of the mix—you'd find green grains and red in the main body of white of the *nasi minyök* that came with a dab of ground chilli and chunks of meat cooked in light Malay *gulai.*

In coffee shops and tea stalls they served bread that stood like rows of terraced houses, baked in tins in the Chinese bakery in Ladang or in Pulau Kambing. This was plain all-purpose bread, sliced, toasted then eaten with *kaya* spread. It was dipped in curry sauce, and hot drinks, of course, and its soft inner dough was dug out and rolled into a ball between the thumb and index finger to serve as bait for the *cicak* gecko.

We bought our *roti bata* piping hot from the bakery by the cemetery in Ladang, but a better loaf reputedly came from the other side of town, from the bakery of Pulau Kambing that served the best tables in Kuala Trengganu and did even better than that. In a story that many swear is true, a young would-be *ustaz* was interviewed by Tuan Haji Salleh

'Misbaha' bin Awang (a well-known local historian and official at the local department of Religious Affairs) when the Tuan Haji pulled a surprise.

'What do angels eat?' he asked the aspiring *ustaz*.

'Why, *roti* Pulau Kambing, of course!' said the interviewee.

Putus of Cassava

DURING A BREAK FROM THE RAIN, as gusting winds lifted sodden paper scraps along the breadth of Jalan Pantai, clouds of charcoal grey reflected themselves in the puddles, and our little town was steeped in melancholy.

In a gap between the tall bamboo panels that made her fencing, on a raised platform sheltered under *nipah* fronds, Mök Möh sprinkled a bed of cassava flour into a concave dip in the thin china lid of a bowl. She pressed the flour gently to take the shape of the mould, then, in the dip in the flour, she sprinkled coconut sugar, brown as the fishermen who came ashore. She heaped another layer of white over the brown, pressing it tightly into shape with another topping mould, concaved above as below. This she removed quickly to reveal a bulging top heap. Then, upturning the bottom dish and tapping it a little, out plopped the compact shape of a cassava meal, like a mini flying saucer, into a muslin cloth that she now folded into a wrap that would soon lie alongside other wraps in a head of steam in her steamer.

The monsoons imbued us with deep *pilu* wrapped in bright sarongs that village men slipped into, top end hooded over their heads as their hands grabbed the hem below to trap some warmth around their body. *Pilu* and melancholia were close cousins, but they came in chilly winds sodden by the spray of the roaring sea. In atap houses the rain poured in torrents down the pointed *nipah* tips, cascading down in a curtain of glistening threads of rain water. A sudden downpour clattering on corrugated roofs—clattering as it did continuously—mesmerised already dozy heads into an afternoon of deep slumber.

Sometimes during a lull in the cloud break, as haziness melted in the light, I was sent out with a ringgit note in my pocket to Mök

Möh Merah's stall near the *surau* of Haji Mat Kerinchi, across the road from Pak Mat Senani's morning stall of *nasi minyök* and *beluda* bread. The continuous lashing down of rain chilled the weather that shrank stomachs, and hunger gnawed on our entrails. It was Mök Möh who quickly warmed our hearts' cockles, opening lids and pulling *putu*s from her steamer, peeling off their muslin wraps, shedding them like ectoplasm that she'd just plucked out of the air.

She made *putu ubi* from a meal of cassava, she made crumbly *putu* from finely ground rice flour; then, for the discerning few, she made *putu halba* that came out piping hot in their fabric wraps, yellow as the fenugreek she'd mixed into the rice flour. Before they cooled down she stuck on each a little square mat of banana leaf before placing them on the tray. The mat kept them from sticking to each other when packed together, six or seven *putu*s to the ringgit, in a newspaper parcel that you clutched and hastened home before the next downpour.

Putu is, I believe, a Tamil word for cakes made from peanuts or rice flour. In Trengganu we have extended our *putu*speak to embrace the fenugreek and the cassava, but largely the *putu* convention is still observed because our *putu*s are still generally flat, and generally crumbly in nature.

For some reason when we travelled to Besut we always came back with stacks and bags of their *putu*. There were *putu*s the size of twenty sen coins, there were white ones and diamond-shaped ones, and others were made to look like they were the plume of mythical birds. There were round *putu*s that fitted snugly into your palms, that crumbled and settled in the bottom of your glass of hot Milo. *Putu*s were dunk-intolerant by nature and came with patterns, passed down from many generations carved into their wooden beds of *putu* moulds. These were the *putu beras* and *putu kacang* of Besut, and another that came with the curious name of *putu kua*.

Mök Möh made discs of moist *putu* that sulked and curled when left out in the cold. These were steamed *putu* not baked, that came unadorned with embedded flowers or tendrils.

Growing Up on The Beano

NEAR THE OLD CEB (LATER LLN) BUILDING opposite the old bus station with the big sentul tree, they came and turned the earth and built another 'modern' building in Kuala Trengganu, the Bangunang Pejabak Ugama. Before it, Father's office looked just like a little bungalow, with an open public counter behind which Father no longer tinkered with dots and dashes but a newfangled contraption that buzzed in one part of the country then burred in another. The sound of telegrams had changed from the *dee-dee-dit-dah-dah* of the old Morse Code to the new wonder of teleprinter technology.

Our town, too, was slowly changing. After doing my lunchtime after-school chore of cycling furiously in the afternoon heat to the Telegraphic bungalow with a hot glass bottle of Father's post-prandial Nescafé, I'd cross the road to the back of the new *bangunang,* into the newest bookshop in Kuala Trengganu. One day I came out from it with a paperback collection of horror stories put together by a man called Herbert van Thal. But mostly I cared little for books, preferring instead the zips and zaps of *The Beano* and *Dandy*, and the gripping exploits of *Battler Britton* or *Spy 13* and other war adventures that Father bought in compact comic books from a cluttered bookshop named Chee Seek of Kampong China.

Father was a secret comic book addict, hiding under his calm exterior a fierce penchant for war stories. He brought home a paperback once with the grand title *Sink the Bismarck!* which I dropped after one little paragraph at sea and which I think he did too. But coming home from work he frequently stopped at the town's mosque before taking a cycling detour over the *titiang* of Banggol to Kampong China. In the cabinet below his writing desk he kept stacks of Chee Seek-stamped DC comics that took me away on rough terrains during many afternoons, deaf to all the ambient noise for the cries of startled German soldiers ('*Donner und blitzen!*'), bombs and gunfire. From the Chee Seek bookstore too Father bought the US *Reader's Digest* which was thicker and glitzier than its English counterpart. It was from here that I got introduced to the condensed O. Henry, Robert Benchley and James Thurber.

Chee Seek was different from other bookshops in Kuala Trengganu.

In it were hidden pearls, paperbacks, and magazines dangling from the ceiling on thin wires; and in the back chamber of the shop, hidden from public view, were steaming plates of *kerepok lèkor* dipped in home-made chilli sauce, and a salad dish called *ceranang* bathed in a thick sauce of crushed peanuts, coconut milk, sugar and hot pepper. This was the domain of the matriarch Mök Mèk, who fed our hungry bodies after we'd feasted our minds on those stacks of printed matter. After Chee Seek, if you had money left, you'd stop at the first stall in row of zinc roofed stalls run by a grumpy man called Sumbu, in that lane that took Jalan Kampung China into the narrow back street of Lorong Jjamil. You'd be lucky to find an empty stool or space at a wobbly table, where for twenty cents or so you could scoop into a bowl of the best *ais kacang* in town to extinguish the heat of war from the comic books in Chee Seek and douse the fire of Mök Mek's chillied *kerepok lèkor*.

In the heyday of our years there were six bookshops in Kuala Trengganu. There was one in our corner of Tanjong by the *surau* of Haji Mat Kerinci where we waited every morning for the appearance of the yellow and red livery of the Trengganu bus company. Further down the road, past Padang Malaya, stood a little shop facing the sea, with racks of Jawi newspapers and periodicals by its door, behind which sat an eccentric with bottle-bottom glasses and a toothbrush 'tache, a man called Che Mat Dök Dèk for reasons I never knew. When his business folded in later years he packed the books, got rid of the mags and rags and opened his doors again as a driving school.

Escaping from the heat one day I walked into a new bookshop at the other end of Lorong Jjamil where it curved into Jalan Banggol. An elderly lady sat scowling behind the counter and as soon as I pulled a big, expensive book from the shelf to see if it was as good as those DC comic wars, she threw a remark that exploded around me like a dozen bazookas: '*Dök söh ambeklah bok besör tu, bukang nye nök beli!*' ('Don't touch the big one, you can't afford it!') I have abided by this advice since that day.

Father read *Qalam* and *Mastika* that he sometimes picked up from the Saudara Store, a quaint little 'bookshop' near the Masjid Abidin that was owned by his friend Ustaz Su. *Qalam* was a hard-hitting political-cum-religious magazine that I found very absorbing, and *Mastika* then had a writer named Othman Wook who penned spooky stories, the fore-runner to the magazine's present day obsession with apparitions, ghosts and ghouls. When Father finished reading those magazines, he'd send them to his friend Mat Jar from the Government Printing Office, and they came back bound in burgundy. Our staple then was the weekly *Utusan Kanak-Kanak* that Father picked up with his daily newspaper from the shop Pök Löh Yunang. I remember reading it (in its Jawi edition) under the lightbulb that hung from the rear verandah of our house while I waited for Mother to lay the dinner table. Sitting there on the floor in the dim light and long shadows, the comic strip adventures of the *Utusan* cast a weird and eerie spell.

Keda Pök Löh Yunang was, of course, our favourite bookshop. It was a bright place, abuzz with people, full of religious tomes and *kitab*s lining its hard to reach shelves and lighter reading material on its tables and at floor level. There was the ever-smiling Pak Yassin who I met for the last time in the shop many years ago when he took me to the coffee shop in the shadow of the clock tower for a breakfast of tea and satay. I had a vague suspicion then that Kuala Trengganu was the only capital in the world that served satay for breakfast, but that wasn't what we were out to celebrate. It was for all those years of the *Utusan Kanak-Kanak, The Beano* and the *Sunny Stories*, and for the good ship Pök Löh Yunang and all the good people who sailed in her.

Murder by Dope

IN TANJUNG MENGABANG was the grave of a man who became infamous in Trengganu folklore; he probably died in the first half of the last century. The British did not start extending their tentacles into Trengganu until 1909 when the Bangkok Treaty was signed, and this effectively put Trengganu under British control, a fact that infuriated Sultan Zainal Abidin III who refused to accept a British adviser, so an adviser they gave him by another name, an agent of the British Counsel. It was another ten years before a proper adviser was appointed to Trengganu in the shape of one J.L. Humphreys.

I wrote before about Tanjung Mengabang, and it was there that a man named Pök Mat Mengamök was buried after he was shot under British orders, so that must've been after 1909 but before 1950; otherwise memories of the incident would've been fresh in the minds of Trengganu people, but my mother, who mentioned him many times when referring to people who'd lost their cool, said she'd heard the story from her elders.

Pak Mat Mengamök, as his name implies, ran amok or amuck, a peculiarly Malay attribute, supposedly—says who? I do not know, maybe it was said by those same people who ordered him shot. From vague stories I've heard, Pak Mat lost control after hearing that his domestic life had gone awry, so he went for his keris and then threw himself into a crowd of innocent people. The result was a trail of bodies of unfortunate souls.Yesterday, while walking in Covent Garden in Central London, I began to think of Pak Mat because there, near the famous London piazza, is an address that constantly reminds me of my alleged identity. In 1821, when Thomas De Quincey was broke and desperate, he obtained lodgings in a house there and started to write *Confessions of an English Opium-Eater* but did not finish it there as urgent matters were pursuing him in the shape of his creditors. But his *Confessions* appeared later in the *London Magazine* where it received much acclaim. By its publication he also brought to the attention of the wider public that Malays were prone to running amok as a people.

Well, De Quincey, though penurious most of his life, was an educated man who must've gleaned this from some Euro-centric ethnographic work while he was at Oxford University, so he must've merely been repeating what he'd read. But his encounter with a Malay was real, though I have doubts about the latter's choice of headgear unless, of course, he was Trengganu or Kelantan born, in which case he'd then be wearing the turban-like east coast *semutar*.

Though a fine writer by his own mettle, De Quincey had a fixation for Wordsworth, his hoped-for father figure. For this he moved to Grasmere in the Lake District, to be near the man he regarded as the greatest poet of his time; but while Wordsworth was intoxicated on poetry, De Quincey was high on dope, a habit he'd acquired in London to cure his little headache. So there he was, in his cottage in Grasmere one fine day, with Kant spinning in his head, longing for discourse with someone Oxbridge educated, when 'a Malay knocked on my door'. De

Quincey guessed that he must've been a sailor on his way to the nearest port about forty miles away.

There the Malay stood, De Quincey said, in his rustic kitchen, wearing a turban and 'loose trowsers of dingy white ... with sallow and bilious skin, enamelled or veneered with mahogany, by marine air'.

If you're wondering, so did De Quincey: 'What business a Malay could have to transact amongst English mountains, I cannot conjecture.'

His servant girl, 'born and bred amongst the mountains' was confounded too. This Malay stranger's 'attainments in English were exactly of the same extent as hers in the Malay', De Quincey said. So, not surprisingly, she passed him on to De Quincey who did his best to savoir faire:

'And as I had neither a Malay dictionary, nor even Adelung's *Mithridates*, which might have helped me to a few words, I addressed him in some lines from *The Iliad*; considering that, of such languages as I possessed, Greek, in point of longitude, came geographically nearest to an Oriental one.'

The Malay man replied in what De Quincey thought was Malay, but he was probably saying, 'It's all Greek what you're saying to me,' in Trengganuspeak, but no matter, he soon lay on the floor for nearly an hour before finally saying goodbye.

Before seeing him off, De Quincey pressed into his hand a piece of opium which he'd divided into three parts, which the Malay, said De Quincey deploying a schoolboy phrase, 'bolt the whole ... in one mouthful.' Or as we say in Trengganuspeak, *pölök selalu*. Then De Quincey became worried for such a quantity could have killed three horses, so, for some days afterwards he felt anxious, but to his relief he 'never heard of any Malay being found dead'. I'm telling you this in case you've heard tales in your family of a seafaring relative who'd wandered into the Lake District in the nineteenth century and never found his way home again. If so, I've solved the mystery and found for you the murderer, or at least the man guilty of manslaughter.

Now out of sight, the Malay was never out of De Quincey's mind because he was to come back to haunt him in dreams for months, taking him to Asiatic scenes, pulling him into veritable nightmares. De Quincey wrote:

'This incident I have digressed to mention because this Malay (partly from the picturesque exhibition he assisted to frame, partly from the anxiety I connected with his image for some days) fastened afterwards upon my dreams, and brought other Malays with him worse than himself that ran 'a-muck' at me, and led me into a world of troubles.'

As a footnote to this I'll just add that De Quincey, when summoned downstairs by his young servant to examine the Malay wanderer, took stock of his 'oriental tongues' and could only come up with two words: the Arabic word for barley (which he didn't state in his book, but which by the way, is *sha'ir*) and the Turkish word for opium. Coleridge probably used *madjoon* which sounds close to the Trengganuspeak *ma'ajong* (from the Arabic *ma'jun*), a medicinal paste that is normally black in colour. What would a man who'd been sitting still for some time on your kitchen floor, probably because he was under the weather, do when proferred something that he'd recognised in his ears as *ma'ajong*? Why, swallow it whole, of course, in the hope of getting better.

* * *

Coleridge will probably be delighted to know that the house in Covent Garden where he part-wrote his famous book is now a ... Turkish restaurant.

Egg on a Stick

A KAMPUNG IN TRENGGANU isn't complete without the *ccuri ayang* character. He's the resident chicken thief. The chicken is central to *kampung* life: cockerels wake the faithful at dawn, make the hens lay the eggs and fight pitched battles in inter-village cock fights where the *kampung* itself is lost or won. A little province of Trengganu is said to have been won this way when one ruler beat the cockerel of a neighbouring state.

Many Malay proverbs are centred around gambling and losing. For example, *Biar alah sabung, asal menang sorak* (Never mind the quality, feel the width) is not altogether good advice, but perhaps it is meant to be ironic. And there's a minefield of irony in the Malay vocabulary.

But back to the hen that laid the eggs that played a central role in *kampung* life. Recently a friend from Blighty who's married to a Trengganu girl told me of an experience he had at a wedding. And then he asked, 'Who comes first at a Malay wedding, the groom or the bride?' The answer is neither; it's the egg, on a stick. If you've been to a Malay wedding you'll know about this because you'd have been given a hard-boiled egg, coloured bright red or green or yellow, that's been pierced through its base by a long thin stick that comes out through the apex with a crown of some hand-made flowers or leaves. There's symbolism here, presumably, and the only explanation I can think of is fertility, the one that always comes to mind when the egg pops up. This friend from Blighty, after an initial period of puzzlement, parked his egg on its stick at a place he thought was safe so he could leave the room awhile. When he came back all that remained was the long stick and the shell of an egg that used to be on it. *'Siapa makan telur saya?'* ('Who ate my egg?') he asked, raising a laugh from the wedding company and a nudge from his Trengganu wife.

Now there's no doubt that eggs do have special qualities for ill or good. 'Swallow a raw egg on a Thursday morning,' an old Malay book on *tibb* advises an impotent man, 'and do it again on the Friday morning after that, then again the following Saturday.' On Sunday, I suppose, he's expected to lie back and think of cakes, probably the *apam* which, besides being a *kuih* or cake, also has lascivious word-association qualities. Here then is a mother lode of the association between the Malay *kuih* and the proverbial fruitcake, but we'll leave that for now.

So in a *kampung* the egg is food for folk, decorates a stick and is also the paraphernalia for magic. When summoned to attend to a sick person, a *bomoh* or shaman will ask for an egg which he (or she, there are lady *bomoh*s too) rolls onto the ailing parts. The egg is then ceremoniously cracked before the assembled relatives, and out pops from the shell a rusty nail, or some bits of glass, or snarled up hair from some distant ill-wisher's head. Here in an eggshell, says the *bomoh*, are the causes of your discomfort, all extracted by a process that in Trengganu we call *aleng* with the egg of your everyday chick.

Old people will tell you of even older people who spoke of sand, gravel and lime being mixed with the binding power of the egg white. Indeed some old mosques in Trengganu were reputedly built with glue made from many hundreds of litres of egg white mixed into the mortar. Buckets of yolk were simultaneously despatched to the ladies' quarter to turn into *akök*—boat-shaped ones for a quick mouthful or magnum-sized flower-shaped ones for a gang of hungry builders.

Trengganu folk eat their eggs hard-boiled or *aröng* with pepper and a dash of *kicap*. In the morning a Trengganu man, bleary-eyed after his visit to the *gok* would make a beeline to the man at the griddle who'd make him a *roti telor* with his home-laid egg, and griddle man would charge him an extra five sen for that. There's egg for healing or egg for building or egg for food in Trengganu, but no cosmogonic egg that tells the history of the universe. But for some weird reason the egg is also capable of speaking not of creation but quite the reverse. If you accidentally smash your mum's china or break a dinner plate, you'll probably hear her reproach you twice for effect: '*Ah, döh ttellör döh, döh ttellör döh!*' It's difficult to explain here how the egg has come to that, as *ttelör* here is a verb, and all she's telling you is … you've laid an egg.

Göng With the Wind

THERE WAS A MAN IN TRENGGANU named Cik Mat Dök-Dèk probably because he was a fluent Tamil speaker. There was another called Pak Mat Bbiang—well, that's a hard one for me. *Bbiang*, it turns out, comes from *pebean* (that's how it was spelt) and means, I think, the collection of excise. There was a noticeboard at the harbour near the customs warehouse in Kuala Trengganu, opposite the post office, near Pök Deh's *röjök* stall. On it was the legend: *Kastam dan Pebean*.

Well, there was also Cik Ali Pailét because he was a pilot on a ship. But at school we used the Pilot (pronounced 'pee' and 'lot' to rhyme with 'boat') fountain pen that was, of course, the *pötipeng*. Those things made our world go round.

Notisebar was the man who served you notices from the court, and you didn't want to know him at all. The rest are easier to guess—Cik Mat

Terapik (Traffic [policeman]), Cik Jusoh Sobia (Surveyor), Pak Mbong Pos Masta (Postmaster) and Sulong Jang. You may have problems with the last one if you're not Trengganu bred and born because this man repaired watches—and that's *jang* for you for the standardspeak *jam* that gives the hour. Did I say bred and born? Is it not the other way round? I don't think so because being a Trengganuer starts from the inside, when you're sitting quietly in the dark, deep in amniotic fluid and then you're *böng* (born) to this world.

When a Trengganu person says, 'Göng with the wing' he is not talking of Clark Gable but about a storm over high ground, and he probably means Göng Kapas. There are many other göngs in Trengganu and they are all elevated land, but not quite hills. And have you heard of the *meng wi' de goldeng gung*? He, I'm afraid, was born not of Trengganu but only came via cinema posters, with his number seven and his Oh-Oh. This probably explains his demeanour, which lacks the inner calm of Trengganu. You'll have to look at how a house is built in Trengganu to understand: first they raise the bare essentials, the roof all tiled, then the floor, then everything goes quiet for a long while as the family sleeps behind a wall of mats, then maybe a few years later will come the planks for the walls. But Trengganuers are competitive too when the mood takes them, and in this they do the *bbadi dang*, which is a race for competitive people to 'reach a goal'.

Somewhere close to us was a bicycle shop run by a man called Tökeh Jing, and opposite him was another run by a man called Tokeh Luga. *Luga* is a calamitous word as it relates to *lapör belepeng* and if you're that, you'd have had your last meal a long time ago. So the Luga man should've been quite hard up, but he didn't seem so. He was a well-padded but shorter-than-average man, and he worked on many bicycles. About his counterpart I can't be sure as *jing* is Trengganuspeak for *jin* or Djinn, but I don't know many who become bicycle *taukehs*. That rules him out of this mighty breed so the only explanation I have is that his Chinese name must've been Jin but was altered by our Trengganu ways.

When Tökèh Luga died he was succeeded by his formidable wife who became known to us as Mèk. Most girls of a certain age in Trengganu and Chinese women especially are Mèks, but if older than that, Mök Mèk.

Chinese business people are all *taukeh*s in deference to their business skills, but there was one Malay man who made the grade. He was known as Cik Mat Tökeh and, if I remember it right, he dealt mostly in scrap metal.

And oh, by the way, we also had a national class singer whose name was Adnang Osmang, and I wonder where he is now.

Walking With Ghosts

'Fresh in my mind, late Sixties walking through Kg. Ladang Taik Lembu, Jèrat China and crossing the paya *to Lorong Mök Pé before heading to Jalan Sultan Omar, Göng Kapas. No public transport available at that time besides* téksi (béca roda tiga) *or bus.'*

—Mek Jarroh

Mek Jarroh, in the late Sixties, walked from Ladang to Göng Kapas via the Chinese cemetery and a *paya*. That was some journey!

As I remember it, there was a long and winding road called Jalan Wailis running through the Chinese cemetery in Kuala Trengganu. No, *wailis* wasn't some expatriate figure but Trengganuspeak for wireless, the Neanderthal man of our present day Wi-Fi. My Father was a wireless man who used to tell me how he cycled back from work in the dead of night, through the dark, long road that ran through the cemeteries— Hindu, then Chinese, then Muslim—before finally seeing the dim streetlights of Jalan Paya Bunga. The person who built the wireless station there in necropolis then made it work round the clock had a ghoulish sense of humour!

For a while Father worked in the annexe of the general post office on the edge of Padang Malaya as a telephone, then telegraph, operator. These were days when Trengganu telephone numbers ran into all of four digits, and every call had to go through the operator. I remember something that Father said whenever I think of that. It's a Kelantanese phrase: *buak gelak mato.* He heard that one day when he was working as telephone operator.

A very important person in Trengganu made a telephone call to another very important person in Kota Baru and, as it turned out, the latter owed money to the former. In their conversation the Kelantan dignitary asked his Trengganu counterpart if he'd received the $2.50 he'd sent him through a mutual friend in repayment of the debt. The Trengganu man replied, 'No.' And so, out of shock and exasperation, the Kelantan man said, *'Ambo, duö ria pong demö tu buak gelak matö!'*

Buak gelak matö is the act of making the eye not see, but the closest English expression to it is, I suppose, 'to pull a fast one'. 'It's only two rial for goodness sake, and he's already pulled a fast one!' And we laughed so much, not because the story was exceptionally funny but because we knew who those very important people were. The amount loaned by the Trengganu dignitary to his Kelantan counterpart was measly, even for those days, but it painted a hilarious picture of the rich and their money.

When Father moved to a new telegraph office opposite the old bus station, I had the task, soon as I got back from school, to deliver a bottle of hot Nescafé to his place of work. It was quite a feat pedalling a small bike while trying to hold a hot bottle of drink with one hand on the handlebars. But still I was thankful that I wasn't of cycling age when he'd been in Jalan Wailis in those wee hours.

The *paya* marshes of Kuala Trengganu were wild and wondrous, with frogs a-croaking, water lilies floating on the shimmery surface and long reeds springing out from under the water. Many types of fish, and leeches galore, lived beneath the floating mats of those broad leaves and grasses that tagged into each other and wove themselves a wide raft over the water. I never saw anything like it again once we left Kuala Trengganu.

Lorong Mök Pè was a short walk from our primary school. I remember that because Pök Mang, the old school gardener, lived around there. One day I went to his house with my friend to pick up some picture books that he'd collected from somewhere. On the way out the friend walked hastily from the junction where Lorong Mök Pè met the main road, then told us that, on some nights at that junction, there stood a mystery lady who'd look at you and deign a smile if you looked into her bloodshot eyes.

For the most part Kuala Trengganu was very dark at night, and some roads even darker. Not far from that junction, turning right to the foot of the hills, was a spot where people, including Father's friend Ali, were shot summarily by executioners of the Triple Star (Bintang Tiga) Communist forces when they took control during the hiatus immediately after the Japanese surrender.

Walking further along Jalan Cherong Lanjut, with the barren hills on your left, there was hardly a lamppost in sight, except for the flickering lights from houses to your right and the occasional headlights that glared into your eyes. We had an outing there one night with our class teacher, walking bravely in the dark, listening to her explain the meaning of 'given the sack' while I looked forward to seeing bright lights again on the other side. It's a funny phrase to remember from a walk in the dark a long time ago, but strong feelings make you remember strange things and weird tales.

Thank you, Mek Jarröh, for your memory.

Accounting for Taste

IN THE OLD PADANG MALAYA in Kuala Trengganu, under the shade of the flame-of-the-forest, sat a man named Ku Awang who sold *air serbat*—a word which sounds very suspiciously close to the Arabic *sharba*—to drink. It could have come to us from those Yemeni folk who travelled down to spread the Word and paused awhile to quench their thirst. Ku Awang's *serbat,* I was told, contained *halia* or ginger, and sugar for sure, and maybe a shred of pandan too.

Sometimes, encouraged by the crowd that stopped by to squat and drink, Ku Awang would upgrade his menu items to include another. It was a mixture of many things, including Horlicks and Milo, and a teaspoon of what could've been Nèscafe. I used to watch him scoop out the powder from various cans and mix them all into a paste with condensed milk before adding boiling water. As the drink slid down his customers' throats it must've given them quite a feel—milk, cocoa, sugar, malt and instant coffee. I don't think he became the talk of the town for that though, for when I saw him again coming down the street he was still known as Ku Awang Air Serbat, not as the inventor of Neshormilocafé.

I tried to define the taste of Ku Awang's recipe when I read that the Japanese, some time ago, had had to invent a word to describe the taste of *aji no moto*, which is monosodium glutamate to you and me. All along I'd thought that MSG merely enhanced your taste buds besides making you feel very thirsty, but how wrong I was, as I'd missed the taste of *umami*, which is described as 'savoury'. *Umami*, they say, is the reaction of your taste buds to food with 'savoury, broth-like, meaty' qualities. The Chinese know it as the Xien Wei taste of glutamate, and our Trengganu *budu*, it's said, is *umami*.

Now it strikes me as something circular when a taste's described as savoury, which itself floats in uncharted waters. 'What's savoury?' I once asked an English person and I was told that it was anything that wasn't sweet or bitter. That was good enough for me to describe chips and morsels of meat that flitted twixt lips and plate of my everyday meal. Then the word 'spicy' was added, and I could live with that too, but the reality is that savoury means many things to many people. So *budu* is *umami* savoury as I can recall, with a salty, fishy, sound-of-*nobat* quality.

Then another English person came my way via some distant shore to ask the number of words there are in Malay to describe taste. It was merely rhetorical really as all he wanted to do was talk about his long stay in Bangkok and the number of words available in Thai to describe the taste of their food there. He mentioned six or eight, I think, which started me counting the number of ways in Trengganuspeak or in standardspeak to describe the taste of our daily meal. So far I've come up with eleven that are worthy of consideration, a lot better than the four that are considered primary, if you don't count *umami* that is, as I am now wont to do.

First we have the basic four: *masin* (salty), *masam* (sour), *manis* (sweet) and *pahit* (bitter). Or in Trengganuspeak: *masing, masang, manih, pahik*. And then I counted seven more—and it's about now that I wander into the 'Here Be Dragons' area in my Map of the Taste Area—for I have *pedas, pedar, tengit, maung, lemak* and *hanyir*. And for good measure, I've got *tawar* too, which isn't a taste at all, I hear you say.

You'll also tell me that *pedas*, the heat of chilli, isn't a taste either as it's a sensation that assaults not your taste buds but your trigeminals. And maybe I'll agree with you on that, but who now will say that the 'taste' of chilli isn't a *rasa*? But you'll probably accept *maung* which Winstedt describes as 'bitter' and 'smelling musty', while to Haji Zainal Abidin Safarwan* it's something with a taste and smell that induces nausea. The *maung* that I remember is a raw vegetable taste that's not pleasant at all, so I'll go very quickly now to something more palatable and that's *lemak,* which in English is perhaps best described as a 'rich' flavour but which plays a more important role than that in Malay, both in Trengganu and elsewhere.

Lemak, you'll agree, is the taste of coconut milk, *ghee*, butter, some bananas and *teh tarik* under a shady tree. In other words, it's not just a description but a taste per se. Then there's *pedör (pedar)* which is a problem for me as it's been said to be rancid, pungent and bitter. *Pedör* to me is quite revolting, like gall or bile, and needn't be rancid at all. It may be just my memory here as once I saw a man produce a shrivelled-up thing in the market to prove the efficacy of some medicine he was selling, and he said it was *pedu beruang,* the internal organ of a bear. And he said it tasted very *pedör.*

But can you taste without your smell? *Tengit* and *hanyir* appear to be two qualities that can be both savoured and smelt. *Tengit* is the rancid smell (and taste) of cooking fat that's gone off, and *hanyir* in Kuala Trengganu is everywhere, being a town by the sea. It's the fishy taste of *budu* and *kerepok lekör,* and the smell of the fishmonger if he sits too close to you in a Kedai Payang café.

So that's the taste of life, and you'll hear most of them every day, varying perhaps only in their quality, for in Trengganuspeak they can take on the added intensifiers of *manis lleting, masang pperik, masing ppekök, pahik llepang, pedah nnaha* and *tawör hebber.* Then you'll know that they're more than what they are normally.

* * *

*Kamus Besar Bahasa Melayu, Utusan Publications & Distributors Bhd., Malaysia.

Hui Hui and Other People

ONE DAY IN OUR afternoon religious class, my friend L surprised me by saying that he'd been enjoying some Chinese New Year cake his family had received from mainland China. L was a pretty ordinary chap, fair of skin and voluble in his Trengganuspeak. In our daily dalliance he was very much like one of us, but it was when he started to talk of his yearly bite of this exotic cake that I realised that he was one of us and more. He was from the al-Yunani clan, a prominent Chinese Muslim family in Kuala Trengganu.

The al-Yunani family of Trengganu were not strictly from the Yunnan, but were the Hui Hui people from Guangdong Province in China. Members of L's family, who were early settlers in Kuala Trengganu, adopted the family name Al-Yunani (of the Yunnan) to signal to the local Malays and the Chinese community that they were Muslim people, though they were not themselves from there.

The Hui Huis were generally Han Chinese, but in later classification of the Muslim community in China the name was used to embrace other Muslim ethnic groups too, including Turkic Muslims and even the former Nestorian Christians who converted to Islam many, many years ago. But the al-Yunani Hui Huis of Kuala Trengganu were Guangdong people who shared the same ethnicity as their non-Muslim cousins in Kampung China.

The journey of L's Al-Yunani family to Trengganu started in 1903 when Haji Ali bin idris (later known as Pök Ali Yunan), his wife Hajjah Halimah and his mother-in-law left Palembang where they'd been settled and travelled to Singapore.There they found another person, whose name was to become famous in Kuala Trengganu, Abdullah bin Sulaiman, or Pök Löh Yunang, and another man from Guangdong named Musa (Pak Musa). From there they looked for another place to go to, and finally decided on Trengganu, a state once visited by Cheng Ho (Zheng He). And so, joined by Pök Löh's wife, Khadijah (Pök Musa's niece who joined them from Guangdong), and another man, Daud, they settled in Kuala Trengganu.

Pök Musa became an itinerant medicine peddler, Pök Daud became a general trader in Jalan Kedai Payang, while Pök Löh went to prospect for gold in Hulu Trengganu. While he was away, his wife and daughter opened a laundry shop in Kuala Trengganu called Kedai Abdullah Al-Yunani. When Pök Löh came back from the sticks, having failed to find much gold in the Hulu, he began to spend his days in the laundry shop, adding other items to its inventory, religious books on the shelves and rice bags on the shop floor. Soon, in an act of trimming down, he stopped taking in dirty linen and stopped the trade in rice entirely. He concentrated on the book trade, and for a long time Abdullah Al-Yunani became the most famous bookshop in Kedai Payang in Kuala Trengganu.

According to the historical records of the al-Yunani family of Trengganu, they have seven pioneers who came down to Trengganu from China, the first five under the reign of Zainal Abidin III (1881–1918): Musa Li, Ali Zhang bin Idris, Abdullah Dong bin Sulaiman, Daud Dong and Hassan Liu bin Salleh. Then two more under the reign of Sultan Sulaiman Badrul Alam Shah (1921–1942): Muhammad Yusuf Xiao bin salleh and Haji Ibrahim Fu bin Muhammad.

Now the Yunanis are completely absorbed into the Malay community of Trengganu, though occasionally they do look back to their roots far away.

Trengganu On the Mind

PÖK LÖH TUK CAME FROM SEBERANG TAKIR across the river, every morning, wielding a stout staff and a heavy burden. The first thing he did when he arrived was to walk a few paces, then freeze his footsteps in between before twirling his alarming twirl while mouthing some wild mantra. And so he did every minute of his time until the shutters were closed and the shoppers had gone away. He was a regular man in our Tanjong market place, distinguishable from the milling crowd by his white beard and tatty headband, and a look that told little about him or what he was on except that somewhere along the line, perhaps when he'd been very young, he'd veered right off the centre.

There was a man called Haji Chik who wrapped himself in a *batik sarung* above the one that he was already wearing. He was a scribe from an unhinged place that was somewhere removed from the hubbub of our town. He scrawled and scrawled in his fine Jawi, then he'd stick his daily despatches to telegraph poles or the walls of his house near a *surau* a short distance from where we were. It was a sad story I heard of Haji Chik, born into a well-off family. When the money had all flown away his mind too decided to go, leaving him still on sordid earth to scrawl his sad tale in wiry Jawi.

There was Encik Omar who daubed walls with his pronouncements that he dished out from a bucket of whitewash and his sign-painting brush of who? what?, why? and where? He'd been, I heard, a court interpreter when he was an altogether man, but in the manner of many sad things, some parts of his thinking became disassembled, and he became detached from daily reality. And so he addressed most of his thoughts and pains, throughout most of my childhood, to the walls of Kuala Trengganu. For a while he lived in a grand house on a high aspect that had been empty for a long time. So he looked down on all of us walking along Jalan Tanjong. He lived in there with his loyal mate, a lady known to us as Cik Puan, and together they inhabited that crumbling place, in a world that was indicated by most with a shake of the head that translated into how far they'd gone into the beyond. That said, Encik Omar, a Chinese man by birth, was an amiable person who nodded his head whenever you hailed him in the street, but there was not a glimmer in his eyes as his mind was obsessed by many things.

While Encik Omar was busily scripting those messages on the murals of his home, and walking the streets with his bucket of white paint and a brush, his consort, Cik Puan, was quietly roaming our streets with some other burden in her head. Sometimes I saw them meet in the corner of a street like two ships passing in the night, and Cik Puan would nag him. Then Cik Omar would be driven back to the wall with his who?, what?, why? and where?

Those were dark days for troubled men, and women too, I must say, though we didn't see them very often. There was a fenced-off part of the General Hospital in Kuala Trengganu where they had a concrete outhouse enclosed by a tall meshed-wire fence. There they kept people of disturbed minds who'd shown some tendencies for untoward behaviour. On good days they were let out to wander in the little open space surrounded by the see-through fence, and sometimes when I walked past I'd look at them with great sorrow.

In the Masjid itself were men who, while not stark-raving mad, had mannerisms most peculiar. They sat quietly in dark corners and smiled at unseen things going by. Some just kept chanting esoteric words in a very showy way. One quiet man we knew as Dol simply sat on his mat and propped himself against the back wall by a side entrance. He'd rise for prayers and retreat again to his patch where he'd been sitting, smiling and mute, for as long as I could remember.

A Short History of Tun Long

FOR A LONG TIME we had a short, bony man with black-rimmed spectacles come to our house for our dirty linen. I remember him for being long in the tooth (though he couldn't have been more than fifty-five then) and for his distinctly olde-worlde ways that came with a ready smile. His workhouse was in Kuala Trengganu, but his speech belonged twenty-five miles away, in Kuala Brang, the ancient Trengganu capital. His name, Tun Long, was one that stood out even in a tangle of laundry because with it came an old title.

The history of the rulers of Trengganu is something that I've been looking into for some time now through my less-than-perfect binoculars. As I twirl the focusing ring left and right, the vision alternates between definitions and blurs, but I keep reminding myself that I'm looking at things far away and from long ago. I have long held onto the belief that the Datuk Bendahara Padang Saujana, Tun Habib Abdul Majid, arrived in Kuala Trengganu in the eighteenth century and clambered up Bukit Putri. But I have yet to come across a concrete source to show that this was true. On the contrary, most records I turn to seem to state that the old Bendahara never actually went there, although he intervened directly in Trengganu affairs from Johor.

In 1725 his son, Zainal Abidin I, became the founder of the present lineage in Trengganu, taking a circuitous route through Patani to Kuala Brang (Tanjung Baru), Langgar, Pulau Manis and Cabang Tiga, before finally settling in Bukit Nangka (Bukit Keledang), a place now known as Kota Lama, the old fort on the hill.

Before Zainal Abidin came down from Patani to be sultan, Tun Habib was already deciding the fate of the state by remote control. He sent three men out there: Paduka Laksamana, Paduka Seri Rama and Paduka Raja. But things didn't work out too well with them, feuding followed and

Paduka Seri Rama became the sole ruler. Bendahara Tun Habib then sent another man, Bendahara Hassan, to hold the fort in Trengganu. After him came four more to continue the line of control: Tun Zain Indera and his three sons, Tun Yuan, Tun Sulaiman (aka Tok Raja Kilat) and Tun Ismail. The centre of power was then in Kuala Brang, although at the time of Zainal Abidin's arrival the *Tuhfat al-Nafis* (written by the Bugis Raja Ali Haji) reported that Tok Raja Kilat (Tun Sulaiman) held power at the mouth of the Trengganu.

Our man Tun Long could have been a descendant of any one of these Tuns of the sixteenth century or, I shudder to think, even earlier from the blood of the Tun Telanai people who once ruled old Trengganu.

There's still much of Trengganu history coursing through the veins of its people. The three Padukas were sent out by the Tun Habib to wrest power from the Megats, who were not really sultans as we now know but chieftains who had local control. The Megats had an anomalous pedigree: some say they were born of morganatic marriages, some say they were

Megat Panji Alam by Adzakiel.

commoners with remarkable powers. There are Megats still in Trengganu who perhaps still look at the moon and wonder if it had not, once in the remote past, shone on their most famous ancestor, Megat Panji Alam, as he and his entourage of a few thousand men marched towards Pahang to take back the lady he was affianced to, Tun Teja. At that time there were Melaka men in Pahang trying to whisk the lady back home for their ruler. The Megat lost his life in Pahang, unfortunately, stabbed in the back as we've been telling young Trengganuers then and now.

The Megats were not royals as we understand them now, so who were they? Panji Alam's father was the local strongman in Trengganu at the turn of the sixteenth century, and there may be some hints of their provenance when we learn that Megat Panji Alam learned his fighting skills in Perak under another famous man, Megat Terawis, who, it was said, was especially skilled in the art of the *lembing*. (The depiction of Megat Panji Alam you see here is from the imagination of my talented young friend Adzakael.)

Before that, in the fifteenth century, Trengganu was ruled by a man called the Telanai. We are uncertain if the Telanai was his name or his title, but most probably the latter. The Telanai was a very old title, some say dating back to well before the eighth century to the early rulers of Palembang. But the Trengganu Telanai could have come from Bentan, where the Telanais married into the family of Tun Perak, Melaka's most famous Bendahara.

The *Sejarah Melayu* (*Malay Annals*) sheds some interesting light on the Telanai and gives him a fix in history. The poor man was murdered by one Seri Akar Raja, sent to Trengganu by the ruler of Pahang Muhammad Shah as punishment for having gone over his head to seek the protection of Sultan Ala'uddin Riayat Shah of Melaka. Ala'uddin, the fourth sultan of Melaka, was another unfortunate soul who departed this earth prematurely—probably poisoned—in Pagoh (on the Muar River) in 1488 after only a year on the throne. Interestingly all the Telanai's children who fled to Melaka when their father died were Megats: Megat Sulaiman, Megat Hamzah and Megat Umar.

The past beyond that is hazier still, though some may have been etched in stone. The Batu Bersurat (Inscribed Stone) had on it the names of Raja Mandalika and Seri Paduka Tuan who, I expect, were one and the same person as *mandalika* was not a name but a job description, so perhaps he was the lord of the manor. And the stone had a date on it of the Muslim year 702, which was 1303 in the Christian calendar.

The East Was Red

LIVING AS WE DID ON THE SHORE, we were sometimes submerged by rising tides. We'd wake up of a morning to see tell-tale tidal marks on our fence and on the shophouses, and the rats all lying dead, drowned perhaps in their slumber. There were rats so big under those shophouses that even cats were loath to walk unaccompanied in the night. But still we were a joyful community. We had *mawlid*s in the *surau* by our South Indian shopkeepers, community bathing at the well with the huge *timba tembaga* powered by a tall cantilever and counterweighted by a huge piece of lumber. And there were folk going hither and thither in the morning *pasar*, and goods coming ashore from the interior.

There were three *pasar*s in Kuala Trengganu, according to one Captain Labe who came ashore in 1769. There was one for Malays, one for the Siamese people and one for the Chinese community. And the one for the Chinese community was the biggest of all. When Abdullah bin Abdul Kadir Munshi visited Trengganu in 1836, he visited the Pasar Kampong Laut which was near us and which he disapproved of for its roaming cows. He probably preferred the Kandang Kerbau of his native Singapura.

But cows notwithstanding, our community was cleansed many times a year by the *air pasang,* the tidal water, not the *air bah* of the floods from an oveflowing river and unending rainfall. We had rainfall aplenty in Kuala Trengganu, but the muddy *air ulu* just swelled the river mouth before flowing out to sea. Further up, in Kedai Payang, the water could've stayed awhile and submerged the thoroughfares, but that's something that I remember only vaguely, perhaps it was from an old photo that I saw.

In 1926 there was a big flood in Kuala Trengganu, known as the *bah merah,* and the town was submerged for three days causing havoc in the community, with people running to the hills seeking shelter in Chabang

Tiga. The sky remained dark for five days as the water rose, and the populace left home for higher ground:

> *'Lima hari limanya malam,*
> *cahaya langit bertambah kelam*
> *air makin bertambah dalam*
> *susah sekelian rakyat dan alam.'*

> 'For five days and nights past
> the sky remained so very overcast
> the water came and rose so fast
> the people and earth suffering the blast.'

The picture painted of these refugees from the flood was one of chaos as they clambered to the top of a small hill, and the ensuing noise was like the din in an eastern bazaar: *'Bukit kecil bukannya besar/riuh laksana dalam pasar'*.

This poetic picture I've quoted was penned by Tengku Dalam Khazaki in his *Syair Zainal Abidin Yang Ketiga Trengganu*, published in Singapore in 1936.

People seeking refuge on a hill from the great flood, Bah Merah, in Kuala Trengganu.

It was like Judgment Day, the poet said, with peals of thunder under a darkened sky, and the people exposed to the elements: the water, the wind, the cold.

> *'Di atas bukit orang berumah*
> *ada berpondok setengah berkhemah*
> *ada yang segar ada yang lemah*
> *sejuk tak boleh nasi dimamah.'*

> 'They were gathered on the hill
> some in huts and some in tents
> they were the healthy and the ill
> too cold to eat even their meal.'

They were all there in makeshift huts and beneath tents, the able-bodied and the sick, teeth chattering so badly from the cold that they couldn't even chew their food (rice) properly, so said the poet. As they looked down they saw their belongings afloat in the water, boxes and trunks they'd left behind: *Harta benda jangan dikata ... tong dan peti ... merata-rata.*

Rumour had it that a hill called Gajah Terum, upstream of the Trengganu River, was washed away by the flood. Tens of hills, the poet said—perhaps exercising poetic licence here—were washed away, their red earth torn asunder and washed to the rivermouth in Kuala Trengganu:

> *'Hingga ke laut di luar Kuala*
> *semuanya merah rupa terhala*
> *beberapa bulan kubilang pula*
> *tiada hilang merah segala ...'*

> 'Into the sea beyond the harbour
> All was red to the seeing eye
> For months it went on from that day
> The red just did not go away ...'

And so it was, the Red Flood, and how it came to be.

Döh Nök Wak Guane ...

A MAN FROM JOHOR came on behalf of the then Parti Negara to Kuala Trengganu and stayed briefly in the Istana Kolam; a *taukeh* peddling assorted wares came to Kuala Trengganu and he too lived there awhile. The Istana Kolam was an *istana* with a chequered career.

It was a fascinating place, with carvings and royal regalia laid out over a wide space near the bend in a road with a mighty tree. The tamarind, if I remember, because beneath it lived a woman we knew as Mök Nab, and her husband, Mang—well, Mang Not-So-Clever, for some reason he was called. I saw the *istana* almost every day on my way to the Masjid Abidin on my journey home from school, in the trishaw (our *tèksi*) pedalled by Pök Mat. It looked distant and mournful, haunted even by many ghosts of yesteryear. It had a wide audience hall standing on low stilts and it sprawled a bit more, perhaps, to the back of nowhere. It was not known to us because few dared to venture into the grounds of the *istana*, and I had no reason anyway to be walking in there alone.

The Istana Kolam has probably since died of neglect, which is a shame because of all the old *istana*s in Trengganu that were still there for me to see this one looked quite special. I am reminded now of the day when a friend and I ventured to the innards of Jugra to look for the old *istana* of Sultan Abdul Samad, a man who, more than others, was synonymous with Selangor. And, oh yes, the old *istana* was still there three years ago, in ruins, in a cluster of undergrowth and trees, in the grey light of the fading day. And looking out from behind its walls were two or three wretched vandals, hacking away at the carvings, bringing further ruin to an already ruined old treasure. When approached they explained sheepishly how valuable those bits and parts were. And they stayed on when we withdrew in disgust and despair.

The Istana Kolam—which I hope is now reclaimed—sat in Kampung Petani, an historic area in the story of how Kuala Trengganu came to be. Its denizens were many wandering souls, I'm sure, and I wonder, even now, about the people who lived there and how it came to fall by the wayside, destitute and in disrepair.

To Each a Quarter

YESTERDAY, while browsing through Trengganu items stored in the system at the British Library, I was astonished to learn that among records, books and manuscripts kept there are the annual magazines of the Sultan Sulaiman Secondary School. I suddenly remembered the lament of a sickly old codger: 'If I'd known I was going to live this long, I'd have taken better care of myself.' In my brief stay at the SSS School I managed to pen a few thoughts for the school annual, and to paraphrase the old codger, if I'd known they were going to end up in such a place, I'd have given them greater care. But to spare myself the embarrassment, I shall say no more about that now.

I had a friend then, in my schooldays, who lived in Lorong Jjamil, which started life as Lorong Haji Jamil but matured on the lips of Trengganuspeakers as Lorong Jjamil, with a *shaddah* on the 'j'. The *shaddah* is used in Trengganuspeak to denote a verb, to attach a preposition to a noun (as in *Ddungung*, for *di Dungun*), or to make a word more manageable and shorter (e.g. *buöh ppisang* for a fruit that must've started life as *buöh mempisang,* or *buöh pisang-pisang*). But the only reason for the *shaddah* in Jjamil of the Lorong that I can think of is that it leaps out better from the Trengganu tongue than the inert Jamil, or perhaps it sounds better that way to our ear. Which reinforces another thing that I have against strict grammar: that language starts as words and rhythm, and grammar follows thereafter. Often rhythm overrides grammar. Who would be silly enough to say 'five items or fewer' (even if it's grammatical) when 'five items or less' sounds much better?

So back to Jjamil and my friend who lived there. He was a talented artist who composed a picture of a Malay warrior with a lady waving from behind him by merely sticking tiny coloured squares onto paper. The work was published in the school magazine, and I thought of him yesterday when I saw that his work had been given a safe haven in the library.

After his display of talent, I began to see my friend's part of town as the artists' quarter in the Kuala Trengganu of my day, Lorong Jjamil. In doing so I wasn't just making up a place for him in the wild for, not far from there in Kampung China, came another artist by the name of Chew Teng Beng who, after Sultan Sulaiman Secondary School, became

145

a painter of national calibre. And that, in fact, was how early Kuala Trengganu was laid out, into different quarters for different people.

Just days ago, in response to my query, my brother charted out the various sectors of Kuala Trengganu according to how it was peopled. There was Kampung Keling near the Pasar Kedai Payang (now Pasar Payang) at the foot of a familiar hill, Bukit Putri. The Kelings were people from Kalinga in India, so they must've settled there quite early in Trengganu's history. And it made a lot of sense too as the *kampung* was near the harbour, so convenient for them to jump off ship straight to shore for a piping hot *roti canai* among their own people. Cheek by jowl with Kampung Keling was Kampung Datuk, reserved for the family of the Datuk Amar, a prominent player in the Court of Trengganu. Kampung China, further up, explains itself, and the history of Chinese people in Trengganu is something that I'd like to look into later.

The royal quarter in Kuala Trengganu started from the gates of the Majid Abidin down to the shore of the harbour, taking in the Istana Maziah, Bukit Putri and the Padang Malaya (now Padang Maziah). In this quarter was Kota Lama (Old Fort), just opposite the Masjid, and an area known as Dalam Kota (Inside the Fortress) continued from there. The royals actually moved down there from higher up, on Bukit Putri, as the hill was said to have been cleared for a base by Tun Habib Abdul Majid Bendahara Padang Saujana (d. 1679) when (if?) he arrived in Kuala Trengganu to father the present dynasty. He was, I think, of the al-Eidrus clan, of good Hadhrami pedigree.

With the arrival of those who became the royalty of Trengganu came hangers-on and other people: the Patani group, for instance, settled in Kampung Petani, through which ran a road once called Jalan Kampung Petani but now known as Jalan Isaac after the man who started the grammar school on a hill about a mile from there. The people of Daik were in Kampung Daik, but of the followers of Sheikh Abdul Kadir of Patani, some were placed in Pulau Duyung Kechil and some on the mainland in Kampung Tanjung Pasar where there is a *surau* or *madrasah* that bears his name still. I don't know how or when the sheikh arrived in Trengganu, but there were a few men of his ilk who settled in various quarters: in Chabang Tiga, Paloh and Pulau Manis—all great centres of scholarly and pious people.

And then there was Kampung Hangus in the town centre—perhaps someone will tell me what happened there.

* * *

My friend Tengku Ali Bustaman (Pök Ku) wrote in to point out my error:

> '*Kota Lama is where Standard Chartered Bank is now, at the foot of Bukit Keledang. You can get there easily from Kampong Tiong which could be an extension of Lorong Jjamil. Chew Teng Beng is Chew Kiat Lim's older brother, I think. Both are superb artists.*')

Tigers of Trengganu

BY SOME MAJOR FLUKE, when I was at primary school in Kuala Trengganu, I was given a book prize for something that I've forgotten now. But the book was *The Tigers of Trengganu* by Col A.E. Locke (and if you're reading this Mr Ravindran Nair, thank you, thank you!*). Locke was the man they sent out to do the shoot, after many complaints from the *Orang Darat* of tigers roaming wild. The tigers were interfering with their livelihood so this chap Locke shot down quite a few—the tigers I mean, not the *Orang Darat*s we all loved and knew.

But still a shame it was as tigers are such magical creatures, eyes so bright, burning in the forests in the night. I think even Locke had to admit, with grudging respect, that it was a pity to have to shoot them all.

There was a Chinese circus that came to town in those years that had elephants, snakes, monkeys and tigers sitting pathetically in their little cages. I hated circuses even then and never knew what they were for until a neighbour married a man for the Circo Brasil (Circus Brazil) that came to town. Then I began to take notice of them, but only in a prurient way. As for the tigers, I actually saw one of them in a cage with a tamer who kept waving a long stick at it that was painted red at the tip. I was told that that was to remind the tiger of how it had become compliant, via a red hot poker. I hoped then—as now—that it wasn't true.

There weren't many tigers in Kuala Trengganu when I was there, though rumours were rife of stripy stalkers. Malays have a healthy respect for tigers, or *tok belang* as they're called even now. The title *tok* is reserved for a revered elder, and generally for someone of deep learning and remarkable skill, such as our renowned anti-colonial folk heroes, Tok Bahaman and Tok Mat Kilau. In the early Seventies a mysterious old man surfaced in Pahang who identified himself only as Tok Peramu, and said no more. At that time there was an old exponent of *silat* in Kuala Trengganu by the name of Che Wan Muhammad, who learnt his art in the Pahang of old. When the elderly Che Wan saw Tok Peramu looking sanguine in those newspaper pictures, he sat up and said: 'This is Tok Bahaman, you know!' But Tok Bahaman is another story.

Back now to the tiger *tok*s of the jungle.

One bright Trengganu day, when I had a little bike, a couple of friends suggested a ride around town but unbeknown to me they had planned a journey to the interior, to Kuala Brang about twenty-five miles away in old measure. I remember passing through Wakaf Tapai, and a muddy place called Atas Tol which Father once translated into Arabic as Ala Tul in his punning way, to mean both Atas Tol and the Arabic expression, 'go straight ahead'—*ala tuuuuul,* as they would say. (Father sometimes took us along strange linguistic routes, occasionally regaling us with tales of the Japanese Momo Taro.) But what I remember most distinctly about this cycling trip was when we reached a stretch of road that was flanked by some wild trees. One of my friends suddenly put his finger to his lips at this juncture, then we cycled and cycled for perhaps another mile without saying a word to each other. When we saw houses again, the friend said that that was the stretch frequented by Tok Belang, and Tok Belang didn't like people who blabbered too much, and to mention his name was strictly taboo. I was pleased when we decided to cycle home via a detour.

Outside of captivity I saw the tiger only once, and that must've been the last tiger of Trengganu. It was during the school holidays when I was sitting with my mother in a packed bus that was lumbering down the road towards Jerteh, on our way to Kampung Raja in Besut. The bus suddenly braked and everyone kept very quiet and still. In front of the bus was a solitary tiger, crossing the road to the other side of the jungle. We muttered not a word until we reached Kampung Buluh just a few minutes from there. That was the kind of spell tigers had on us ordinary people.

There must've been many tigers in the jungles of Trengganu, perhaps, not too long ago, maybe until the early second half of the last century. In or about 1809 the sultan of Trengganu, Sultan Ahmad Shah I, sent a Trengganu tiger to Brunei as a royal present for Sultan Muhammad Kanzul Alam (1807–1826). The gift provided more than just amusement to the people of Brunei as, not long after that, the tiger escaped but was recaptured by a man named Pengiran Muhammad Daud who, by all accounts, was a fierce warrior. The Pengiran—who was given the title Pengiran Pemancha after another act of heroism involving some Spaniards who visited the state—single-handedly brought home the Trengganu tiger.

After my bus trip with Mother to Kampong Raja I never saw tigers again outside captivity, but there were things laid out on the cloistered pedestrian walkways, the *kaki lima* of the shophouses in Kuala Trengganu that reminded me again and again of those mighty beasts and the spell they had on the lives of people. Strange pieces of dried meat, coiled like rattan bits sat in front of bored-looking street peddlers. There were other bits and bobs too that they laid out for sale: Buddhist amulets, semi-precious stones and jungle herbs of unknown powers. Those coily bits were things that we took notice of but were seldom mentioned by polite people as they were, reputedly, tigers' pudenda. I never saw anyone picking up or taking home those tiger bits plucked out—and God knows how—by those intrepid people, but I guessed that by some powers of sympathetic magic, they would have been sought after by men who wanted to be, well, like the mighty tiger.

In a moment of great curiosity I once asked an elder who told me what he thought with a loud guffaw. It was then that I began to take an interest in the male dogs of Kuala Trengganu, to see if they'd had things taken from them by intrepid people, all in the name of ... the magical Tiger.

***

Eyes on the Istana

IN THE SURUNG FRONT PART of our house in Kuala Trengganu was the portrait of a man of serious mien in full Trengganu regalia, and he looked very distant from us all.

We looked up to him, literally, and said no more. Sometimes during his conversations with friends Father would mention his title, Datuk Mmata, a strange name for a child to grapple with. For a long time I bore the notion that he must've been precious, as *mmata* was Trengganuspeak for *permata*, meaning precious jewels. Then one day a quack practitioner came to the house and spoke of his prowess with diseases of the eye. As a testimonial, he pointed to the portrait of our man: 'The Datuk had problems with his eyes.' Then the shyster continued: 'One day he had it so bad his eye plopped out.' When he'd gone with his bundle of herbs and

Istana Hijau in Kuala Trengganu.

geegaws, and was a safe distance from us, Father could not contain his glee and my elder brother, whose biology lessons at school had already reached the level of the eye, made a meal of the man's knowledge of anatomy.

But it struck a chord with me—*mmata* was close to *mata,* Trengganuspeak and standardspeak for eye. Maybe there was something in it after all. So for a long time afterwards I began to look closely at the portrait, and I examined especially the poor, sad, faraway look in those eyes.

And then I thought no more of him until I began to travel away from town to my school in Kuala Ibai. On the bus I'd often look out to a palatial-looking building en route that housed the new Sekolah Sultan Zainal Abidin, the premier Arabic school in Kuala Trengganu (that was later to transform into a college with the outlandish acronym of Kusza). It was a strange building set amidst the wooden houses of Kuala Trengganu; it looked grand and old to a Trengganu child, and possibly contained many stories; and then I was told that it was the only house in Trengganu that had a cellar. And when someone told me that it was probably the former residence of Datuk Mmata, it was like 'wow!'

I came across Datuk Mmata again recently when looking through the history of the Istana Maziah, at the foot of Bukit Putri. The *istana*, to me, was a mournful place with only a ceremonial purpose, whilst most of the time it looked forlorn and empty with shutters closed, and so removed from our daily activity. Yet at festival times, when roofed platforms were placed over barrels on what used to be known as Padang Malaya, folk came milling around from the outer reaches of Kuala Trengganu for the *rödat* show, or the *bangsawan* theatre. The Istana Maziah took on another shape, flooded as it was in light and decked with twinkling bulbs of many colours. The *istana* that stared at us mutely in our workaday lives had suddenly come aglow. And so it'd done in Trengganu history, looking and absorbing all: the ceremonies of *mandi safat* for pre-nuptial royals, the sweet voice of the opera starlet Ruhani B and voices of politicians that bellowed their cause on platforms in Padang Malaya, including the late lamented Datuk Onn Jaafar who, towards the end of his life, became the voice of Kuala Trengganu South in the People's Chamber (Dewan Rakyat) in Kuala Lumpur.

151

Datuk Mmata was not *permata* or *mata,* but Mata-Mata. The name that perhaps described his role, for the *mata-mata* were the seeing eyes of policemen or people who played a watchful role. So Datuk Mata-Mata was probably the man in charge of state security; and he was connected with the Istana Maziah that now looks across the harbour of Kuala Trengganu.

The *istana* was built in 1897—some say 1895—during the reign of Sultan Zainal Abidin III (1881–1918). What's beyond dispute is that it was built on the site of the old Istana Hijau (Green Palace) that was built by Sultan Baginda Omar in 1870 and later destroyed by fire, some say in the heat of battle when the Japanese came to Kuala Trengganu. This latter claim is patently untrue as the Japanese did not arrive in the town until 1941, while Istana Maziah was built at the end of the previous century.

For this new palace, the sultan entrusted the role of planner and supervisor to his brother-in-law, Tengku Chik Abu Bakar bin Tengku Abdul Jalil. There were other men involved in it too, and among them, in charge of its design and interior decor, was our Datuk Mata-Mata. Wood for the construction came from Dungun, under the supervision of Tengku Panglima Besar Tengku Muda Kechik, and students of building construction material will be interested to know that it was built from a mixture of lime, clay, sand, egg white and palm sugar. (In building his fortress on Bukit Putri, Sultan Omar did one better. He mixed his mortar with honey.)

The old Istana Hijau was a grand palace from a different era, and the old Istana Maziah too had understated beauty, influenced, no doubt, by European architecture. Both were grand buildings, so more's the shame then that the Istana Hijau was destroyed by fire, and its replacement, Istana Maziah, is now disfigured by planners with little notion of the purity of memory.

Folks Who Lived on the Hill

ON A DAY WHEN THE RAIN was lashing down in heavy torrents, I was looking out through our window to the distant light blinking through the haze on Bukit Putri. It was probably early afternoon, but the dim light in a town enveloped by the heavy downpour raised uneasy feelings about the *tuk wah*, for that's what my uncle named it, that distant beacon flashing and dimming, flashing and dimming incessantly. Unknown to me then it was merely his spur-of-the-moment onomatopoeic word for that light on the hill—*tuk* for when it dimmed, and *wah* for when it came aglow again. Not surprisingly, in my first year at school at the Sekolah Melayu Ladang, as we were discussing the landmarks of Kuala Trengganu, our teacher, when he heard my contribution, began to look very puzzled. '*Tuk wah?*' he asked. '*Tuk wah tu apende?*' ('What is it?') The *tuk wah* was one of the wonders of Bukit Putri that commanded the harbour of Kuala Trengganu. It was a beacon on a tall platform that winked out to the outer reaches, to boats coming ashore, to fishermen back from the sea. It looked down on the harbour from its place on the edge of the hill. It had a steep ladder that rose to its height, though we were never tempted to go up there.

There were two ways to go up Bukit Putri in those days: via the footpath that was beaten into the hillside facing the sea, or the proper way, up the steps that started at its foot by the *istana*. Up these steps to the count of a hundred and a half, maybe more, you're confronted with the edge of mystery, of bushes, tall trees and old graves that had lain there silently since the beginning of memory. To our left, just before the graves, I remember, half buried in the ancient earth, a heavy piece of time-worn cast iron known as *bedil beranak,* a mother cannon that reputedly begot another. It had another one beside it, much smaller, presumably the by-product of this parturition in heavy metal. Many a time I must've stood there wondering how the mother—known as Sri Buih—could have raised such a baby boomer.

The Malays had a thing about the cannon and its surrounding aura, giving it near-mystical qualities and some inexplicable power. I remember being told, when researching some aspects of the state of Selangor, of a mysterious cannon whose appearance was foretold in the dreams of a royal *pawang* or shaman, and then making its actual appearance as an omen for the state at the appointed time in the mouth of the Selangor river. This mystical cannon is now on a hill in Kuala Selangor, wrapped in yellow, the royal colour. The Trengganu cannons weren't draped in such regalia, but I wonder if they're still there now, mother and a grown-up, loud-mouthed child.

My mother used to tell me stories of Bukit Putri, of the princess who lived up there and who looked favourably on folks below by lending them her crockery for their banquets or nuptials—some say it was silverware, others say it was just ordinary china. The princess or *putri* who gave the name to the hill was of the fabled *Orang Bunian* of Malay folklore who had one foot on this ordinary earth and another in the spirit world. But one day some careless borrower failed to return her silver or chinaware, which made her take flight in anger, never to come back to Kuala Trengganu.

This story that Mother told me must have been handed down to her by her own mother, and God knows how or when it first began in folk memory. When Mother passed on, she was laid to rest not far from an older grave that seemed to have been given special care. My brother told me recently that it belonged to an old sultan of Trengganu, Mansur II, of whom he knew very little. When I began to look further, I made a familiar yet still surprising discovery: how we live in our past shadows, how linked we are to one another.

I had to go back to Bukit Putri.

It was there, on the hill, that a battle was fought between two rival factions for the throne of Trengganu in the first half of the nineteenth century. Baginda Omar, a claimant to the throne, had built a fort there to stake his claim against Tengku Mansur, whose base was in Balik Bukit. After early negotiations, Tengku Mansur took the Trengganu throne in 1831 as Sultan Mansur II, while Tengku Omar became the Yang di Pertuan Besar. But that didn't settle the matter. In the Trengganu civil war that followed, Tengku Omar lost his positon yet again and had to leave his fortification in Bukit Putri (said to have been built by him from bricks held together by a mixture of lime and honey), fleeing first to Besut then to Daik in Riau.

Mansur II died in 1836 to be succeeded by his son, Sultan Muhammad I, who used Bukit Putri as his base. Three years later Tengku Omar came back with his men and, after a pitched battle on the hill, drove the incumbent away to Dungun. Omar was once again back on Bukit Putri. A few months later the unfortunate Muhammad made an attempt on the *bukit*, this time aided by Tengku Hitam of Dungun, but failed.

Sultan Omar Baginda Shah reigned in Trengganu for thirty-seven years until 1876.

Balik Kampung

IN A SENSE the *kampung* is the womb of the Malay body and soul. The mentally damaged curl up in a foetal position, and the insecure and the uncertain go back to the security of their mums. It's one thing or a mother, but the Malays always go back to their *kampung.*

I was talking to a sage person about the plight of young people who grow up in towns. In his day, he said, it was unusual to hear a Malay person saying that he or she was from Kuala Lumpur or Petaling Jaya or Shah Alam. The Malays were always from some *kampung*, hence the stock opening line when meeting a new person: *'Kampung di mana?'* ('Where is your *kampung?*)

Nowadays it would be extremely presumptuous, churlish even, to ask a person you've just met that same question, especially if he or she is young. The young lad or lass may be brash and uncertain, but chances are that he or she grew up in a big mansion with Doric columns, awoken in the early evening by the gentle purring of a magnificent car, and was probably bathed and dressed by compliant servants. He or she may still be uncertain for all that, but townsfolk are strange people.

Not too long ago the *kampung* was the country, but now it is becoming *another* country. The Malays have lost their home, they no longer have a *kampung,* said my sage friend.

The way I remember Kuala Trengganu it was very much a *kampung,* even if it was right in the middle of town. If this was an anomaly, it was one that ought to have been preserved. But folk thought differently, and so it was in the Nineties that some of my people woke up in their fine houses in the middle of town to an order for them to go away. The state government was planning to modernise Kuala Trengganu, and they must have decided that all these folk who had lived there most of their lives, and many who were born there, were stumbling blocks for the planners. There was a massive programme of evacuation in the old town. Houses were demolished, people uprooted and families torn up. Then they began to move in: the bulldozers, mechanical rollers, house-builders and town planners. Parts of Kuala Trengganu today are just masses of shophouses. Many parts of the old Kuala Trengganu—the old houses, the communities and especially the village folk—were moved along to places like Chabang Tiga, Wakaf Tapai, and some have even moved back to Kuala Brang, the old capital.

The planners started to build the hotels, the motels and other forms of recreation that they thought tourists dreamt about as soon as they deplaned and went past passport control.

I remember my uncle's magnificent wooden house—it may not have been magnificent but to a young boy, any tenement that could house more than two families, had a concrete frontage of steps and a car port was a magnificent house. It stood next door to the Masjid Abidin, and that was our first stop on Hari Raya (Eid day) once the prayers at the mosque were done. It had a spacious lounge with deep sofas, and what impressed me most were two hefty volumes on Uncle's overhead bookshelf—the Malay–English dictionary of R.O. Winstedt. As it is now, so it was then: Winstedt dictionaries have a way of transporting you to a place that was beyond your everyday world. Its base was basically rural, and the language it showed was the very essence of being Malay. I think it was Winstedt who gave the definition of an 'express train' that was distinctly *kampung* in character. It was, he said, *kereta api sombong*. I remember reading that and giggling at the picture that it conjured up in my mind, of a market-trading *kampung* lady carrying a bundle of things on her head, wrapped in a bright sarong. She was hailing a passing train that would've taken her to town, except that it wouldn't stop. It was, of course, an express train. *'Kereta api sombong!'* ('Proud train!') she muttered beneath her breath as she spat out residues of betel nut and *sireh* leaves she'd been chewing all her waiting while.

The house that my uncle and auntie lived in was transported in piles of beams and slats of wood to another place, out of town, and there it was rebuilt in a sad community of displaced folk while that part of Kuala Trengganu that was left as an open field braced itself for a brave new world. My uncle died soon after that, his wife, my auntie, followed suit, and I hope the two Winstedt volumes are well cared for somewhere safe, quietly mourning the loss of soul.

Kuala Trengganu wasn't much to speak of by the standards of peninsular towns. But it had what most didn't have, or had lost as they moved along: a thriving community that lived and breathed the place and air, and who gave back to it something more. We had our own *paung* maker, *roti canai* kneader and *nasi dagang* sellers by the score. There was Mök Teh 'Spring' who made *rojak* of green papaya, Pak Löh Yunang who sold newspapers, *kitab*s and secular books all laid out on a table. There was Che Mat Nobat to whom they turned when they found old gamelan instruments in an old *istana* in Kampung Kolam who still had old tunes singing inside his head as he made his other claim to fame: the technicoloured *nasi minyök* of Trengganu.

These were people that made you glad that you were part of the whole. But as my uncle and auntie moved on to another place, lock, stock and house, so did hundreds of other people, all ordered to uproot and go away. Nowadays, I'm told, the old Masjid Abidin finds it difficult to form even two *safs* of the faithful at ordinary prayers. The community is now no longer about the people, but about shops and polluting motorcars. A sad thing that is to befall a town when it has lost its civic community and is transformed into a soulless shopping centre. The Trengganu government then, which was rolling in petroleum cash, never found it attractive to retain the people that helped build the town: the butcher, the baker and the brassware maker. Other civic-minded communities would have devised a housing programme for them in the centre of town, subsidised housing perhaps, but that was far too visionary, and visions are found only in the dreams of common people.

And that is the trouble once we've moved out of our *kampung*s, physically or mentally, we lose the power to dream creatively.

* * *

When I wrote recently about yearning and remembering, Anonymous sent me this poignant advice, in the Minang dialect, from a grandfather to a grandson who's about to leave the *kampung* for the glitzy town:

'Ingat posan atok, ingat baik-baik yo,
Jangan tinggal solat, kecuali terlupo,

Jangan bergaduh kecuali dalam bahayo,
Jangan mencurik kecuali terpakso.
(and, of course, to make it livelier,)
Jangan pulang kampoeng kecuali dah kayo.'

I'm no expert in the Minang dialect, but until someone else comes up with a better translation, we'll have to make do with mine:

'Remember my child what grandpa's saying:
Unless you forget, do not stop your praying,
Do not pick a fight unless it's for your saving,
Don't take what ain't yours without matters compelling,
(and the modern addition:)
Don't come home till you're worth more than a shilling.'

And Anonymous rightly cites R. Azmi on passing time and severe longings.

'*Kkenang* is thus a serious disease. What is the *penawar* or antidote?' she asks (why do I think it's a she?). Well, you've got me stumped there. I've looked in *Tajul Muluk* but can't find a suitable remedy.

An Inlet by the Sea

PANTAI TELUK DOESN'T EXIST anymore. Its name, at least, has vanished. It was an inlet of tranquil water, sheltered from the lashing waves by a sandbar that ran until it dissipated in the harbour. From there you could stand and look at the narrow strip that met the sea from the downward roll of Padang Malaya. You would have heard the traffic coasting along the road that held the edge of Kuala Trengganu, enjoyed the view of the post office and the *istana*, the Chartered Bank and, of course, Bukit Putri on the other side of the water.

Behind you was another world: the sea-eaten remains of an old boat sticking proudly from the loam, an empty *töngkang* barge standing still, a *perahu bèdor* of Trengganu merchant sailors, sails rolled up, maybe after a long journey from Senggora. On the sandbar meeting the sea the sand was white, but in this inner calm there was a different earth, dark and clayey in consistency, smelling of the *teluk* and breeding its own family of coastal creatures—the *ikang ddukang,* a riverine type of catfish, was most feared for it carried a nail-like sting on its back. You stepped on it, as I once did, at your peril. But mostly its other inhabitants ran shy from you, the interloper. They were little crabs with over-sized claws that waved enticingly then scattered away to their bolt-holes as you drew near. The dark, slimy shore on this side was pockmarked with little holes. We sometimes scooped them out, hole and creature, and kept the captives in a bottle.

This was an area of dead boats decorated with long service medals of barnacles, beachcombers gathering driftwood and fishermen dabbing a fresh coat of paint on a fishing *payang* pulled ashore. If it was a Friday morning there'd be many fishermen stretching their legs along the coast, exchanging fishermen's banter and perhaps taking time off too in the shade of trees while other village folk sauntered off to Friday prayers. Going out to sea for the Friday catch was unthinkable, though some did in violation of this. And they were turned into monkeys, so we learned from our folklore. This was the first rule we learned, in case later in life we opted for a life at sea.

There were not many trees, though, on the sands around the *teluk,* except for the unfussy coconuts that grew almost everywhere. There was

A view of Pantai Teluk, looking towards Bukit Putri and the post office.

159

a low tree with branches well spread out which was much sought after by retiring fisherfolk for its deep shade, and desired by the coastal goats that chewed on its broad-leaved canopy.

The Pantai Teluk also served the Tanjong market as its tradesmen's entrance, where boats from the *ulu* were parked and tough, no-nonsense men from upriver, skins darkened by the sun, jumped ashore with bundles of firewood and portions of fermented *tapai* wrapped in pouches of broad leaves and hung together in a cluster. Their women brought fruits plucked from the jungle: *ngekke, perah, pulasan, salak,* strips of *petai* beans and *jering* for eating as a vegetable side dish with rice and fish. Maybe there was also a bit of *belara* which my friend Tengku Bustaman Ali (the blogger Pök Ku) described as fish preserved to an alarming, gooey consistency.

On a morning when the market was at its peak, the Pantai Teluk would have dazzled with *batik* patterns and loads of fruits in primary colours, the shawls of women coming out for their daily needs clashing with the red, green and blue sheets of plastic stretched out above the stalls to keep out the heat of the day. There were voices from the *ulu* and the chatter of the Kuala people. Medicine peddlers in full flow extolling the powers of their concoctions of herbs, an Indian magician 'slitting' the throat of his turbaned son, beggars in full voice drawing attention to their physical afflictions, the gaggle and cackle of street theatre.

Wan M, who grew up just a stone's throw from there, wrote in to tell me that Pantai Teluk is no more, and even if there's anything left, it goes now by another name, Pantai Taman Selera. Taman Selera was an idea, thought up in the 1970s when the market was dead, to transform the area into a gluttons' square. But I suspect that Pantai Teluk would have died too from the acts of men with the construction of a dam upriver. The Teluk now is a diminishing remnant of its former glory, eaten up by the changing flow of the water that has deposited a mound of sand in the rivermouth and extended the coast opposite, Seberang Takir.

A journalist friend from a national newspaper once gave his bright idea to the then *menteri besar* of Trengganu on how to unblock the harbour: blast it with explosives, he told the man. I can't imagine what that could have done, but I expect the big noise would have rattled the boat skeletons in Pantai Teluk a little and woken up the barnacles.

The Kapitan and the Admiral

WHENEVER I WALKED UP THE MAIN STREET of Kampung China in Kuala Trengganu to a bookshop there to look at the latest comic books or magazines, I could do a roll call of friends I'd meet along the way. There was YCK, a little lad from Batu Rakit who lived with relatives in a shophouse on the bridge, TPS who lived in a house that looked like a temple with pigeons brooding in the forecourt, GWB whose father was a car dealer further up the road and KSF in her father's corner studio and photo shop.

Kampung China was a bustling world compared to the quiet of our own corner near Pantai Teluk, and even though the air in front of our house was abuzz with the noise of petty traders, wayfarers and lorries carrying fresh deliveries of goods, in the afternoon it became almost still as the centre of commerce shifted back to the Kedai Payang area that was close to Kampung China. Kampung China means, essentially, Chinese village not town, so perhaps it portrays a town as it was described by an English eighteenth century traveller. Then it consisted of groups of houses, one cluster quite distant from another, in a sprawling area known as the *kuala* or mouth of the river.

The Chinese, or *teng lang*, of Kuala Trengganu have a long history. They came in their junks way back in the eighteenth century, maybe earlier, bringing goods with them and taking goods back to China. They settled and became cultivators, and would have also been part of an even older settlement, if speculation is correct that the Fo-lo-lan—referred to by the Chinese chronicler Chou Ch'u-fei in *Ling-wai Tai-ta* in 1178—was indeed Kuala Brang upstream of the Trengganu River. To the Chinese, Trengganu was variously Ting Ko Nou, Ting Ko Lou and Ting Kia Lou.

There is said to be a well in Kampung China known as the Low Tiey Well, reputedly owned by the Chinese translator Lim Keng Hoon (Low Tiey) in 1875. Translators served the sultan as well as their own community as Kapitan China. These *jurubahasa,* as they were known, were not paid by the state, but were given powers instead to issue their own token coins, known as *jokoh*. One prominent Kapitan China was Wee Sin Hee, whose father, Wee Kiat Kheng, arrived in Trengganu from the Fuxian Province in the eighteenth century. Sin Hee served as a translator to Sultan Zainal Abidin III (1881–1918) and became a very successful trader who built many of the historic shophouses of Kuala Trengganu. In his *Pelayaran* in 1836, Abdullah bin Abdul Kadir Munshi named another *kapitan* in Kuala Trengganu, Lim Eng Huat.

My friends from among the Chinese community in Kuala Trengganu spoke in Trengganuspeak with us, and a brand of Hokkien at home that was coloured by the local vocabulary. They'd been arriving and settling among us from time immemorial, scores at a time maybe, but the biggest number of Chinese people came to Trengganu not as settlers but with their most famous Admiral Zheng He on a mission of goodwill in the fifteenth century. According to Chinese records, the admiral sailed with sixty-two vessels and 20,000 men to Southeast Asia, and among the many places he visited was Kuala Brang in Hulu Trengganu.

I used to sit with friends at dusk near Pantai Teluk to watch ships coming in—the *Hong Ho* or some other—and it was a great moment of awe when we saw the lights on the ship and the crew waving to us on shore. I can't imagine even now what a jaw-dropping moment it would have been for a boy—the son of a sea gypsy maybe—sitting in the same place in the fifteenth century as sixty-two vessels, or even half that, sailed in from China, bedecked with flags and banners fluttering in the air. And there on deck, in the robe of the Imperial admiral, the man Zheng He himself, taking his bearing from Bukit Putri then checking his map for the journey ahead to Fo-lo-lan or Kuala Brang, further up the Trengganu River.

Times of Day

WHILST LEANING ON THE LEDGE on top of the stairs of the *surau* Haji Mat Kerinci in Tanjong, and looking out to the road on most mornings of the week of my Trengganu days, it hardly escaped my notice that there was time and time; and thanks to the early buses that rarely stopped for us, we were late for school on most days.

The morning and the buses moved on, the former with the lengthening of shadows, the latter packed nearly to the gunwales. When I looked into the old *surau* thinking whether to turn back home or to wait for the next bus that trundled down, time seemed to move in different ways. There was time that ticked away on the old clock in the *surau,* and there was time outside that was slipping away with the day. And then I remembered there were two times in Trengganu: the time *waktu* and the time Malaya.

I don't know how it came to be or how long it had been so, but in Trengganu then prayer times were set to the *waktu,* which was tautological time because both time and *waktu* meant much the same thing. Shops and businesses worked according to the time Malaya, which was the time of the country—and it remained so even after we became Malaysia—because that was the standard time that we always knew. So while the country rotated on standard horological principles, the mosques and *surau*s of Trengganu worked on *waktu* hours. This meant that the noon prayers were always fixed at midday, whilst on ordinary clocks it kept moving throughout the year, from twelve-thirty to one o'clock to just a few minutes after. That was the constant of our *waktu* clock, that the midday prayer was always in the middle of the day.

This caused confusion, needless to say, to those who were not regulars of the mosques or *surau*s who happened to peep in to find out the time of day. Which probably explains why people were often found snoozing in the nearly empty *surau*s outside prayer hours, because they'd suddenly found that they had time to spare. When out again in broad daylight they'd, of course, find that a part of their day had moved away, not to mention the people they had appointments to see.

Unbeknownst to hoi polloi, a close watch was kept on the *waktu* hours by the men in charge of prayer times in mosques, local *musolla*s and indeed in our local Haji Mat Kerinci. Once a week or so the man in the Masjid Abidin in the town centre—normally the *bilal* who shouted out the *azan* call to prayer—would take out the mosque's astrolabe to measure the sun's altitude. Then he'd set the mosque clock accordingly for the time of the *zuhr* noon prayer. I expect adjustments were also made to the satellite *surau*s or *musolla*s.

The *surau* Haji Mat Kerinci was an eponymous *surau* like many other *surau*s in our part of town. Kerinci is a place in South Sumatra, so Haji Mat (Mohammad) of the *surau* must've hailed from there. Closer to us was the *surau* Sheikh Abdul Kadir, a religious scholar who came to us from Patani. Further north from there was the *surau* Haji Mat Lintar, a *hafiz* with a deep knowledge of the *tajwid* or the correct recitation of the Qur'an. He had a voice that carried loud and clear to the back rows in the Abidin Mosque when he led the prayer, hence the word *lintar* in his name to denote 'thunder'. And between him and us was the Surau Besar, which means, simply, the big *surau*.

So with each passing of the hour in a Trengganu day, there were pockets of time zones in those mosques and *surau*s that were out of synch with the outside world. And that was the *waktu* that has faded away from us now.

Sticks of Old Trengganu

KUALA TRENGGANU must have been the first town to have its breakfast of satay. The smell came wafting down the cloistered walkway of Kedai Pök Löh Yunang, the Fernandez shop for posh watches and the old *kedai* Yamada, which later became Redi Photo Studio. The satay man stood in the narrow lane between the walls of two shop ends and there he fanned billowing smoke from his satay all laid over a bed of glowing charcoal. It was an early time of day as the trishaws arrived with loads of *kangkong* freshly harvested from the *paya*, and the lopsided clock faces on the *jang besar* showed times in various places in this world, except that we couldn't connect them to world cities that we knew. Three o'clock it would be saying on one side, and maybe five on another. I can't remember what stood there before this big *jang* took over, perhaps just a few concrete-filled metal drums or *leger*.

Sometimes Pök Yassin, Pök Löh Yunang's shop manager, took me to the coffee shop for sticks of satay as a reward for being the son of a man who'd been a lifetime subscriber to his *Utusang Melayu* and loose-leaf *kitab*s that came encased in folders with which to face the Tuan Guru. The Tuan Guru also sometimes came by in the people's *tèksi* otherwise known as the trishaw, or the *beca*, on his way home to Tanjung Kapur after a session of post-dawn pedagogy at the Masjid Abidin further up, past the *gertak* or what Mother called the *ttiang* bridge, past Ah Chin the tailor, past the delightful *kedai bbunga*.

Another peculiarity I noticed about this early-morning satay under the clock tower was that the satay was served with toast from the kitchen of the coffee shop owner, whose name I cannot now remember.

When I posted on my blog a picture of boats by the shore opposite Padang Malaya (taken by Mr Chung Chee Min, a teacher at my former school, Victoria Institution in Kuala Lumpur, during a break in his sixth form year in 1960), fellow Trengganuer Tengku Ali Bustaman (the blogger Pök Ku) wrote in to remind me of another Kuala Trengganu satay man who'd slipped from my memory. It's a strange thing because Che Muda Satay lived near Surau Besar by the Kelab Pantai which was in my daily route of travel. Later when we moved to Kuala Lumpur the name appeared again as, if I remember it rightly, he owned a restaurant and lodging house in Jalan Raja Muda in Kampung Baru. This was the place where you went to in those days to meet the likes of Pak Sako, the socialist writer Ishak Haji Muhammad, who penned the famous novella *Anak Mat Lela Gila.*

If, as another correspondent (Long Ladang) and Tengku Bustaman have pointed out, Che Muda made the most excellent meat-on-sticks in Kuala Trengganu in a coffee shop that stood just to the right of the picture,

The mouth of the Kuala, taken in 1960 by my schoolteacher Mr Chung Chee Min when he visited Trengganu in his sixth-form year.

I'm afraid I've missed out on that too. Which is a shame really, as the coffee shop they speak about was actually next door to the permanently closed residence-cum-shophouse of an elderly man who always walked in a T-shirt that Father called the *kanciperat,* and the *sarung pelikat* as his daytime wear. He was the grandfather of my good friend C.H. Lim who came down from Dungun to read whatever it was that we read at the Sultan Sulaiman Primary School.

At the end of the school day, C.H. Lim and I would rush to the awaiting *tèksi* pedalled by our man Pak Mat, and off we went, past the *paya* marshlands of Batas Baru, past the Chung Hwa Chinese School, then to Lim's grandfather's house, before arriving at Tanjong where I alighted in front of Kedai Pök Löh, another coffee house of the town.

I used to pop in at the coffee shop where Che Muda's boys sold his satay sometimes to buy a tiny frozen block of butter that the shop kept in the freezer compartment of their Kelvinator. That cost ten cents in those days, and the cholesterol was a treat for me. Then I'd go back to the house to read another comic book or two from C.H. Lim's collection in his grandfather's doorway.

Burying the Past

HALF OF KUALA TRENGGANU, it seems, is a necropolis. There are more cemeteries in this town than in any other.

As a child I used to walk, in daylight, of course, to a place called Nesang Pak or Four Gravestones which, as the name tells, had a grave there with four stone markers instead of the usual two. They were there in the shade along with those of many others who were buried there beneath a cluster of bamboo trees that creaked all day in the slightest breeze. It was an old burial place that no one visited. No one remembered those who were laid there in the graves.

There was a vast expanse of cemetery next door to—and in the back of—the Malay Sekolah Paya Bunga; there are old gravestones on top of Bukit Putri, Bukit Kecik and in Kampong Keling, where lived the family of the Datuk Amar; there were many old graves on the slope of the hill.

Behind the Arabic School, the old Madrasah Sultan Zainal Abidin, in the sandy soil that stretched a long way, were graves too, the dead of long ago, now in their last, nameless resting place. Old grave markers were large round stones picked from the sea, unlike the new ones whose roundness or flatness would tell you if the dead was male or female. May God have mercy on them all.

My mother was buried in the old Sheikh Ibrahim Cemetery, quite coincidentally, near the grave of an early sultan of Trengganu. It was in a stretch of burial place that extended further up into other burial places to accommodate Buddhists, Christians and Hindus. You could walk there till you saw the mast of the 'wireless' station from afar, where Father cycled to in the wee hours when he was a young rookie. This was then a long, dark road, before the complete electrification of Kuala Trengganu.

Near the Sheikh Ibrahim is another, called the Tok Pelam, where people still bury the dead of Kuala Trengganu. Both the sheikh and the *tok* were old luminaries, two learned men who must've had many followers. They built a structure over Tok Pelam's grave to house those who stayed up late at night to read a *surah* from the Qur'an or two; and to passers-by it looked like a house and many tales were spun around there. I was told in my Sekolah Ladang days that an egg of the *buraq* was kept there, and the *buraq* if you don't already know, is a bird that travels multi-dimensional paths.

Cemeteries make sobering thoughts, beckoning us to the end of days. We're all dead now, as someone said, the living are just dead people on holiday. Needless to say, the cemeteries of Kuala Trengganu are silent records of its past, its repositories of old. On Bukit Putri are old sultans, past royalty, people killed in battles for ascendancy. In the cemetery of Kota Lama are remains of the sultanate and their entourage who moved to the Kuala from the *ulu*. Many old graves and burial places in Kuala Trengganu are not tended and forgotten, though they're still highly visible. The cemetery near the Sekolah Paya Bunga, for instance, is near what used to be known as Kampung Petani, where people from that now southern Thai province lived and were perhaps buried when they came down with the founder of the present Royal House of Trengganu. There was Kampung Daik too, near the Masjid Abidin, and the *kampung* where you can still see a cluster of houses belonging to the family of Datuk Amar and Datuk Mata-Mata.

Those long forgotten graves could have been the last resting places of people who came down with people who became the rulers and royalty of Trengganu, from Daik and Patani and other parts of the archipelago.

Datuk Mata-Mata was the old commissioner of the Trengganu police force, and Datuk Amar was an important court official, perhaps the prime minister, descendants of the entourage that came with the sultan who came from Johor on the orders of Pak Habib, the grand old Bendahara. Father used to have many friends from the Datuk Amar family, one of whom was known to us as Che Long, an oldy worldy Malay gentleman (and I used the word advisedly) who always dropped in on us on Friday mornings for a cup of hot Milo. His grandfather, Datuk Amar, was a fluent Arabic speaker who used to sit on the *wakaf* by the little *surau* in Kampung Keling opposite the Pasar Payang to practise his language with seamen from the gulf area. Hadhrami sailors have etched many chequered marks in our history.

In Kampung Dalam Bata, near our *kampung* of Tanjong, lived a grand old man who trekked his slow but steady path to the Masjid Abidin in my day. He must've been well over ninety then, but was still brimming with many stories, and the name he went by was Datuk Balai, an old court official at the fin-de-siècle. One thing that never failed to fascinate me about this Datuk was that he was part of the Trengganu that went over to Bangkok with the *bunga mas*, the gold flowers that we made for the Thais every so often to keep them in good humour. Datuk Balai once told Father that as soon as they walked the streets of the metropolis with the flowers, assorted Thais prostrated themselves immediately in every nook and in every corner, for such was the lure of gold and their respect for their ruler. I shook his hand once at the urging of my father, and I'm glad that I did so, for I shook the hand of Trengganu's past.

But such is the transience of life, nothing in it lasts forever, even cemeteries themselves do die. The last time I visited Mother many years ago, I saw a notice posted by the gate. 'Burying the dead is forbidden here,' the notice said, a strange note in a cemetery, but the place was full and there was no more room for burial.

Man With the Pomponed Hat

A MAN ONCE TOLD FATHER his darkening secret. He was of a great age, walked with the measured gait of a man of *silat* (though I'm not sure if he was an exponent of it). He wore the *kain pelikat* and his *baju*, and a woollen hat with a little pompon atop his head. There was nothing unusual in that except that he was then maybe a score of years or two from a hundred, and he walked the fifteen-minute walk from his house to the mosque when others maybe a little over half his age were ferrying themselves by the local *tèksi* because of a crick in their necks, or a pain in their backs, or were never out in the streets without a walking stick to prop up their troublesome gammy legs.

Beneath his pomponed hat he had hair that was darker than the night. He called it *sirang dalang* in Trengganuspeak, which meant watering from the inside, and that, he said, was his secret. Father, as far as I knew, never took this advice to heart for it involved watering the inner parts with a daily glass of milk, a practise that was unknown to the denizens of our house. And oh, we took our daily milk all right, but it came thick and condensed white from a can that carried a picture of the milkmaid. We called it, in Trengganu, *cap junjung* because the milkmaid carried a little wooden tub on her head, and that was *junjung* as we saw it done in our market.

One day Father came back and told us of the *du'a Haikal* (the supplication of Sayyidina Haikal) that was another one of the secrets of our grand old lad. Read that daily, he once told Father as they adjourned from their morning prayer and were dispersing into the street. The pompon bobbed up and down on his head as he continued his early morning walk, taking the streets with his familiar gait. Then, with a twinkle in his eye, he looked at Father and reminded him of the *sirang dalang* that worked, for him at least, a treat.

I am reminded of Datuk Balai when Ganukite placed his comment on what I wrote about the *bunga mas*, the flowers of gold that were sent to Siam by our Trengganu sultan in those days before the British signed the treaty that took the northern Malay states of Trengganu, Kelantan and Kedah under their wings and still did not give Patani to the Thais but left it to its own fate. And the rest, of course, is history.

Datuk Balai loomed large in my mind as he was a link with what was then to me our 'ancient' past: when Siamese might came down to Langkawi and burnt the locals' stores of rice as punishment for something the Langkawians did or did not do; when northern sultans bore Siamese titles of Phraya this or that but the Trengganu sultan did not because, as Ganukite points out, Trengganu did not send those *bunga mas* in deference to some Siamese might, but more as a token of thanks for favours done in the past. I wonder if there's any proof of that.

At the mosque Father was always bumping into Datuk Balai, a man he respected greatly. He was also a close friend of the junior Datuk, an amusing man, I remember, who wore thick glasses and drove one of the few Morris Minors in the street. It was obvious where he got his humour from—the senior Datuk Balai had his way with words and was adept in what we Trengganuspeakers called *mengayör*, speaking with irony and looking at things with a light heart. When he came home to tell us of his meetings with the Datuk it was always with awe that Father narrated his words, and a little bit of glee too for that matter. Even in his later years Datuk Balai was a man of great resource. He once retreated into the sticks to breed a gaggle of ducks, Father once told us, but the venture soon floundered.

But the story that most captured my imagination was of his journey up north to deliver the Trengganu *bunga mas*. Whenever the subject came up for discussion in our house, that was what Father would bring up. That Datuk Balai was a member of the Trengganu royal entourage to Siam that guarded the *bunga mas* with their lives en route to the King of Siam's court. And with glee, Datuk told Father that in the streets to The Great Palace, the Thais would throw themselves at the feet of the entourage to prostrate before the sacred gift to their royalty.

Down Our Way

WHEN ABDULLAH MUNSHI arrived in a Kuala Trengganu of puddled waste water and lanes of no more than an arm's width, he was irked by the lack of purpose in Trengganu males. This was March 1838, on a Sunday if my calculation's right, and it was a dirty old town he saw with unkempt bushes, coconut husks piled beneath houses and many, many coconut trees.

He followed the lanes and what lanes they were, running between houses that stood higgledy-piggledy, curving and twisting like snakes knocked senseless into twists and coils. *Macam ular kena palu*, (wavy like a snake that's been beaten with a stick) as he put it, were the lanes of Kuala Trengganu. Of course, Trengganu town planning left much to be desired, even I knew this from my days there in the latter part of the century after Abdullah had gone. There were houses that faced the road, those that turned their backs to it, those that looked at one end of the road from their front doors, and others that viewed the road from their rear. There were bushes, little trees and snakes too, Abdullah then observed, living in lanes that snaked through this little old town.

I didn't meet many snakes in the streets in my days over there. But I did see goats, sitting alfresco on the roads, taking in the warmth released by the nighttime tar. The goats that Abdullah saw were tethered in the market, sold on four legs at the price of one ringgit—cheap, I thought, even for more than a hundred years ago. But then goats were unfussy creatures if I remember them well, mostly left to roam freely to chew on odd bits of paper for supper on their tarmac table. There was another defining feature of goats of Kuala Trengganu that I recall, and that was that they nearly all had a piece of stick about the width of their body that dangled horizontally from a ring of rope around their necks. Abdullah Munshi didn't mention this in his 'journey'. Maybe he was too busy to notice because he was too engrossed in the width of those passages that twisted and turned between the higgledy-piggledy houses of Kuala Trengganu. Some of these passages were just wide enough for one man to pass through, he observed, getting ever more irritated by how unkempt and unruly Kuala Trengganu was compared, perhaps, to Singapore.

But please don't misunderstand me. I'm grateful to Abdullah Munshi for having written such an engaging account of Kuala Trengganu in days of yore. I only wish he'd paid a bit more attention to those goats when they'd not been tethered to their posts in the *pasar* because I've often wondered when the idea of dangling sticks around their necks started. If he did, the idea would have been taken and patented in Singapore to goat-proof the houses of the Tuans Raffles and Farquhar. In Kuala

Trengganu rice, flour and those delightfully coloured cuts of *agar-agar* were spread out daily to dry on mats in front of our houses. But goats that tired of their paperfests and were longing to nibble on grains of rice or crystal-coloured bits of *agar-agar* would have had their ideas thwarted by the sticks because horizontal sticks wouldn't have let them go through the picket fencing that surrounded those drying houses that sat higgeldy piggeldy in the town of Kuala Trengganu.

Like goats, the Kuala Trengganuans of 1838 were afternoon people. On entering the market—the Pasar Kampung Laut, which, I think, was not far from the Kampung Tanjong that I grew up in—Abdullah asked: 'Where's the market?'

'All this before you is the market,' replied an idle bystander. 'You come back later in the afternoon and you'll have all that your heart desires.'

The men of Kuala Trengganu, if you can imagine it, were not just bystanding strangers. Local princes and their henchmen hung on every corner, 'each man carrying four or five throwing instruments, a keris and a long sword; and that's all they do, walk up and down the street carrying their weapons.' Now if I were there, just off a ship for a day's recce, I wouldn't have been so brave as to put smart-alec questions like 'Where's the market?' to men armed to the teeth when I could see the market before me, and an empty one at that. And even if I were so brave as to ask such questions of them, I'd have prepared myself to bolt the other way at the slightest movement, especially out of reach of those throwing things.

But Abdullah Munshi did survive intact, and went home (after visiting Kelantan) to write his tale. And in the market, when the womenfolk came out, he saw goats, sheep and poultry, and noticed that all the food, vegetables and fish were cheap and plentiful. But alas, the folk of Kuala Trengganu were not keen eaters of meat or *ghee*, preferring to feast themselves on fish and food that was distinctly foul, like *tempoyak, pekasam, petai, jering* and herbs that were found everywhere.

No mention by name though, of *budu*; but the man who missed those goats with their neck sticks would have missed out on this one too.

Egg on Tracks

STANDING ON AN ALMOST EMPTY train platform in the middle of nowhere (which was near Thetford), feeling the chilly preludes to the gusts of Yule, my mind drifted to Sura Gate. It was a strange day, dark and cold and still snagged in the pale remains of an extended summer: a woman was looking at the screen on the platform and bemoaning the 4.12 that had become the 4.45. At 4.45, a veteran train-travelling man was making known to all five of us standing on the platform that the signal had not been activated yet, and it had to be activated at least five minutes before the train's arrival. 'There's no way the train's coming now,' he announced to one and all.

And then, at 4.50, the 4.12 that became the 4.45 vanished from the screen altogether.

I was counting the ports of call in the chilly darkness before reaching home: Thetford, Ely, Cambridge ...

It was very hot in Bukit Besi. 'Heat of the metal, you know,' someone said. Then the train wended its way between banks filled with trees, stopping at Luit, Pinang, Padang Pulut. Then it travelled somewhere into the darkness of Bukit Tebuk, the bored-out hill, then Kemudi, Kumpal, Serdang, Binjai and Che' Lijah before we reached Nibung. Then the train stopped at Sura Gate, the station among the shops in the Dungun town by the sea.

It was at the final barrier on the sea front that the train, if it was carrying iron ore, finally stopped. From there its wagons emptied glittering contents of hard Trengganu rock onto ships to be taken to God knows where and transformed into mystery objects.

Sura Gate plopped itself among the noise of ordinary people, between the small Dungun shops that you saw if you turned left or right at the main road (depending on your direction of travel) as soon as you saw the cashew trees. There were shops there that served the bustle of people who came up from the sea, or villagers that Kuala Dungun served before it took its afternoon siesta that lasted into the following day. I could hear Sura Gate like the eggshells that we cracked as we waited for the train to arrive to drag us up to Bukit Besi.

Mother was a great believer in hard-boiled eggs that she carried in a knotted handkerchief whenever we had the need to travel. 'Eat these eggs to power your knees,' she'd say. And so from very young I learnt about *lembèk lutut,* the syndrome of buckling knees that became the dread of Trengganu-travelling folk. Even today the taste of a hard-boiled is, to me, the taste of travel: Sura Gate, Padang Pulut, Bukit Tebuk on the hill.

Before the Japanese bore a tunnel into the hill the journey took longer and, to save time, the ore was dumped onto boats at Che Lijah to be taken out to sea. Yes, it was a Japanese geologist, Kuhara-San, who discovered tin in a place called Cemuak in Ulu Dungun in 1916, but it wasn't until 1929 that a mining lease was formally granted to the Nippon Mining Company (NMC), successor to the Kuhara Company that had already started mining there two years before.

The trains started to arrive at Che Lijah in 1930, then six years later, under Japanese supervision, local labourers dug with their hand-held implements into the hill that soon became Bukit Tebuk. The journey to the bottom was shortened and Che Lijah became just another stop en route to a new off-loading place called Nibong, before the trains moved even further to the edge of the sea at Sura Gate.

The journey upwards to Bukit Besi was interminable. Every station was a stop, and at every stop people milled about. Some got off with great relief, nursing headaches contained by Japanese koyo plasters stuck steadfastly to their temples. New passengers got on, heaving baskets and heavy sacks, accompanied by the incessant murmur that people carried along in their travel.

We had a cousin working in Bukit Besi for a company that had become known as the Eastern Mining and Metal Company (EMMCO). We stayed in a house that was part of a line of many others that housed workers for the company. I was dazed by then by the weight of travel so I remember little of Bukit Besi beyond the strange colour of its earth and the bits of rock everywhere that bore metallic specks of iron ore.

I heard the sound of a distant train and an awakening signal in the winter chill. A funny place to be dreaming of the smell of boiled eggs and to remember the light at the end of a hole in a hill. It was a slower and warmer day on that hill made of iron; right now it's brass monkeys, as they say over here.

À la Recherche du Temps Perdu

THERE WERE CLOCK FACES on the tower of the Pejabat Jam Besar, high over the needle-leaved casuarina trees, but it was elsewhere that time's shadow fell.

Kuala Trengganu had a sundial that sat on a plinth opposite the police station at the intersection of Jalan Paya Bunga and that long and bucolic stretch that led to Sekolah Sultang Slèmang Primary. There was a padi field there on the left side of the road as you moved towards Cherong Lanjut, and a *paya* marshland as far as Batas Baru on the right-hand side. Frogs, leeches, water hyacinth and lillies thrived there, and on the other side, on the road against the afternoon light, you could sometimes see the cycling silhouette of Mah Babu. But, of course, they are all gone now.

The sundial was an intriguing bit of metal, so we sometimes stopped there if we walked home from school through the hinterland of Pejabak Jang Besör. There was a vast expanse of old Trengganu graves there—round marker stones lying on white, sandy earth, forgotten over the years and overgrown by *lalang* and bird-nesting trees.

We had to raise our legs over a stout chain that hung around the concrete plain raised three steps high, but a cursory examination of the curved intersecting metal of the sundial gave us no inkling of its purpose, nor did it give us the time of day. Sultan Sulaiman Badrul Alam Shah (standing, right, in the picture) appears to be as bemused, the other

Unveiling of the Humphreys Memorial.

gentleman in the dark Malay *baju* appears to be giving it an equally polite nod and the man in tropical suit and topi appears to be shielding it with his palm, the better to see the figures on the dial. Now, what advice can you give to a man who reads a sundial by shading its light away? He was probably the state's British adviser.

I don't know when this photo was taken but I presume it was the official launch of the Kuala Trengganu sundial, so our KT police force could set their clocks by it and the referee in the nearby Padang could start the kick-off at the exact time of day. Mat Sprong (the famous Trengganu Private Dick of my imagination) would've stopped there, I'm sure, on his way to crack another case in the maze that he walked in the Trengganu underworld. His office in the pantry of the coffee shop was just a stone's throw away.

Trengganu folk may have been bemused by this device of the shadow clock, but telling the time by light and shadows wasn't unknown in Trengganu. While the town moved along to the time kept by their watches and clocks, corrected against the time checks on the radio, the mosques and *surau*s of Trengganu kept their movements according to what was then known as the *jam waktu*. *Waktu* time was kept in the prayer houses and, if I'm not mistaken, set the noon prayer time close to noon. This was confusing to a person unaware of the different audits of time that were practised in Trengganu, especially if you kept check on your time by the clock in the Surau Haji Mat Kerinci as you waited for the bus that was to take you to school.

Once or twice a month, when the sun was clear in the sky, the *bilal* of the Masjid Putih of Sultan Zainal Abidin the Marhum Haji would take out his astrolabe and check the alignment of the sun to get a reading of the hour. And so was set the *waktu* clock that moved in a continuum that differed from the other clock that was generally known as the *jam* Malaya.

View From the Wakah

WE DREAMT UP THINGS in our waking hours and went to sleep on a *nyiur kömèng*. That about sums up life on the *wakaf*. My brother once told me of an old school friend he sent out on an errand when he was back in Kuala Trengganu, and the friend came back—he did—but well after dark because, he said, he'd fallen asleep on the *wakah* in Pantai Teluk.

The *wakah*, as we say it, had a well-worn floor from regular games of draughts, and a gentle breeze blew across its boards, interweaving between the four pillars that raised the roof above the head, terracotta-coloured Senggora tiles and rafters of chengal wood. Fishermen stopped there on their way home from work, beachcombers piled their day's collection at its foot. There was no alfresco music then, thank God, so the *wakah* was an ideal place for a chat as the world walked by, as a game of draughts continued apace moving pieces shaped from the tops of bottles of *air lamnid*; what jollity went there by day, what mischief passed there by night.

The *wakah*s were the landmarks of Trengganu, put up by anonymous donors along public roads, in the middle of *sawah*s, on beaches, under big trees and in the middle of nowhere even, always sheltering people from the rain and heat, always a place for them to rest their feet, to rest their heavy heads on the *nyiur kömèng*. *Nyiur kömeng* was a dud coconut that had no flesh and little weight, so a dip was carved into its dried outer husk wide enough to take the back of the head. And that was where my brother's old schoolfriend rested his head as dusk crept slowly over his feet until he was totally draped and lulled to sleep by the gentle sea breeze and the dark, while the items he was sent out to buy for the evening's *kenduri* sat forlornly by his ankles, still in their plastic bags.

There are places in Trengganu that are known by their *wakah*s, Wakah Ppelang and Wakah Tapir to name but two without looking at a map, but there must be scores more in their wake. They marked the land, adorned a place, kept the weather out, rested the weary feet of travellers or sheltered them for the night. But a *wakah* by the roadside in a remote place was best avoided, for you couldn't tell who'd be looking down at you from the rafters in the middle of a moonless night as light rain fell to the earth below.

*Wakah*s were landmarks in philanthropy, for you could judge the disposition of a community by how its landscape was filled by the *wakah*. From the Tanjong in Kuala Trengganu where we lived I can still picture three *wakah*s in my head. But we were not really *wakah* kids so

I can't tell you what transpired there among the *wakah* crowd besides the regular chorus of *dang* terms that came to us as we passed by on our way to another place. Terms such as *makang* and *bahang,* the *aji* and *darak*. Poor was a community without a *wakah*, and lonely a traveller that walked its place.

But *wakah* was more than just a stopping place, it was a vehicle for dreams and thought. A proper *wakah* with elaborate fretwork and wood carvings was first envisaged in a benefactor's head, then passed to the master woodworker by word of mouth. Then the latter gathered wood and craftsmen from the village to chisel, saw and nail dowels as the patron saw fit without benefit of written notes. As the last tile was laid on its roof, the workers would probably find cause to congratulate themselves by sitting there for a few days.

It is said that the haunting sound of the Trengganu royal *nobat* ensemble came from noises in the sea, but I suspect that they were heard not from the Trengganu *perahu besar* that sailed along the coast to Senggora to buy the tiles, nor from the fishing *payang*s that daily left our golden shore, but by sharp-eared men sitting quietly watching the waves from the comfort of a seaside *wakah*. Moo, the sea said and he kept a mental note. Waaah came another sound, and that went straight under his *söngkök*. Then there were the wooos, the lilts and the mewling sounds that could only have been the wailing of our mermaids.

It is difficult to sit in the *wakah* on a moonlit night with eyes firmly fixed on the landscape without also hearing a distant call that causes a local pain in the heart. In Trengganuspeak, as in the standard lingo, this is the *sayu* of one's longing, for another time, another place, and the pain, the *pilu* is the tugging of the heart's melancholy. This is the pain in the heart of standardspeak's *menyayat hati*, whose meaning is closer to the original meaning of 'nostalgia'* rather than its latter meaning. And what is the longing and the pain all about? Well, it's a feeling that probably has primordial roots, an atavism that no longer knows what it's for—for times past that really went perhaps, or that were presumed to be. It is difficult to pinpoint the extent of this *sayu* except by defining it as a distant call, as people are often attracted by a 'past' that may not have been real at all. Trengganuspeak has no word for this, but the Portuguese *saudade* may sum it all up: a longing for a whimsical present or past.

*'The word "nostalgia" was invented on 22 June 1688 by Johannes Hofer, an Alsatian medical student, by combining the word *nostos* (to return) with *algos* in his medical thesis *Dissertatio Medica de Nostalgia* to describe the sickness of Swiss soldiers kept far away from their mountains.'

—Alberto Manguel, *A Reading Diary*

Taxed by the River

IF YOU LOOK IN an old copy of the AAM's guide to driving in Malaysia and take the road that wends and bends up Bukit Kijal, you'll see, as you're coming down the other side, a breathtaking view of Kemaman beach, the sea framed by steep hillsides, coconut trees with leaves waving so nimbly and the sun shining brightly in a cloudless sky. This was the view I saw many times on our journeys home from Kuantan by bus or taxi, and maybe a few times more on our trips from Kuala Lumpur with Father when he drove us home in his ailing Hillman Minx. And again later from inside a tank called the Volvo 122S that Father picked up from the yard of a second-hand dealer.

In 1936 the young colonial officer M.C. ff Sheppard, delighted to be re-posted to Kemaman, found the beach there as beautiful and alluring as when he'd left it in 1934, so much so that he wondered how his fellow countrymen—coming as they did from a 'nation whose youth has been spent on holiday at Margate, Broadstairs, Filey or Bude'—could have left it alone and unspoilt.

Kemaman may have been beautiful and the place for one to be, but it was not a view espoused by all of Sheppard's fellow officers. In 1923, G.E. Clayton, a man who survived the Great War mentally and physically intact, found the solitude and the quiet life in Kemaman just too burdensome to bear. He took out his gun and just blew his life away. His successor had much the same view about Kemaman, but instead of pulling out his gun he took out his pen and wrote a resignation letter just a week after being condemned to this life of beach, sea and sky.

I had no view of Kemaman except that it was a stopping place after the stomach-churning roller-coaster roads that we knew as *jalang ulör* after Kuantan and the Kemaman ferry, the floating platform that bobbed up and down from one side to the other of the Kemaman water. Kemaman looked to me like a vast place, with villlage houses sheltering under coconut groves and miles of mostly straight but potholed tarmac that led to Kuala Trengganu. Then, of course, there was Geliga, that enchanted stone on Kemaman's shore.

A boy who was our cousin, or maybe in a position further removed in the kinship line, went on a bus ride to Kemaman one day and came back with other unfortunates stretched out in the back of a lorry. They were all laid out fully clothed, with lungs still drenched in brackish water because the bus had lost its brakes during its journey down the steep slope to the Geliga ferry. It plunged straight into the swell. That was a very long time ago but I can still see them all stretched out on the tarpaulin when the lorry stopped under the streetlight just after dusk so that the bodies could be collected by grieving families.

It marked out Kemaman as a distant place in my mind's eye, with loopy roads and deep rivers in the shadow of a steep hill. It was, after all, nearly a hundred miles away from Kuala Trengganu. Then there was a town called Chukai, its reflection shimmering in yet another body of water. Chukai was allegedly named after *cukai*, duty collectors that kept their posts on the riverbanks, but Mother told us a different story. There was in times past, she said, a crocodile in the Kemaman River and because of its habit of regularly snapping up local inhabitants for food, the place came to be known as Chukai, the place where the crocodile exacted its toll.

When crocodiles no longer swam in the river and drill platforms rose along the shore, the trunk road from Pahang through Kemaman was lit up at night by a tall gas flare that signalled that one was entering oil country. It seemed aeons ago now since Tuan Separd (Sheppard) left his local idyll to take up further posts in the rarefied air of Kuala Lumpur, then stayed on after Independence to become the first curator (I think) of Muzim Negara before moving on to distinguish himself in other things, not as M.C. ff but as Abdul Mubin Sheppard, writer, historian, socialite, Tan Sri, Dato' and Haji.

Kemaman had its way of luring people. As the historian Heusseler put it: 'For bachelors who were not overly reliant on clubs and European society, it was a paradise of vast, empty beaches and tiny kampongs dreaming under a tropical sun, peopled by *ra'ayat* who were as attractive as they were shy and suspicious of outsiders.'

Distant Göngs

A MILLION THANKS to John Roberts who sent me the photo below of two pith-helmeted colonial enforcement officers rummaging through the belongings of some natives to impose the 'göng tax'. John originally suggested to me that they could be searching for Weapons of Mass Destruction, and those round objects with a bulge in the middle do look to me like massive landmines. But göngs are my best bet, as the Brits imposed a tax on land in Kuala Brang (that led to uprisings known as the *perang ulu*), so why not a tax on göngs too for good measure to keep locals lively and hopping mad during their post-harvest *ronggeng*?

Göngs in Besut.

This photo could have been taken in Besut in the 1920s. There's a reason for my saying that, as it came from the collection of a lady who was married to a colonial officer who served as District Officer (DO) in Besut around that time. His name was Mr (later Sir) Patrick McKerron, who you can see below standing in front of the DO's residence in Kampung Raja, Besut. If you've driven along Jalan Tengku Long in Kampung Raja you will have noticed this impressive house with, perhaps, the ghost of Sir Patrick lingering in the foreground; but my informant tells me that a tennis court has been drawn into that bit of lawn where he is standing.

I mentioned the *perang ulu* in my spurious whimsy about the göng but McKerron, being the man on the spot and of the moment, did go to Kuala Brang to look into this small matter of the unrest. John gave me an amusing insight into the conduct of colonial diplomacy between McKerron and a rebel leader from Kuala Brang, but I'd like to do a bit more research in the archives to shed more light on the man (and maybe the despatches of) McKerron. So I shall hold onto this for another time.

Looking again at the picture of the Göng people, I am impressed by the smart attire of the villagers and especially the well-turned-out youth sitting in the foreground wearing a neat Haji's turban. So I believe the villagers must have been waylaid while travelling to some special occasion, and I don't think, as John alternatively suggests, that the Tuans

Mr (as was) Patrick McKerron standing in front of his Besut villa.

were each buying a göng to take home as a souvenir to Blighty. But then again, John tells me that a Malayan göng was indeed found among the possessions of his mother, the late Mrs McKerron.

Once on a Hot Day

THIS PHOTO SHOWS TRENGGANU CIRCA THE 1920s. It is a very hot day, and a procession of school children is moving away from the river during a ceremony that must've seemed interminable: sun beating down, adults palying their adult games and dignitaries looking and perspiring under their little marquees and umbrellas in the background. Handkerchief on head time: don't you remember that from your school sports days? Even the man in the

A Trengganu ceremony in the sun.

foreground, who looks to me like one of the event organisers, looks hot and bothered, and has just produced his hanky to mop his brow. If you sweep your eyes further to the right you'll see a man in a trilby, a Tuan perhaps, about to unfurl his umbrella that looks like the green type that weathered many moonsoons in our day.

Now, what is going on here? This photo comes once again from the collection of John Storm Roberts, left to him by a close family member who lived in Kampung Raja during that time. Written in ink on the back of the photo, in handwriting that you don't see anymore these days, is the short word 'Treng' (Trengganu); but was this Kampung Raja or the *kuala*? The river in the background reminds me of both places, but the neat long road rising to the town, the well-trimmed lawn and the surrounding trees make me want to opt for the latter. But what ceremony is this that seems to be rising from the river? What are those emblems that sit on top of those huge canopies in the background? Love those policemen with their *topi jjambul* (pomponed hats) but I never saw a policeman with a *lathi* in my day (as in photo). Then they only had short, well-polished *ggandeng*s (truncheons) dangling from their belts. But even then I never saw the *ggandeng*s swung in anger.

If you have the slightest clue about what is happening here, please do not (I repeat, do not) hesitate to contact me.

John, who lives in New York and is at the moment incommunicado because of a 'plague' on his computer, wrote this note to me re the göng tax photo on page 181 (also from him):

Greetings,

I am still deeply suspicious of your göng tax. It smells strongly of a Goneng fantasy! In case it is not, I thought you might like the following, written by the great Sydney Smith in the early nineteenth century.

'The schoolboy whips his taxed top, the beardless youth manages his taxed horse, with a taxed bridle, on a taxed road; and the dying Englishman, pouring his medicine, for which has paid seven per cent, flings himself back on his chintz bed, for which has paid twenty-two per cent, and expires in the arms of an apothecary who has paid a license of a hundred pounds for the privilege of putting him to death.'

Of course, things are just the same today, only we call it the VAT or sales tax.

Suggested caption for the göng police—'göng fishing'.

Nice one, John, I wish I'd thought of 'göng fishing' myself. And of course, thanks for sharing the photo.

Hot on the Bus

RECENTLY, WHEN I MENTIONED to my friend Atok the glory of the old Bah Net (the North Eastern Transport) buses that trundled daily down our roads in Kuala Trengganu on their journey from Kota Baru to Kuala Lumpur, I could see tears welling up in his eyes. The Net bus company was the showpiece of our east coast travel culture. Its buses had bodywork that stood like jet engines before our locally crafted wooden-frame-on-a-chassis vehicles, and even their sprinting *kijang* logo seemed to be cocking a snook at our *bah bberer* that was pushing it to Kuala Manir.

We were proud of our very own Trengganu buses, though sometimes we carried this celebration a bit too far. Like the time when we hurled stones and fistfuls of other objects (mostly hard) at the sprinting *kijang* on the bus's mud-splattered green body, but this was all done in good spirit or to chase away the bad. We were convinced as we did it that those self-satisfied passengers—especially those *semutar*-wearing ones—and their so-called football players, had won the match against Trengganu by the injudicious use of their Kelantan *bomoh*s.

In a town where traffic was sparse, minor reverberations came on our roads mostly from the mini lorries that bore the name of Murtuja (bin Mohammad Salim, God rest his soul), and by the tarpaulin-covered lorries of the Pahang Mail that tipped our daily Richter; but Trengganu moved and shook mostly from the transport of our own Trengganu bus company. These were charabancs of red and yellow, with four parallel aluminium tubes fixed by screws across the outside of their windows which, as Kookabooras wrote in to say, were push-up-pull-down frames that were bolted from within by the passengers. The bars were, I think, to keep our passengers jovial and prevent their heads from sticking out

185

of the windows.

One feature of our buses, if they had one at all, was that of being irregular. You would wait patiently under a *tembusu* tree or on the *wakaf*, then wave and wave as soon as a white-topped apparition appeared mirage-like in the shimmering heat of Kuala Ibai. Needless to say, the bus just wheezed past with the disconcerting feature of driver, conductor and all the passengers looking at you as if you'd fallen out of a nut tree.

Bèkèng, as Kookabooras pointed out to me, was the endearing characteristic of the company workers. *Bèkèng* is a Trengganuspeak description for dogs that barked at passing strangers, or humans who wouldn't talk to you if you asked them the time of day, then poked you in the eye for your sheer gall. We called the bus conductors *kelèndang,* same as we did those drivers' assistants who sat glumly and sometimes fell off the back of our lorries. I thought the word would have originated from the standardspeak *kelindan,* but as *kelindan* has more to do with sewing than driving it is just possible that our *kelèndang* came another way, via *attendang,* from the English 'attendant' of our buses and lorries.

Once Kuala Trengganu had a clock tower and our buses had to turn around a turtle before heading for the town centre. Our bus station also moved to a place that Kookabooras said was near the Lorong Bumba (Bombay) and the Kedai Kobo (cowboy). I remember vaguely the former and even more vaguely the latter, but a little plot of burial ground remains clear in my memory because if you looked at the luggage-laden crowd in the station awaiting their time to go, then swept your eyes across the road to this little plot of quietude, it brought home clearly what they say about the living being dead people on holiday.

But the bus terminus hasn't always been next door to Panggung Cathay. It once stood on muddy ground on the long road that sloped down to the taxi stand in a part of town called Kedai Binjai. I don't know what stands there now, a bank perhaps or some concrete paeans to the modern soul of Trengganu. If so then it is worth remembering that the ground on which they stand was made of a collection of mud, earth and bits and pieces of distant grit that stuck to the wheels and under the soles of the *kelèndang* and *derebar* of our *bah Teganu.*

Fair Weather and Fowl

BY THE HEALTH OF CHICKENS are our times measured. In these times of mass-driven mania and waste aplenty, when farms are turned into factories and weather cocks spin wildly in the unseasonal winds, is it surprising then that our birds are feeling ... er ... under the weather?

We had not farms in Kuala Trengganu, but front yards, littered with *dedök* or the *hampas* of the sago or *nyiur*, and chickens or ducks pecking in their pecking order. Then a housewife would appear from somwehere with her hair still *jerebèk* to scatter rice that'd gone off in the pot during the night. She would make a song and dance in her steps, saying *kur, kur, kur!* and *deee, di-di-di, dee-dee!* The latter, as you know, is duckspeak in Trengganu, for 'come hither, come hither, come hither', said in tones of ululation that would rise higher and higher. Only women and pre-pubescents were good at that, while men opted for the lower calls of hens and cockerels. These were days before tight trousers, mind, when sarongs were the mode casual. All men, and boys, slipped into their sarongs at the start of day and walked, with *timba* in one hand and toothbrush in the other, to the community well. The feel of the sarong was, as our Pök Wang Mamat used to say, '*lega macang sura*' ('spacious as the *surau*').

Chickens were a precious possession in (or under) Trengganu homes, whether it was for the eggs, the pot or for the bits that dropped out of their backs that were collected and passed on as manure. Chilli plants thus fed were *pedah nnaha* (very hot) but the hottest chillies came from Marang because Marangers were hot-tempered people. *Lada Marang* were chillies that you doffed your *söngkök* to in the *pasars* of Kuala Trengganu. But we must now go back to our chickens in the yard waiting impatiently for their first meal of the day.

So you said *kur* and *kur* but it was all very quiet. So you twisted your sarong first this way then that, then you heard a feather drop so you shook and scratched your head a little. With unease, your fellow front-yard feeder gave you a knowing look with his eye. It was Pök C***k, the village chicken thief. It could've been that times were hard, it could've been the weather, but a rise in chicken stealing was always indicative of the state of the local economy. And our Pök C***k, guilty or not, was like a straw in the wind of our financial weather.

187

Chickens come out in Trengganuspeak in all miens and manner. There was a man who sometimes walked past our patch from the direction of Ladang who was always greeted with hoots and calls. He seemed to enjoy it as he waved and smiled to acknowledge the calls as he continued his exaggerated amble, the only man, perhaps, who could have raised a call in the right pitch to rouse the ducks of Kuala Trengganu. He was J, but sometimes called Che Awang Che Mek to indicate the ambiguity of his gender. There was Mèk B**ng, the *ibu ayang* whose deeds were not staple for talk in polite company. Then there were the *ayang bapök* who were lads who passed the night in idle talk that often led to ungodly acts, then slept away the remains of night not at home but on a flat slab, atop a box or in the empty stalls around the *pasar*. Late risers they were who blinked and scratched in the morning light as men were emerging from their coffee-shop ports of call after they'd done their dawn prayer. If someone known was met in that state, the post-prandial person would greet him with words that often went: '*Hör, mung ning macang ayang bapök!**'* which was a disapproving message wrapped in a hello.

The expression used for a sickly person was *macang ayang keték ttunga*, like a chicken bitten by the *ttunga*. For a long time I puzzled about this beast or mite, and then I discovered in Winstedt's** that *ttunga* was *tungau* in standardspeak, a mite with the posh half-Japanese name of *trombicula akamushi* that infested both man and fowl and was also probably a typhus carrier.

* * *

*'Well, well, you're just like the cockerel!'

**Unabridged Malay-English Dictionary*, 2nd ed., 1957; Marican & Sons, Singapore.

Seeing the Light

WE HAD A MAN IN TRENGGANU called Che Ali Pailét. I think he was a pilot on a ship, and the lady with the lamp in the sand on the shore was helping her husband, the *pailet* of another boat, to navigate the *kuala* and come home safely. I never found out who he was, though we often spoke to the lady as she waited patiently for the light to blink from her husband's boat on the horizon. Then she'd wave her hurricane lamp and placed it on the pole. Then it was time for us to go home as it was *ggarék*.

I was talking yesterday to an Englishman about our problems in Malaysia with the English greeting, 'Good evening'. Malaysian speakers of English generally don't know what the phrase means and, of course, our *'Selamat Malam'* is now troubled by their 'Good night' (which is a goodbye). So, in the Malay language now (but not in Trengganuspeak) people are uncertain when to say *'Selamat Malam'*, unsure if they're coming or going. (In Trengganuspeak we just say *'Hör guane!'* when we meet acquaintances at any time of day, and *'Nök gi döh!'* when we wish to depart). But back to 'Good evening'.

'Maybe,' the Englishman said, 'the problem arises because you don't have an evening as such.' In summer in England the light peters out very slowly as it gradually gets dark at nine o'clock. Even in winter it takes awhile before the light is completely out. This poses a curious problem for Muslims who are observing the fast of Ramadan which ends at sunset. The sun may be setting, but there's still enough light in the outer 'dark'.

In Scotland they have the term gloaming, a beautiful word to describe this twilight time of day. The closest we have to that is our *senja* or the Trengganuspeak *ggarék*, which is borrowed from the Arabic *maghrib*. *Senja*, alas, is too short, and *ggarék* conjures up all sorts of activities at a time when *setang dök tengöh gelibuk* (when the devils are busy doing their work). I have dwelt on *buöh ggarék* too often so I shall just give it a passing mention now, but *ggarék* is actually the peak time before the night. And nights were not very raucous in Kuala Trengganu then because we spent them mostly winding down. Folks walked to Kedai Payang to catch the shops before they closed with loud clatterings of wooden slats. The Kedai Pök Löh Yunang stayed open till ... well, till the newspapers arrived on their long journey from somewhere behind the hills. And that was how we got the day's news, when we were ready for bed. Sometimes the rivers burst their banks in Dungung and Kemamang so the papers never arrived, and all the news we had was carried by the winds of the *jo'ong* that brought the chill from the north-east.

In the waning light of *ggarék*, if it was a Thursday night, we'd look out for cigarette packets and fold the thick paper into chevron shapes to use as bullets for our *lastik*. Then *zap! zap!* as they impacted against the slats of the closed shops, paper chevrons on the backs of the gecko *cicök*. This was a strange ritual that was supposed to be virtuous, especially if done on a Thursday night; but I'm glad that the practice is now dying out or completely dead as it manifested nothing but the hunter–gatherer instinct that was still lolling around in our Trengganu heads.

As an endnote I shall say that I used to catch a gecko lizard in my palm before shaking my sister's hand, and seeing it jump out of her hand as she screamed and screamed was more delightful than seeing it dead.

Fruit of the Loom

BUÖH PERÖH came in enamel metal basins carried on the heads of the *Orang Darat*. They were dark-shelled seeds soaked in water, heaps of them like dead beetles, pre-cooked till their shells cracked.

We bought *buöh peröh* at ten sen for ten or maybe twelve, wrapped in newspaper that soaked up the brine. We imagined the *Orang Darat* picking the *peröh* fruit from a shrub, or the branches of a medium-sized tree on the edge of the forest, then sitting on their haunches while the seeds gurgled over the fire in a *lègèr* drum that'd been trimmed to half its industrial depth.

How wrong we were.

I know now where the *buöh peröh* came from, and they were not a fruit at all but seeds of a three-valved fruit that grew in the branches that spread out like arms from a tall-stemmed tree (Elateriospermum tapos) with leaves of many colours. One source says that eating too much *buöh peröh* can make the world around you spin a little, but twelve must have been a safe number as we never saw our Tanjong spin when we finished our ten sen's worth wrapped in newspaper. The *Orang Asli*, the same source says, pound the seeds, bury the paste in the ground and there it stays until they come back again to retrieve it, fermented, to use as a condiment on their food.

My friend in Kemaman, Wang Ripeng, tells me that *buöh peröh* still makes an appearance in his local market, and are yours at twelve seeds a ringgit, wrapped in little plastic bags.

I am also thankful to Wang Ripeng who, even as he eats his *buöh peröh* and feels slightly dizzy in the head, is still able to take some delightful shots of the local trees before they disappear from this earth. He sent me a picture of the *pohong bbaru*, which I must've mentioned at least three times à propos the diet of Kuala Trengganu goats. When we lived in Tanjong (in Kuala Trengganu), says Wang Ripeng, we kept a goat beneath our house, so we planted the *pohong bbaru* near our kitchen door to keep the goat supplied with its favourite snack. But in Kemamang, adds the crestfallen Wang Ripeng, the goats care little for the *pohong bbaru*, preferring to chew on tufts of grass, bits of yesterday's newspaper and whatever's available in the market.

If Winstedt is to be believed, the *pohong bbaru* is actually *pohon baru* in standardspeak, so the *shaddah* emphasis in its Trengganuspeak version of *bbaru* must've been put there for balance, as we do sometimes in our speech. It is, says Winstedt, from the family of the hibiscus.

I've mentioned the *buöh terajang* a few times as a fruit from our Kuala Trengganu childhood (and here I pause to shed a tear for Long Ladang (page 236) who used to write in to say how lush his Kampung Ladang had been, with fruit trees from the Sekolah Arab to Kampung Paya, *jambu arang*, and *buöh terajang* ...). I am pleased to record here that my attempts to find out more about the *buöh terajang* has borne fruit, and that far from being near-extinct, it is flourishing still throughout the land, even lending its name to a famous town in the peninsula. Yes, Bukit Mertajam is the town of our *buöh terajang*, and *terajang* (*Lepisanthes rubiginosa, Eriglossum edule*) is indeed the *mertajam* of standardspeak.

Sultans and Scholars

I'VE BEEN RAPPED ON THE KNUCKLES for having left a gap in my last blog. Someone with the venerable title of Tok Pulau sent me an email saying:

'You said that Sheikh Duyung Wan Abdullah died in 1890 after serving two sultans, Sultan Baginda Omar (1839–1876) and Sultan

Zainal Abidin III (1881–1918), so who was sultan between 1876 and 1881?'

Well, let me linger awhile on Baginda Omar. *Baginda* is a word of Sanskrit origin, meaning 'the fortunate', a title usually applied to a conqueror in those days of constant strife. As I've written elsewhere on Bukit Putri, Omar, a man who was by all accounts quite remarkable, was banished to Daik in 1833 during the reign of Mansur II. Mansur died the following year and was succeeded by his son, Sultan Muhammad Shah I, who was remembered after his death as Marhum Tèlor. Omar took his nephew by surprise in 1837 when he returned and took possession of Yam Tuan's palace, holding out there until the fourth day when an attempt to dislodge him was repelled quite easily. Yam Tuan—an ignorant young man who was not only lacking in administrative skills but also burdened with a *tèlor* (a speech impediment)—lost his life in this struggle. Omar crowned his triumph—as foretold by a *wali* known as Habib Sheikh in Daik—by setting up his base on Bukit Putri before coming down again to build another on the ruins of his predecessor's *istana*.

His victory was easy as the the people of Trengganu had little regard for the young son of Mansur II. Furthermore, as Clifford observed in his report on Trengganu and Kelantan in 1895:

'[T]he peaceful artisans of Kuala Trengganu and the fishermen of the coast villages had little inclination for fighting, and evinced far more anxiety for the safety of their possessions and for the welfare of their trade than zeal for the preservation of the existing régime.'

Trengganu prospered under this strong, enlightened ruler who valued learning and spent much energy on the development of the state. Clifford said that it was he who built the 'handsome stone mosque' in the town, which I take to be the one now known as the Masjid Abidin or the White Mosque (Masjid Putih); but I could be wrong here.

Clifford, who was no doubt sent there on an 'expedition' for the British, also made the following remark which looks now, in hindsight, to be more 'precious' than casual:

'With the exception of a rebellion in Besut, which was speedily and ruthlessly suppressed, no internal trouble impeded the progress of Trengganu during this reign; and though the British government bombarded Kuala Trengganu in 1863 no serious damage was done, and this incident represented all the external trouble which interfered with the prosperity of Trengganu while that state was under the rule of the Baginda.'

Baginda Omar was succeeded by his nephew Ahmad who became Sultan Ahmad II in 1876. Upon his death Sultan Zainal Abidin III ruled Trengganu till 1918. Zainal Abidin was not an astute man like his great

Sultan Zainal Abidin III with his son, Tg Ahmad.

uncle Omar, but like him he loved learning and learned people. Like his great uncle, he too chose Tok Duyung to be his tutor.

Omar returned to Trengganu with an entourage of about fifty people, half of them women, Clifford noted. I believe these were the people who settled in an area in the town centre, between the Masjid Abidin and Bukit Putri, which became known as Kampung Daik. Trengganu has many pockets of settlements that reflect much of its history. The first sultan of Trengganu, Zainal Abidin ibni al-Marhum Bendahara Seri Maharaja Tun Habib Abdul Majid, arrived in Trengganu via Patani in 1725. (He was there to marry his second wife, Nang Rugayah, better known as Raja Dewi Perachu Nang Chayang of Patani. Later he married another, the daughter of another remarkable man of Trengganu, Sheikh Abdul Malik bin Abdullah, the man widely revered as Tok Pulau Manis.) He too arrived with an entourage, from Patani, and they, I think, settled in an area next door to the Istana Kolam that is still known as Kampung Petani.

Soon after writing about Duyung Island I met (in London) a Trengganu man from Chabang Tiga who told me that in the village where he lived, they were all related to one another as they had all come down from Patani. Chabang Tiga, like its neighbouring Losong(s), was a seat of learning for many *pondok* and many exits that were used in the internecine wars. Losong, I'm told, is old Trengganuspeak for 'escape route'.

I would hazard a guess and say that the Patani peple of Losong and Chabang Tiga arrived during the time of Tok Duyung Sheikh Abdul Qadir in the 1830s. This was the time of rebellion in Patani and Kedah, to shake off the yoke of Thai rule. Trengganu sent an expedition under the leadership of Panglima Tengku Idris to help the sultan's forces in Patani. When the rebellion was quelled, Trengganu and Kelantan had to surrender their partisans under threat of attack by Siam. Some 4,000 fighters were taken as prisoners to Bangkok, including some members of the Patani royalty who had fled to Kelantan.

The rebellion changed the course of the Patani sultanate and started the diaspora of Patani scholars southward, to Kelantan, Trengganu and beyond in the Nusantara.

These Blessed Isles

SOMETIMES IN EXASPERATION Mother would say, 'Seberang Takir is just across the river from us, but the people of Duyung are better by far.'

Now, before I get irate letters from the Seberang people, please allow me to make this clear. We were connected to many people in Seberang Takir, with a few branches—but not roots—over there from the family tree. This was what Mother was getting at, for being let down, perhaps, by our own side across the water.

Seberang Takir was sun-dried fish, the cries of fishwives and nets extended out to dry. A long strip crossed by winds reached out to us, like a dagger over the water, to our side of the Kuala. The other side was reached by *penambang* boats, clinging to the breeze then paddled ashore by grumpy men in khaki shorts kept beneath their *batik* kilts, hemlines pulled above their knees. There was an airstrip in Seberang Takir—the first I could remember in Kuala Trengganu—with the name of Telaga Batin that could easily trip from the unwary tongue and be transformed into Tenaga Batin (Sexual Energy), in one mad rush of the *kundalini*. Seberang Takir gave Trengganu Ibrahim Fikri, our first elected Menteri Besar. Then in 1961 A. Rashid Ngah, another son of the Seberang, wrote a novella called *Di Bawah Alunan Ombak* (*Under the Rolling Waves*) that won him a national award from the Dewan Bahasa.

Upstream from the rumbustiousness of this shore, the islands of Duyung, both Kecil and Besar, reflected themselves with quiet dignity on the surface of the Trengganu water. These were the homes of craftsmen, boat makers and scions of saints and religious scholars, islands of erudite and gentle people, unharried by the rush of fish to shore. A cool place, as Mother would say, this *tempat sejuk* that nurtured many remarkable men.

Among these was an eminent Shafi'i scholar, Sheikh Abdul Qadir bin Abdul Rahman al-Fathani, who became known as Tok Duyung. Many scholars of renown on the east coast then bore the tag al-Fathani, which merely indicated their original home of Patani, a Malay state that is now under Thai rule. The ease of movement between Trengganu/Kelantan people to Patani and vice versa was a continuation of links that has existed since the latter Kingdom of Langkasuka that moved its hub over there.

The date of Tok Duyung's arrival in Duyung is unclear. An account I've read says that he was great uncle by familial rank (though younger) to another eminent scholar of the region, Sheikh Daud bin Abdullah al-Fathani. After studying in Mecca and Medina, Sheikh Abdul Qadir returned not to Patani but to Trengganu, to Pulau Duyung Kecil, where he planned to set up a *madrasah* similar to those found in his homeland. With this 'blueprint' for a religious school he returned to Patani to get teachers and the necessary funding, but his plans were torn asunder by a rebellion against Siamese rule that broke out in Kedah and Patani. Muslim scholars were involved in this rebellion, including members of his own family. So Abdul Qadir had to backtrack to Duyung where he continued to give religious instruction and became its Sheikhul Islam, the local religious luminary.

From these events I gather that Sheikh Abdul Qadir would have travelled between Trengganu and Patani in 1831 at the earliest, and his return to Trengganu was probably no later than 1834. With Duyung as his base he extended his reach to Bukit Bayas where he set up his 'academy' on the Patani model. Little wonder then that in later life he became known as Sheikh Abdul Qadir of Bukit Bayas. He died in Kuala Trengganu in 1864.

Tuk Duyung had twenty-one children (twelve daughters and ten sons). Of these, Wan Muhammad Saleh bin Sheikh Abdul Qadir, a religious scholar, was awarded the title of Datuk Sangsura Pahlawan (Tok Kaya Pahlawan) by the sultan of Trengganu. Among his students were Sultan Omar (1839–1876) and Wan Abdullah bin Muhammad Amin al-Fathani, who himself took the mantle of Tok Sheikh Duyung after the passing of his mentor.

The Second Sheikh Duyung Wan Abdullah was also a trusted adviser to Sultan Omar. In 1874 at the behest of his sultan, he journeyed by elephant to the Royal Court of Kelantan where he successfully persuaded the sultan there to stop aiding disgruntled elements in the border district of Besut.

In 1853 he became the Mufti of Trengganu just as his predecessor, the first Tuk Duyung, had in his time. This wasn't the last Mufti of Trengganu to have come from these blessed isles. Sheikh Duyung Wan Abdullah died in 1890 after serving two sultans, Sultan Baginda Omar and Sultan Zainal Abidin III (1881–1918).

His children continued their contributions to the religious and intellectual life of the State. One, who took the title of Datuk Kamal Wangsa, was a skilled mathematician and astronomer with a deep knowledge of *tasawwuf*. A grandson, the chief judge, Datuk Bija Sura, helped to draft the Constitution of our state.

I'd like to record here my thanks to Tuan Haji Wan Muhammad Shaghir*, a man who is tireless in his work to keep the intellectual tradition of Patani alive. I have benefitted much from his research.

***

*Since I wrote this, Tuan Haji Wan Muhammad has passed away in Kuala Lumpur.

New Year and Old Umbrellas

IT WAS APPROPRIATE that we ended the year sharing stories on the *wakah* but in the Trengganu where I grew up, the new year meant little to us except for those tear-away calendars that were given by the shops (usually attached to a piece of hardboard adorned with the shop's name and a pouting Hong Kong film star). The more classy ones showed a whole month, with days compartmentalised in little boxes that were marked with not just the date and day but also with Hari Raya, Christmas, Chinese New Year, Thaipusam, Deepavali and Wesak days, as well as race meets in Penang, Ipoh and the Selangor Turf Club (where the KLCC towers stand now).

This was the *kelèndar* that were torn daily or monthly. Then there were the staid yearly affairs published by the Pejabat Ugama (Religious Affairs Department) that was then, I think, on the road between Padang Puléh (the police grounds, or Padang Paya Bunga) and the *kubur*s of Sheikh Ibrahim and Tok Pelam. The wooden office building of the Pejabat Ugama was always mustard-coloured as I saw it from Pök Mat's *tèksi* on those rare occasions when he pedalled us—me and my schoolmates Lim Chee Hian and Tay Huay Cheng—home from SSPS via the Jalan Batu

Buruk/Jalan Tanjong intersection that later became the site of the Turtle roundabout.

Our New Year's Day was always sodden and bleak, always in the blast of monsoon winds and drenched by leaks in the dark clouds. There were floods on the trunk roads that connected us to Kemaman and Kuantan (the Jalan Ular stretch being specially treacherous), or on the other side to Jerteh and Besut. In this blustery season in Kuala Trengganu, the river took the *tèh tarik* colour of the *air ulu* that lapped furiously on swollen banks, rushing downwards to the Kuala of our Trengganu with the flotsam and jetsam of upstream life—*buöh rengas* and fallen logs, carcasses and tendrils entangled in broken bits of an old boat.

Ours was a house that overlooked the open market that sat next door to covered shops, rows and rows of spice vendors and textile traders, rice dealers, purveyors of novelty goods and our man Yahya who kept pencils in his shop and hair cream, combs and multifarious other knick-knacks, plus the odd Terylene shirt. On dull Friday afternoons when shops were closed and the drizzle blew wildly in incessant gusts, Yahya sat, legs folded, on the platform in front of his closed shop and played a mournful tune or two on his harmonium which he lovingly wrapped in a piece of old cloth with memories of his *kampung* in the Tanjore district. After playing a few phrases he'd sing some mournful songs, refrains maybe from an old *qawwali* or some sailor's ditty he learnt as he sat on the deck of the SS *Rajula* or *Madras*. Occasionally he'd throw a sad look at the huge expanse of concrete block that stood between his shop and our house: the overground part of a huge underground septic tank, built by the local council in our midst to put some content and aroma into our lives.

I was an adept Jawi writer then, even before I learnt anything else at the Sekolah Ladang. It was a skill that came from early exposure to the *Utusan Melayu* that Father brought home from Abdullah Al-Yunani—the stationer, newsvendor and purveyor of comic books and *kitab*s next door to Kedai Fernandez in the shadow of the clock tower of Kedai Payang. When Yahya wrapped up his old harmonium and kept it under lock and key as he took his annual trip home to his family in Mappulaikuppam in Nanilam, his brother came down to mind the shop. He'd write copious letters to the daughter he'd left behind in Kota Baru by enlisting me as a scribe. I'd write faithfully in Jawi script as he dictated: *'Anakanda Aminah'* ('My Dear Daughter Aminah').

The New Year came in very quietly as the old one went out. I saw all this from the chair that I pulled out and stood on to look out of the window of our *surung*, towards Kedai Wang Wook when Ayöh Wook wasn't yet a Haji and was still selling rice by the sack and by the *cupak*, when Pök still kept his hardware store next door to that, almost opposite the *roti canai* shop of a Malabari man called Pök Löh. Pök was a jocular man who was very kind to us kids; he kept nails, nylon rope and thread for mending fishing nets, and bamboo poles and planks in his backyard; he had fishing tackle and bamboo rods, and for some reason he kept vinegar in an earthenware jar in his store room so a certain sourness hung in the air of his shop. At five, as the radio music from the government PA system in Kedai Bhiku blared out loud, Pök replaced the wooden slats in front of the shop and put on his loose Malay trousers beneath his sarong. He wound the Haji's turban on his head then, with a *'Bismillah'*, he'd cycle out to the road (later he bought a Honda Cub) past the goldsmith's shop next door to Kedai Wang Wook and past the hairdresser's next door to that. Then he'd take a left turn at the coffee shop at the junction to Kampung Kolam to arrive in time to chat awhile under the henna tree and catch the *maghrib* prayer in our white *masjid*.

From our house we saw many things that marked the coming of the new year as it slipped in through the pouring rain, but what gave us childish delight was seeing women's umbrellas pushed up into V-shapes as their owners clung desperately to the bamboo rods that held them up, as the wind blew sarongs tightly against their bodily shapes and *selendang*s unfurled in the wind's might. This sudden upward push to the umbrella was called *löcöh* in Trengganuspeak, and it gave the name to one woman in town who became known to us forever as Cik Wook Payong Löcöh.

Mother sometimes referred to the *anging tahun baru* (the new year wind) but I think she meant the Chinese new year, not the one that marked the beginning of the month she called *Jandawari*. Then, as we moved up to a higher class in school, the incoming year became significant as it marked the beginning of a new session under a new teacher in a new class, and for the whole of the wet and windy December before that we were already going back and forth to friends' houses with the following year's prescribed texts, in the hope of buying used ones at half the price.

That was New Year in Kuala Trengganu, and I can almost smell it in the air now: dog-eared old books injudiciously annotated by previous owners, crisp new ones from the school bookshop, the smell of ink and virgin paper, the thick red *High School English Grammar, A Garden Book of Delights* and *Lamb's Tales From Shakespeare* (shortened and suitably bowdlerised), and there was one named after Jane Rhys but I can't quite remember what Jane Rhys did and where.

Romancing the Work

IF YOU PICK UP an ancient copy of the *Utusan Melayu* and pull back momentarily as your eyes water in the dusts of time, your attention may be caught by the 'earpiece' lying to the left of the masthead, with its gleaming face of a comely lady urging you to partake of some sticky stuff called *ma'ajun*. *Ma'ajun*, if memory serves, is either Tupai Melompat (Leaping Squirrel) or Kamar Ajaib (Magical Moon). *Ma'ajun* or *makjong* in Trengganuspeak means 'paste', and as a concoction and a word it is borrowed from Arabic.

Magical Moon and its sister, Squirrel, came from the town of Marang, by the sea just outside Kuala Trengganu, but its most remarkable product wasn't *ma'ajun* but pocket-sized romance books under the imprint of H.C. Mohamad b. Abdul Rahman (Cik Mat Marang). Its most famous writer was a man much forgotten now who went by the name of Pak Sako. His real name was Ishak Haji Mohammad.

Ishak had a promising start in life as a magistrate; but then the Bohemian nature in him took over and he opted for a life of greater freedom as a writer and journalist. Unlike other people of his generation he was unimpressed by wealth and the pomp of office so, not surprisingly, with Ahmad Boestamam he started the Partai Sosialis Rakyat Malaya. He left a more enduring mark in Malay literary circles with his novels, poetry and journalism; but his most famous work was a novella called, alliteratively, *Anak Mat Lela Gila*. It was quite the most remarkable book that I picked up from the bookshop of Pök Löh Yunang and which I read in the *surung* of our house in Kuala Trengganu. I remember getting the impression that whilst the first half was written by a man of great skill, the second half seemed to have been written by a man who was growing impatient with his work. He was paid $200 for it by Annies Printing Works in Johor Baru, the highest amount ever paid to a Malay writer of that time.

Ma'ajun and romance sat side by side in those days, for H.C., who produced aromatic men and women's paste, was also the same Encik Mohammad who brought our Ishak 'Pak Sako' Hj Muhammad to Kuala Trengganu to write a series of 'penny novels' for his production-cum-publishing house H.C. Mohamad of Marang that was the earpiece of the *Utusan*. I am told that the series spun around a rickshaw puller, and could have been, for all I know, the adventures of our *tèksi* man Cik Kalèh in *roman à clef*. The *ma'ajun*, as I suspected, was fuel for the men and women living the lifestyle of the romance novellas. Its aim was to inject vigour into their lives, and so it was that literature of sorts got mired with the paste of life in our little town on the east coast.

It must've been a lucrative trade for our Encik Mohammad as he was able to keep the film star Latifah Omar smiling for a long time in his 'earpiece' advertisements that endorsed his products in the *Utusan*.

Ishak was Pahang born, but he had deeper connections with Kuala Trengganu than his rickshaw travelling works of fiction. When in town he was often seen at the bookshop of Encik Mat Dèk. He also had many socialist fellow travellers in the state including not a few of our family members. When in Kuala Lumpur he kept in touch with the Trengganu crowd in the Restoran Encik Muda (the famous Encik Muda Satay of Kuala Trengganu) in Princes Road (later Jalan Raja Muda), not far from another institution in the Malay book-publishing trade, the Pustaka Antara, then a publishing house and bustling bookshop but now, sadly, dead.

Snapshots to the Past

ABDULLAH DONG (pronounced Tung) bin Sulaiman, came to Kuala Trengganu during the reign of Sultan Zainal Abidin III (al-Marhum Haji) in the early years of the twentieth century. In Kuala Trengganu he opened a shop that sold everything from shellac to rice to salt to books and Hari Raya cards. He was assisted in this venture by fellow emigrant Haji Hassan Liu bin Salleh, known widely as Pök Chang Siput.

Soon the shop trimmed its stock and specialised only in stationery, magazines and books. It became the sole agent in Trengganu for the *Utusan Melayu* and the *Straits Times* (later the *New Straits Times*). In Trengganu, Abdullah Dong became known as Pök Löh Yunang, and the shop, Abdullah Al-Yunani, became Kedai Pök Löh Yunang, the famous purveyor of books and religious *kitab*s.

I am fortunate to have been sent this photo of Pök Löh in his shop by Encik Yahaya bin Mohd. Nor, his grandson. Encik Yahaya used to help in the shop in the days when he was still in shorts. He says that in the early days, some of the Hari Raya cards sold there were printed in the back of the shop.

As a very young schoolboy, I remember going there one Saturday morning to enquire about a book. It wasn't the very young Encik Yahaya

Abdullah Al-Yunani in his shop.

202

I spoke to then, but a much older lad by the name of Shukor who told me that they no longer had it in stock. 'That was my elder brother who died last year,' Encik Yahaya says.

Thanks to Encik Yahaya, I also now know that Pök Chang Siput had no connection whatsoever with *siput*, but was a master chef known by his Chinese appellation of *sifu*; so *sifu* became *siput* in Trengganuspeak.

Another man who arrived with Pök Löh, Ali Zhang bin Idris, became Pök Ali Yunang. Pök Ali was the man I describe elsewhere as the alchemist. He had a shop in Jalan Kampung Daik where he sold roots, poultices and Chinese herbs, and also kept a stock of hardware goods and sparklers for the end of Ramadan. Pök Ali's ointment, Minyök Pök Ali, was much sought after for aches and pains.

Another bookseller from this remarkable group of Yunani pioneers in Kuala Trengganu was Abdullah's brother Pök Daud (Daud Dong), who specialised in religious books in his shop, also in Kedai Payang. Among his *kitab*s Pök Daud (Pök Ok) also kept an array of *kris* (made, probably, in Ladang), seeds and brassware (most certainly from the brass workers of Tanjong).

Encik Yahaya also very kindly sent me another interesting photo ('that I saved from my mother's house, before the termites moved in')

A delegation of Chinese Muslims.

from the heyday of the Yunani brothers. This one was taken probably in the early 1940s, and shows a delegation of Chinese Muslims (mostly in white coats) being taken by Pök Löh to visit Sultan Sulaiman Badrul Alam Shah at the *istana*, though I'm uncertain which one. I'd hazard a guess and say that it was Istana Kolam, though I haven't come across any records of fire damage to any of its outhouses. (If you look closely in the background you'll see, as Encik Yahaya points out, that the roof on the left has been gutted).

In the picture Sultan Sulaiman is seated in the centre. Standing fourth from left is Tengku Ismail, his brother, who later became Sultan Ismail Nasiruddin Shah. Pök Löh Yunang is seated second from the left.

Mass Movements

UNDER THE HENNA TREE, on a weather-beaten bench in a compound fenced by a grill of thin metal spears over a low brick wall, sat Pök Mud, wizened by time and jangling with a ring of keys that hung from his Haji's belt that was broad and green with pockets for loose change and the odd dollar note. A Haji would wear that belt to punctuate the middle of his elaborate gear, his trousers underneath his *kain pelikat* dropping to his ankles and an undershirt of silky material, collar buttoned halfway down the chest in a style that Father sometimes referred to as *kanciperat*, a word that's as elusive as its flavour's regal. At a wild guess I'd say that it's a marriage between *kancing,* meaning buttoned, and *sekerat*, meaning halfway, from the style of its collar. Over this *kanciperat* shirt went the *baju melayu* with its two patched front pockets to dip into when the conversation came to a halt. Then there was the turbaned head, tasseled and tailed, that swung round quite breezily when talk turned to raucous laughter.

There were men who wore the *kanciperat* as de rigueur in Kuala Trengganu. Firemen walking around during their off-duty hours wore it too as they loitered in their fenced area in Kampung Daik opposite the 'flowered shop', our *kedai bbunga*. But Pök Mud wasn't a fireman; he was a genial man and a retired warder as he'd tell you. In his working days he carried a heavy bunch of keys on his belt that held up his regulation trousers in the Kuala Trengganu gaol. I saw Pök Mud on his bench under the tree in the compound of the Masjid Abidin for many years before learning the true meaning of that glint in his eye. It transpired that in the last year of his wardering days, he took behind the prison walls some tiny, brightly coloured laxative fruits of a palm tree that was known in Trengganu as *buöh manjikiang* and dosed them liberally into the prisoners' food. It was the day when there was a mass breakout of diarrhoea among the inmates in Kuala Trengganu.

Going back two generations or so before Pök Mud, prisoners were lucky to have found food in Trengganu gaols. Walter Skeat, who went on a 'scientific' expedition for the British in 1899 to Trengganu and beyond, illustrated Sultan Zainal Abidin III's 'original mind and a shrewd sense of humour' by his answer to the question about why he did not pay off his debts promptly. The great man answered that his creditors would be constantly praying for his continued well-being for as long as they were waiting to be paid, deploying, no doubt, the Trengganu penchant for the leg-pull or *nngayör* as we call it even now. Unlike other states, Trengganu did not provide free food for its prisoners then; when tackled on this matter the sultan replied, according to Skeat, that if it were so then the entire population of Trengganu would be clamouring to be inside.

Pök Mud, the prankster warder, would have loved the humour, even if there wasn't enough *manjikiang* fruit to set off the population behind those walls.

Light Over Trengganu

HOW SWIFTLY TIME FLIES. A peek at the date and it's already the eighth day of the new year!

> *'Cepak sunggoh masa jjalang,*
> *dah nök wak guana setarang!'*

> 'How swiftly the time it flew
> Then there's nowt that you can do!'

In 1925, maybe later, they placed an instrument on a raised platform to measure time with light from the sun that travelled over the Trengganu sky. This was near the police station, opposite the Padang Paya Bunga and not far from the Pejabat Jam Besar (Jjabat Jang Besör in Trengganuspeak) that was hidden a short distance away in the shade of casuarina trees.

Sometimes when we walked home from Sekolah Sultang Slèmang (the *rendöh* or primary branch of the school), we'd stop at this monument to peer at the intersecting bits of curled metal with barely a note of recognition for the person that it was trying not to forget, nor the time of day. This was the sundial of Kuala Trengganu, raised over the ground where once walked J.J. Humphreys.

Humphreys was appointed British agent to the court of Sultan Zain al Abidin in 1915, first in a supporting role to Charlton N. Maxwell, then to replace him altogether. Maxwell, grandson of Sir William Maxwell of Maxwell Hill, was a Malayan-bred gentleman who was familiar with native lore; he'd turned his position in Trengganu into a curious anomaly, as an official representative of the British and as member of the sultan's council. Sultan Zain al Abidin was so impressed with his ways that he appointed Maxwell his *mushir*—'an obscurity meant to cover over the fact that it was illegal for a non-Moslem to be on the council,' opines Heussler in his book *British Rule in Malaya, The Malayan Civil Service*

Unveiling of the Humphreys Memorial, Kuala Trengganu.

Maxwell was soon pulled out of Trengganu to give Humphreys more space to swing his role. He (Maxwell) later retired with his Malay wife to the islands of Dinding off the coast of Perak but sadly, as Heussler notes, they were both murdered by their syce just before the Second World War.

I must have seen the photograph opposite hundreds of times in our family photo album, wondering about the quaint ritual that was taking place (judging from the shadows) in the morning light, and it was not until I went to that school, wedged between Batas Baru and Cherong Lanjut, that I got to know that the monument was a sundial erected in memory of one J.J. Humphreys.

I would guess that the ceremony took place between 1925 and 1933 when the flag was replaced by another. The white-suited man with the pith helmet is probably the British agent, and I'm confident that the man in the black Malay *baju* is none other than the Menteri Besar Datuk Seri Amar Diraja Ngah Muhammad bin Yusuf, who, one fine golfing day, gave Humphreys a long memorable lecture on the judgment of Solomon vis-a-vis the claims of two women over a child.

Humphreys was, by all accounts, a tactful man and a competent agent credited with the economic progress of Trengganu. He stayed a long time, until 1925, and is remembered, among other things, as the man who brought golf to Kuala Trengganu. He died in Tientsin in 1929 from pneumonia, aged fifty.

A Well-worn Tale

AROUND CHRISTMASTIME maybe eight years ago, an aristocratic German man from one of the state education authorities told a group of us, while waving at the River Rhine behind him, of the enchanting lady Lorelei, the sad maiden who sat on the riverbank 'just behind me,' he said. Her haunting calls sent many a fishing boat and many fisherfolk down to their graves in the deep water.

As a Trengganu man I wasn't surprised by the lure of this siren's call, for in Kuala Trengganu we too had one residing on Bukit Putri. She was a lady with one foot in the spirit and another in the corporeal world, and to whose door on the hill Trengganu folk beat a well-trodden path to—believe it or not—borrow her crockery. It was a very satisfactory and very Trengganu way of flesh meeting the spirits: we kept her on a higher plane and borrowed from her cups for tea.

This was the tale told us by our mothers at bedtime or by elderly folk with rheumy eyes turned towards Bukit Putri. Some quiet nights, when I looked out of the window from the front part of our house, I saw a light winking from the hilltop, guiding ships coming into the Kuala, not misleading them like Lady Lorelei. And I thought of Tuan Putri wandering there like a demented soul trying to make sense of the unsatisfactory audit of some missing items in her incorporeal household.

Both Lady Lorelei and our Tuan Putri were pushed out of my mind for a while by the petty business of this workaday world until last Christmas break, when, swept to a quiet corner at a friend's wedding anniversary do, I met again a friend who'd in the past been telling me fascinating stories about his corner of Losong in Kuala Trengganu. Now Losong is a part of town about which I know very little, though I was told once that the word actually means 'an escape route', a bolt-hole for one or all of those parties that were intermittently engaged in their little wars. And so what did we talk about, this Losong man and I, after we'd exchanged our *guana gamök* and *dok ggitu lah sökmö*?

Well, we exchanged notes about Trengganu wells.

There was a well near his house, my Trengganu man told me, that was square-shafted and held together not by the standard Trengganu round *kèrèk* or by brickwork as in our own well in Tanjong Pasar. Instead its sides were boarded with ancient lumber. Wells—as you know if you've stood there pouring water on yourself with a *timba*—need to be cleaned once in a while to rid them of moss and lichens and old *timba* that had cut loose from worn out ropes of woven coconut fibre. This was the ritual known as *ranya telaga*, when a man in his *kaing ssahang* goes down into the well to rid it of all its debris before going up again. Then, if it's a family well, he enlists the help of all able-bodied family members to bail out all the dirt to let fresh water trickle once again down below.

'It was during one such ritual in his *kampung* that they found crockery hidden at the bottom of the well,' said my friend from Losong.

And this links us back to Bukit Putri because, as we so often heard at bedtime, Tuan Putri fled the hill never to be seen again after some parties defaulted on their promise to return her pieces of china.

'Folk in my *kampung* said that those were the pieces of crockery that belonged to Tuan Putri,' my friend said.

'Well, let's go back and take another look at that old well then,' I said.

'No that's no use,' my Trengganu friend said. 'There's a house now standing on that well.'

* * *

I have been scouring many picture files for that *pintu gerbang*, that old gateway into Istana Maziah at the foot of Bukit Putri where, as I wrote before, the *hantu kèkèng* stretched his (its?) legs at the chime of the *genta* at the midnight hour.

I am happy to say that I have found one half of it—the *gerbang*, I mean—in this photograph that my brother took out of our old family album. Here Father and his friend Soon (probably from the post office

Father with his friend Soon.

nearby) are seen standing by one of those cannons that were placed in Padang Malaya (now Padang Maziah) under the *pinang gatal* tree. You can see some of its early shoots on the left hand of the picture. And there it is, that old *pintu gerbang* of the Istana Maziah in the background, looking tired and well mottled even in 1947 when this photograph was taken. I hope the *hantu kèkèng* has found a suitable place to haunt, now that this *pintu gerbang* has been dismantled, and I hope too that whichever road it's at now is broad enough for it to bring its midnight stretch to its full potential.

Crocks in the Well

IF YOU'VE EVER RESTED on Frazer's *The Golden Bough* to view the rich seam of folklore in us, you'll find that there's a thread running through them all. A link however remote, however thin, to another, then another, until this tapestry of folktales becomes one collective note on the great unconscious of this world.

But even then I'm still surprised by what I find in there. Loreli, for instance, the singing lady who sings not just on the Rhine, but everywhere. The Malay *nobat* is the music of the spheres, heard by folks at sea then translated into the voices of strings and flutes and the reverberating noises of hard metal. After what I wrote about the princess of Bukit Putri, I was surprised to hear a smiliar story from my friend Atok about Kelantanese people borrowing crockery from Putri Sa'adong for their *bèkwöh* then dumping it into a well. Ah, that word *bèkwöh*, defined in the *Kamus Besar Utusan* as *kenduri arwah*, feast for the remembrance of a departed soul. Is there a possibility that it started life as *berkawöh* then slowly morphing through word of mouth into *bekawöh* then *bèkwöh*? And what happened to Putri Sa'adong? Did she too fly away? Why was her crockery dumped into the well?

Then a gender note: someone—a grammarian, perhaps—wrote to comment on my use of the male honorific Tuan for our princess, Tuan Putri. It is the way of Trengganuspeak, I'm afraid, for Trengganuspeak often makes no distinction between male and female when awarding titles. Even today there are still ladies in Trengganu (and in Kelantan too, maybe) who carry the family title of Tuan; and big sister or brother in Trengganu is, of course, *abang*, and *kakök* is both male and female in our Trengganu world. I believe this is also true in some parts of Indonesia.

But thanks Atok for taking us to your well of coincidental crockery. May your family blossom in their chosen paths and may there always be fish for your *kerepok lèkor*.

Fruits and Needles

WHEN, IN THE EARLY 1990s, the political administrators of Trengganu woke up with the stilted vision that perhaps people should be evacuated from town centres, despatched immediately to the *darat* and their homes replaced with roads and shops—a commercial rather than a civic community—one of the houses that got the demolition order under short notice was one that belonged to the family of my uncle's wife, next door to the Masjid Abidin. This was the beginning of the end of the vibrant community of Kuala Trengganu. Its spirit may have gone when the Tuan Putri left the hill, but now it was the turn of the people down below who were being pushed out by men with moneybags as hoteliers began to usurp their views.

Seventy-nine years ago this month, a poem was penned by a Trengganu lady named Hajah Wok Aisyah binti al-Haji Nik Idris which had these stanzas:

'Pada masa jalan dibuatnya besar
Datanglah notis pegawai bandar
Rumah yang terkena ke jalan besar
hendaklah segera pindah beredar
Manakala mendengar notisnya itu
banyaklah orang berhati mutu
Mulut berkata tiadalah tentu
"Inilah akal orang putih itu".'

'When the roads were to be made broader
A letter came from the town officer

All houses that now stand in the way
Must be pulled down without delay

When word of the notice began to spread
Many people they became so sad
And then they began to natter
"That white man must be behind this matter".'

Pulling down houses (and people) that stood in the way of progress isn't something new: it was done during the time of the British agent/adviser J.L. Humphreys, the 'Tuan Hampris' of the Syair Tuan Hampris I quote above. Now progress continues apace: Kuala Trengganu is a town with banks, hotels, tourist places and the Cup to catch the monsoon wind but, as with planning in most Malaysian towns nowadays, it isn't planning for the community.

Tuan Humphreys wasn't at all a bad colonial officer: he spoke Malay fluently, played *dam* with the *dam*med locals and even made up for the lack of tact of the pompous high commissioner, Sir Lawrence Guillemard, (who went down to Kuala Trengganu in 1923 with a göng for the sultan, the KCMG) by translating his high and mighty address into polite and proper court Malay.

A portrait of Humphreys used to hang in the government administrative offices with that famous clock tower (Jjabak Jang Besör in Trengganuspeak), standing serenely between the wide expanse of old graves of unknown Trengganuers, the padang, the police station of Paya Bunga and that little monument sat in the middle of all that traffic, the sundial memorial to Tuan Humphreys. These offices stood amid clusters of casuarina trees that spread trunks, and shed needles and mini spiked fruits on the tarmacked floor. Casuarinas also shielded another place connected with the Kuala Trengganu of J.L. Humphreys: the golf course along Pantai Batu Burok that he gave to the Kuala people.

We used to stop under the shade of those Jam Besar trees to collect the strange-looking mini fruits of the casuarina and to play tricks with their needles. We pulled them out of their joints then restored them again intact, such were the simple pleasures of childhood to the Kuala people. Then we walked away towards home—leaving the casuarina trees and the clock tower and those government quarters filled with people from states bigger and richer than ours—to emerge in Kampung Kolam by the *istana*.

Up to the Drum Tower

SOMETIMES ON DAYS when we were at a loose end, when adults were well-disposed towards us, we went up the spiral stairs to the loft of the Masjid Abidin where the big drum was housed. Actually we could have dispensed with higher authority completely for such purpose as the son of one of the muezzins was a friend of ours and not only that, he was also the mosque drum beater when it was his father's turn to make the call.

The staircase as I remember it was painted green and spiralled around a pole that propped up the ceiling. In the semi-darkness behind massive doors that led into the closet at the base of the stairs who knew what ghosts lurked there? We ran up the stairs more in fear than enthusiasm, and held onto the spiralling handrail until our heads emerged at the top. The handrail was always bathed in light and dust of many years' neglect, bearing perhaps the footprints of *bilal*s past. This was the drum chamber of the mosque where the *geduk* rested on mighty legs, its hollow body wider than an adult's embrace, its open end aimed like a cannon to the rooftops of Kuala Trengganu. Döllöh, the muezzin's son, always led the way, to show us the *geduk* that he beat with all his might. Then he would take us to the windows to look over the roof of the mosque at the tops of houses afar. How vast Kuala Trengganu looked when we were so high.

Kuala Trengganu was a colony of shops in a large village. The mosque stood among a cluster of dwelling houses opposite the Lay Sing Photo Studio. Diagonally across it was a lumber yard. My uncle's house abutted one side of the mosque perimeter, against a huge wall that fenced in the graves and the mosque outhouse called the *marja'*, where mosque helpers adjourned to between prayers and where the *imam* often dropped in for a chat or a nap. *Marja'* is Arabic for 'a place to consult' and was where the *imam* or someone of wide knowledge would answer questions from the perplexed. But to me it always smelt of left-over food or the scent of hair pomade that wafted from someone's freshly shorn head.

Cik Omar, the cycling barber and mosque congregant, sometimes did his tonsorial work there.

We wandered sometimes into the photo studio to admire the works of the square-jawed man who owned the shop. There were scenes of Kuala Trengganu and the faces of its people staring at us, passport-sized, in black and white. The square-jawed man never spoke nor smiled at us or his dog or his wife, but Ah Leng, his son, was a genial lad who never, as I remember it, wore a shirt.

When I was in upper primary at the Sultan Sulaiman School, it was Ah Leng who taught me how to take passable pictures. We did photo analysis in Trengganuspeak, my under-exposed shots, my overlapping pictures when I forgot to wind the camera after each click, or those dark ones taken against the light. He hired out cameras at just over a ringgit a day, and then took in the film to develop. I still have photos taken in those days with the Lay Sing Rolleiflex—Mother sitting on top of the stairs of our house, my old trishaw-to-school mate C.H. Lim, and K.K. Soh who lived not far from our house, and the Pantai Teluk on a gloomy day.

Just before I left Kuala Trengganu I heard that my friend K.K. Soh had died in a road accident, and that one day, as Ah Leng was tending to his work among the cameras and the tripods, a man walked in and plunged a knife into his shirtless top. He died instantly in his father's shop.

The Masjid Abidin was very much the centre of my life in Kuala Trengganu, not because it was the only place Father went to after work—oftentimes with me tagging along—but also because of my uncle's proximity to it, and an auntie who lived just a minute's walk down the road near the Rex cinema. I knew the mosque and its people well: ate with them during annual feasts, listened to their adult talk in between evening prayers and sometimes I'd stay there to listen to the *imam*'s interminably long talks.

One day after afternoon prayer, while the mosque's leading preacher, Haji Wan Hassan, was giving a discourse on some aspects of a *kitab,* a slightly unbalanced man sitting in the front row produced a wad of ten-dollar notes. Then, with one mighty burst of strength, tore all the notes to shreds. I remember the terror in my mind as I though that he was after us next—but he wasn't—and the preacher, I remember, never even batted an eyelid. The police arrived soon afterwards to lift the poor man out in a straitjacket while torn pieces of money confetti lay strewn in his wake.

Later in life, when we were all suited for adult talk, Father shared with us his observation from a lifetime of mosque-going. 'It's a place,' he said, 'that attracts many types: the devout, the wayward, the scrounger and the sad.'

A Mosque in the Heart

THE GRAND WHITE MOSQUE of Sultan Zainal Abidin dominated the centre of Kuala Trengganu because of its size, height and by the reach of the muezzin's call. The locals knew it as the Masjid Putih for its gleaming whiteness, but I remember it as a mosque of many colours.

A child remembers its deep interior, the massive pillars that reached great heights, and the depth of its *mihrab* in its front west-facing side that was out of the reach of little lads. This square forward position that jutted out from the vast rectangular body of the mosque was the

The White Mosque Masjid Abidin.

215

sanctuary of the *imam* who led the prayer, of local dignitaries when they were present, of men with flowing cloaks and turbans with dangly tails and of a local learned with headgear that looked like it'd been made from reeds. We called him Ku Haji Ambak of the *topi bakul,* the hat of woven basketry; a Ku by title he was, a scion of local royalty. When he passed on his eldest son came to the mosque in similar garb, so we took it to be the regalia of office of some esoteric order of local dignitaries.

In the quiet after the Friday congregational prayer, I often wandered to the front of the mosque, to the *mihrab* where the *imam* led the prayer. It was a confined quarter without the ambience of a wide chamber in the back, but in this limited space one could presumably focus better on meditation and prayer. From this forward position which projected out of the main building I could see—not through windows, but portholes— the tips of tall tombstones outside in the burial ground of members of the royal family.

The Masjid Abidin, as I remember it, was a 'living' mosque that attracted people of many miens and assorted ways, and these were just my little peers. There was Ku Teng, so thin that he was reputedly *beranok ddlang botol* (born in a bottle); there was Pe'ee, who lived in Kampung Dalam Bata; and Cik Wa, whose father had one of the early motorcars in Kuala Terengganu. Some of the people I knew actually stayed the night there after the last *Isha* prayer, to be awoken again at the crack of dawn by the resounding beat of the *geduk,* as we called it, and the gentle lilt of the pre-dawn *tarhim* that was followed by the thunderous *azan* that bellowed out of speakers in the four minarets. There were people who worked in the mosque, people who slept there and a brave man who spent the night behind a closed door in the annexe that housed the mausoleums of past sultans and their close family members. His job was to tend to those tombs and offer daily supplications for their souls. Once, in daylight, I saw the door slightly ajar and peeked in to see him among the pallisade of tombstones of the royals, fast asleep. Those supplications in the dead of night must've made him quite dozy in the day.

The muezzins were known to locals by volume and name. Bilal Sa'id, a handsome man with a mellifluous tone, lived in the vicinity of the mosque; another, Bilal Haji Deraman, lived in the middle of a padi field not far from a romantic place called Paya Bunga, Pond of Flowers. He was a bluff man with a gruff though not unpleasant voice that reached parts that other *bilal*s couldn't, even with the benefit of a microphone. Once on Radio Malaya I was listening to a play and the natterings of Raffles' scribe, Abdullah Munshi, when Bilal Deraman's unmistakable voice boomed out in the background just as Abdullah reached the shores of Trengganu. When I told this to Father he said yes, he did remember a Radio Malaya man coming to the mosque to record the voice.

My father woke up to the sound of the *tarhim* at dawn when he rose for his ablution. Then, by the sound of the *geduk*, he'd be dressed in his *sarung* and *baju* to start his brisk walk to arrive just in time for the end of the muezzin's call. Regulars to the mosque knew this routine very well, and timed their movements to those of the the the *bilal*, taking the gap between the *geduk* and the *azan* to be roughly eight to ten minutes—the time the *bilal* took to walk from the loft of the mosque, where the *geduk* was housed, to the foot of the stairs, where the microphone was placed. It worked out very well for Father unless it was Bilal Deraman's turn, for then he'd rush out muttering something about Bilal Deraman being at the helm. The reason was that Bilal Deraman had a muscle-rippling, *silat*-practising son called Dölloh who did the *geduk* for him as he waited patiently at the microphone by the stairs below. As soon as the beatings of the *geduk* ended, Bilal Deraman went straight to the *azan* without pause, sending many faithful followers scurrying and scrambling down their stairs in twos and fours.

A Burning Village

THERE WAS A BENCH under the henna tree in the north-eastern corner of the Zain al-Abidin Mosque. Here one could sit all day and watch cars zooming past, or pedestrians going by, or throw a look across the road at folk who lived in houses in the area known as Istana Kecil, the Small Palace. Down the road, going north to the harbour front, in his zinc-roofed shed, Pök Dir poured his secret-recipe sauce over strands of mee and tofu bits, shreds of cow's lung and pieces of squid of his *röjök Pök Dir*. The wind blowing in from the sea hit the post office and the ceremonial Istana Maziah, while little nymphets or the spirits of the Tuan

Putri, the legendary princess, hovered on the hill fort of Bukit Putri, with its guiding light for ships coming in and fisherfolk coming home with their haul.

On a busy day maybe ten cars would fly past the mosque in an hour, and maybe a score more cyclists going hither and thither, stirring the dust and breaking the quiet of Kuala Trengganu's sleepy day. The Saudara Store across the road held a small stock of books, mostly in Jawi script, maybe *kitab*s on *ahkam,* the *Taj al-Mulk* or loose-leaved books on the art of *Tibb.* When the store's owner, Ustaz Su, packed up his stock to move to the Ladang of the turtle roundabout with the aim of delving into a different and more lucrative trade in *söngkèt,* Saudara Store became Mansor Press, while the Lay Sing Photo Studio in the back street of the mosque remained where it was, taking the daily blast of the *azan* from the speakers in the mosque towers.

Folk didn't sit for long on the bench under the henna tree, preferring instead the more relaxed and cooler ambience inside the mosque, under the bank of rear windows. They sat on the long grass mat laid out on the marble floor against the wall to chat or take in the view from the many aspects of this hall. This was the very last row of the *saf,* the straight line kept during the *solat,* but the mosque filled up to this brim only at noon on Fridays; on ordinary days the last row of the line-up stopped deep inside and this back row, which looked out to the passing traffic, roads, houses and shops was used as a resting place between prayers, a place to mutter a quiet *zikr* or to indulge in empty talk.

One morning, as we were walking home from the mosque in the early morning light, a cyclist friend dismounted and joined us as we were turning into Kampung Hangus which, from its name, was probably a part of town that had been engulfed in fire long ago. Now it was a cluster of rickety structures among the Trengganu *gedung* houses, atap and unpainted decaying wood amid moss-covered old bricks and mortar.

There was one atap house facing the road that seemed to be tenanted by ladies in figure-hugging clothes and men who always seemed to be leaving in a hurry. We knew this as the house of Mek B***n, and Mek B***n was a woman you wouldn't want to be caught gazing at when you saw her in the market with her comely gait in her *sarung kebaya.* By the stairs that led up to her house was a knee-high earthen jar from which

218

visitors scooped water to wash their bare feet, as was the custom before entering a *kampung* house. As we walked past this dwelling place in the rising sun, paying scant regard to the ladies who were lounging in the curtained doorway, our cyclist friend—a devout lad who was ahead of us in years—began to shout at them something about playing the *bujang* and ending up in a fiery place.

Now, *bujang* was a Trengganu word that went beyond its ordinary meaning in standardspeak. A *bujang* woman was an unmarried person and a demi-monde in the Trengganu world. In his pronouncement, our cycling friend threw in an Arabic phrase that poured out randomly from his mouth, so I asked him if that was the source text for his translation in Trengganuspeak. 'No,' our cyclist preacher-friend said, 'I just want to scare them a little.'

Some weeks later, when I met our cycling friend again, he had a story to tell about the water jar at the foot of Mek B***n's front steps where, he said with a twinkle in his eye, the ladies came down to ablute themselves after work. A neighbouring Haji who was irked by the goings on in the night went to the local grocer for a *kati* of dried chilli that he pounded and mixed into the water of the clay pot one dark night just before life began in Mek B***n's house. Then he waited for the ladies to come down to refresh themselves after work.

There were real screams coming out in the dark that night as the Haji's chillies reached the working parts of Mek B***n's people. It could have been a tall tale that our friend had spun but it gave us a new insight into the meaning of Kampong Hangus, the burning village that we passed through on our way home from morning prayer.

Ornamental Wonder

IN THE FOREST OF COLUMNS in the Masjid Abidin, perhaps ten or fifteen paces from the *minbar*, was a baroque object with protruding parts and dangling baubles. I often sat beside it on crowded Fridays to look at it and marvel at how on earth it had got in there. We'd decided among ourselves that it was a *bekas bara*, a container for the glowing embers of wood charcoal that made a bed so the incense could burn out its cloud of smell on some special nights or days of prayer. But the nights never came for us, not even before or during the Hari Raya festival. I never saw its lid raised to take in the burning coal. In fact, I never saw anyone raise its lid at all.

I'd inspected the object closely as the adults were abuzz with chants and prayers, while waiting for the Friday *imam* to walk up to the pulpit, and I saw many holes drilled between the raised hoops in the lid—escape routes, perhaps, for the sweet smelling smoke from the crackling incense in the fire. There were dangling earrings of beads, and there were leaves, unmistakably of the *paku* variety of Malaysia. The shoots of these fiddleheads (what a nice name) made delicous salads, and as I was ruminating this in my mind, a Tamil shopkeeper came and stuck incense sticks into those holes in the lid. Soon my eyes followed them in the air, thin trails of smoke from their lit ends that rose and burst into wispy clouds climbing to the column tops in the Masjid's main chamber.

This fascinating architecture was of white brass; it came and indeed sprang—I had no doubt—from the minds of Tanjong people.

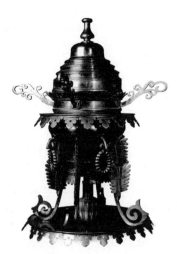

A strange object in the Mosque chamber.

Bits of Old Paper

IN THE GAP BETWEEN our house, Pök Wè's and the *surau* was the tall green *belinjau* tree that was speckled red in the fruiting months when it no longer swayed in the monsoon's blow. The *surung* of our house looked down onto the wide span of the market but in the back it gave us a different view, of houses huddled in *kampung* style: the *surau's* roof an arm's length from our window, and on humid days when I looked beyond the shade of the *belinjau* to the open part of Pök Wè's house, I'd see him sitting on the floor, stretched out till his head rested on hands that reached out on the open deck that we in Trengganu called the *lambor*. In this prostrate position Pök Wè found relief from his frequent attacks of asthma.

Pök Wè's was the old Trengganu house of chiselled bas-relief and cut-through panels that shaped the sunlight filtering through into curly patterns on the floor, *cengal* and hardwood now left to grey and crack into rivulets as wood does after long exposure to the sun and salt spray that blew in from the shore. The *serambi gantung* was just the floor, now exposed to the air, with pillars and lintels now like a mini timber Stonehenge, supporting the air where once—if it did—it would have borne the weight of the roof of Senggora tiles. In the do-it-yourself way of

A Treatise on Birds from Pök Wè.

221

Trengganu houses, things could suddenly come to a halt, and the project put on hold until the money flowed again. But often work carried on to the next generation, as in the case of Pök Wè who lived with his family in the completed main part of the house and spent his time under the sky in the other half, crippled by a bad attack of asthma.

On good days he'd be atop the stairs in the front *anjung* that extruded into the communal hub, exchanging banter with the regulars before the time came for noon or late-afternoon prayers at the *surau*. The daily life of the village was there before his eyes: the brass workers and women cleaning fish by the drain that carried waste water from the well, and discarded remnants from the shed of *kerepok* makers. Pök Wè had varicose veins the size of rhinoceros beetles, and ribs that poked through his slender flesh and ridges of bones in his thin white Pagoda shirt.

'*Wak ape Pök Wè!*' we'd call out from our window. ('What are you doing, Pök Wè?')

'Ya!' he'd say in stock reply.

I was of *wök* age then; we played *wök* in the space beneath the sea-facing windows of Pök Wè's main house, the *rumah ibu*. There were broad rectangular racks out there, woven from bamboo strips and placed on tall stilts to dry sliced *kerepok lèkor*. The taller of us would reach up to pick and feed, normally on the end bits that were thicker than the regular slices before they became dried and dead and then made to fluff out again when thrown into hot oil. This was *kerepok keping,* the fish crackers that served as edible spoons for scooping out *mee goreng* from the plate. Or that were dipped in a concoction of pounded chilli and natural vinegar from the coconut *nira*, and dollops of *gula pasir,* literally 'sand sugar', to give a satisfying taste of fat and fish in an ambience of sweet and sour. Then all overwhelmed again by the bite of the hot chilli that was described not simply as *pedas* but the *pedas nnaha* that takes your breath away.

I looked up sometimes to Pök Wè's windows that were rarely open and imagined the sheltered coolness within that living quarter, behind the greying panels and weather-beaten frames under the great canopy of Senggora tiles. There were probably antique sarongs there in old chests that brooded quietly in a dark corner, and *mengkuang* mats that curled at the edges with criss-crossed patterns of vegetable colours kept aglow in the fretworked sunlight patterns that came through the ventilation panels above the windows; and a thick calendar pad on the wall from which the days were ripped out daily. It was an old house with unsettled matters. A corner box was in there too, perhaps with ancient tools laid to rest when the last dowel (for the time being) was driven home years ago.

One day, as I was walking in the shade of the *belinjau*, Pök Wè was standing there spade in hand, his eyes looking deep into a hole. It was filled with old papers, burning now at one edge, grey and blue smoke billowing around his varicose veins and reaching out to parts in Pök Wè's *sarung pelikat* with hem rolled up to the knees.

'*Wak apa Pök Wè?*' I asked as he lifted another pile.

'Oh, I'm just burning some paper,' he said.

I looked and recognised the cursive flow of hand-written Jawi, some with diacritical marks in the style that I was familiar with from the Qur'an class. 'Oh nobody will walk here,' Pök Wè said quickly when I pointed out that some of those words spelt 'Allah'.

Old writing on old paper—that really fascinated me. 'Can I have them?' I asked.

The pile that I took home were copies from old *kitab*s, Father said, and some were just bits of family history. They were written in *kemkoma*

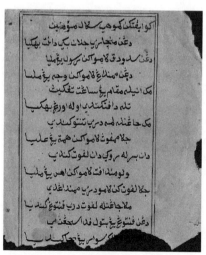

A page from the Book of Mawlid *salvaged from Pök Wè's family library.*

Father said. *Kemkoma* was from the Sanskrit *kumkuma* meaning saffron, hence its reddish-brown colour. Pök Wè was clearing out his past, smoking out the silverfish and the termites from his family papers.

God knows now what has happened to that pile of old paper. I kept them in a locker with some school books and memorabilia. Then our family moved to Kuala Lumpur and I myself even further. I never saw the inside of that unfinished house and Pök Wè's asthma got worse with each monsoon weather. But after that smoky day, I think I saw not just ghosts of old men but workers who had not quite downed their tools, scribes and men in skullcaps stained yellow at the rims that stuck to their brows by the sweat of toil, hunched they were over paper sheets, drawing letters from left to right with bamboo nibs dipped in *kumkuma*.

***

After I uploaded the words above, my brother sent me an email with the following message:

'The drying rack for the kerepok is called the rang. And if I'm not mistaken, the rectangular racks are called acök.

'Coming back to Pök Wè—may Allah rest his soul—I have with me bits of old kitabs of his that I took from our house in Tanjong. One is a page from a handwritten book of berzanji that has been part-eaten by termites, and two pages from a book on the nature of birds. If I am not mistaken, these kitabs were left to him [Pök Wè] by his mother. They were wrapped in cloth and kept in the serambi of his house. When repair works were done to the serambi after Pök Wè's mother passed away it was found that the kitabs had suffered from a bad attack of termites. And that's how [your story above] started.'

Music in the Rubble

LATE ONE AFTERNOON IN JUGRA, in the soft light of fading memory, we walked to the skeletal remains of a house that hid behind a bank of trees. It was no ordinary place; its bones were the decaying remains of the *istana* of Sultan Abdul Samad, a colourful figure in the royal Bugis lineage of Selangor.

Time had been harsh on this historic pile—columns wrapped in the descending gloom and tiles and wood carvings that had seen better days now exposed to the elements and worse. In the shadows were hands that were plucking and hacking at bits and parts of the old *istana*: we caught two men in the act of stealing Selangor's past.

I wrote about that incident in the story *Döh Nök Wak Guane* (page 144) and connected it to a shadow in my own past in Kuala Trengganu the Istana Kolam that sat in an area of some ambiguity between Kampung Kolam and Kampung Petani. It too was an old *istana*, grander than the old 'palace' of Jugra, but wrapped likewise in sad decay and the hazy light of melancholy.

A friend recently wrote to say that he once saw bits of the Istana Kolam laid out in a car-boot sale.

The Istana Kolam in its prime was at the heart of Trengganu's history. It was there that the Trengganu gamelan was born and reborn, and there the Trengganu dissident-scholar Haji Abdul Rahman Limbong was called to meet the sultan for a rebellion that he was allegedly fomenting in the *ulu*. When a rabble-rouser named Garieb Rauf came to revive the Parti Negara after the death of Datuk Onn Jaafar, it was at this *istana* that he

Istana Kolam.

225

first hung his shirt, before coming to live in our midst in Tanjong Pasar. He made much of his being in the *istana,* of course, but he was no Onn Jaafar, so the Istana Kolam outlived him and soon saw him fade away.

Unknown to me then the *istana* had a hidden aspect: a wide living quarter under a roof of Senggora tiles, with porte-cochère and raised on stilts. All I could see from the gap in the wall between the bend in the road and the old tamarind tree each time I walked past that way was the Balai Besar where many royal ceremonies would have taken place in the *istana*'s heyday, where Cikgu Muhammad Hashim bin Abu Bakar, a teacher from the nearby Sekolah Paya Bunga, stood with a group of schoolchildren from the Boy Scouts of Kuala Trengganu to sing a song that he'd composed for Sultan Sulaiman's birthday in 1927. The song later became the state anthem of Trengganu.

Istana Kolam became the centre of gamelan music in Trengganu during the reign of Sultan Sulaiman, but as to how the gamelan came to Trengganu is a contentious issue. One version has it that, like the older *nobat,* it came to Trengganu from Riau—in 1813 says one version of the story—before it moved on to the *istana* of Pahang. What can be said with certainty is that the gamelan as palace music flourished under the reign of Sultan Sulaiman Badrul Alam Syah after his marriage to Tengku Ampuan Mariam, daughter of Sultan Ahmad of Pahang. The Tengku Ampuan, helped by her mother Che Zubedah, developed dances to be accompanied by the gamelan for the first time. It is said that it was Sultan Sulaiman who turned the Joget Pahang into the Joget Gamelan Trengganu (Trengganu Gamelan Dance).

After Sultan Sulaiman's death in 1942, the Trengganu gamelan moved completely from the ceremonial Istana Maziah to Istana Kolam, the official residence of Tengku Ampuan Mariam. There it stayed until the music faded completely away with the passing of the Tengku Ampuan and the decline of the *istana.*

One sad day in Trengganu the municipal workers came with their lorries and their sturdy workers, and without so much as a passing thought for the glory of better days, they pulled down the *istana.*

Singing for the Sultan

CIK GU MUHAMMAD HASHIM BIN ABU BAKAR stood before Istana Kolam in its glory days, leading a group of schoolchildren in the first performance of what was later to be the Trengganu state anthem before Sultan Sulaiman Badrul Alam Shah on his birthday. Some of the children, I am told, were from Sekolah Paya Bunga, a school that must have stood close to a pond with pretty flowers, but not in the days when Father was there. And I don't think Father was among the young people who stayed back after school to *solfeggio* in preparation for the big song day.

If as Peter Newmark* says, imagination has two main faculties— sonorisation and visualisation—then we've all been there and there. I've replayed in my head many times our hot mornings in Padang Paya Bunga (which is some distance away from the *sekolah*), us parading schoolchildren, *söngkök* on heads and flags in hands, listening to speeches and more speeches and then singing. In sonorisation, says Newmark, you normally hear voices in your mind, of people dead and living, and you hear your own voice too.

My sonorised memory of those days on Padang Paya Bunga consists of some distinguished voices, of Buya Hamka, the Indonesian writer and religious scholar, speaking and wiping tears as he narrated the story of what I now think was most certainly the *Qasida Burda*, the *Poem of the Prophet's Mantle*. Father took us there one evening, and all I could hear were hypnotic words (Hamka was a formidable speaker) that I could not relate to any everyday thing, but I remember him saying *selendang* as he wiped his tears. There were many dignitaries who spoke there, and once we heard the voice of a lanky man in horn-rimmed glasses who was known widely by his pen name of Misbaha, the distinguished amateur historian of Trengganu.

I began sonorising yesterday when a Trengganuspeaking friend sent me an email to say that he felt *ssebök* when he saw on television the installation of the sultan of Trengganu as the thirteenth Yang di Pertaun Agöng of Malaysia and the third Agöng from Trengganu. *Ssebök* is the more evocative Trengganuspeak version of the standardspeak *tersebak*, that welling up of emotion, that swelling in the chest and that tissue moment for the eye, in sadness or happiness or a mixture of both.

And, of course, I remember the state anthem of Trengganu, but only in my sonorised way that went, for a long time, like this:

'Allah peliharakang rajakang mi,
Memerintah Trengganu negeri ...

That was probably how I (we) sang it on the Padang, and looking back now on that first line, how wonderfully alliteratively it falls in its Trengganuspeaking way, what sonorous memory!

We were taught that at school, not from a song sheet but by ear, from the mouth of our teacher. My school was in Sekolah Melayu Ladang, built on colonies of *cik ru* on sandy Ladang soil. Traffic went past our front gate: the red and yellow of the Trengganu bus company, the tarpaulin-covered lorries of the Pahang Mail Transport Company, the *tok peraih* middlemen with their cone-shaped *terèndak* hats cycling at speed from one fish market to another with their trademark fish baskets in the back rack of their bicycles. Fish odour, diesel fumes and dust wafted into our grounds at playtime, and the occasional Arabic noises from the Madrasah Sultan Zainal Abidin next door. Walking home via the footpath through the village at the back of the school, we met the putrid smell of dried shrimps, pounded with sea salt and the sweat of labour into grainy-looking dark brown paste that now lay in slabs on the *belacan* racks that were put out to dry in the sun and air.

Allah peliharakang rajakang mi—how wonderfully apt the sound, how evocative the sonorous rhythm of Trengganu.

* * *

* *The Linguist*, Feb/March 2007. Professor Peter Newmark, occasional lecturer in translation studies, University of Surrey.

In a Manner of Speaking

Forgetting to Remember

KKENANG IS DIFFICULT TO PRONOUNCE for non-Trengganuspeakers as it is a difficult word to grapple with. I chose it on the basis of melancholy grounded in memory, for whatever reason people remember. If it's a longing, then it's certainly with a sense of loss, and much that's been relegated to the past has been lost. Yet it keeps coming back, in spirit at least, in acts, sounds or certain smells. That is why the first sentence in Gabriel Garcia Marquez's *Love in the Time of Cholera* strikes a chord:

> 'It was inevitable: the scent of bitter almonds always reminded him of the fate of unrequited love.'

I wrote about *kkenang* after reading Orhan Pamuk's *Istanbul* which, to me, is not so much on Istanbul or the author's experiences growing up, but an essay on melancholy. But melancholy is not the exclusive preserve of any culture, it imbues many. *Kkenang* in Trengganuspeak has a certain resonance and, to me, it conveys best the idea of longing and loss which the standardspeak *teringat* (remember) seems to lack. But you may disagree.

I am grateful to those who have reminded me of that other meaning of *kkenang*: approval. This is, of course, *berkenan* in standardspeak, as opposed to *terkenang;* but in Trengganuspeak they have become more than just homophonic, they have been so truncated as to become identical in form if not in meaning. As things are often remembered with feeling— value, yearning or regret—so remembering is often accompanied with rejoicing or reproach, more often than not it's the latter. Pamuk's version was with a certain sense of loss and regret at the direction the present was taking. Modernist thoughts so overcame the Kemalists of Turkey that they used to gather as amused and detached bystanders as wooden Ottoman houses burnt to the ground, perhaps by arsonist modernists of the day. I am pleased that many share my feelings about what we've lost by our deliberate acts in Trengganu.

In Trengganu we are a remembering people, but often we do forget. Whereas in other cultures a message is given by the parents or friends to 'be safe' or 'take care' before a journey, however near or far, in Trengganu our parents' favourite parting shot is, *'Ingak ingak ya!'* or 'Remember to remember.' Someone who's gone beyond the pale is often reproached with that ominous phrase, *'Ha, dök ingak ke?'* or 'What is it that you've forgotten, what is it that you ought to have remembered?'

Remembrance is in this sense not only historic but also forward looking—you remember the past, present and future. A person who's lost, in Trengganuspeak, is *'Orang dök sedör diri,'* a person who's lost a sense of himself; someone who forgets, a person who doesn't remember. Si Tenggang of Malay folklore was one such, but he did not forget, his obliteration was a deliberate act.

And there's so much that one has to remember: one's Maker, oneself, society and one's people. One's place—insignificant though it is—under the bright and starry sky. In this sense, *dök sedör diri* contains a strange irony—of forgetting who you are, and being interested solely in yourself. This is the root of greed, the kindling spirit of the inconsiderate, the forgetful who destroy for immediate short-term gains, hacking at trees while muttering, 'Damn, damn the people.' It is a sad thing to note, but we see this everywhere.

A Sense of Longing

MALAYSIANS—WELL, MALAYS most certainly—are constantly overcome by a certain longing in their stories, in the quatrains that are props in their daily lives, and in the ways that they see things. But the surprising fact is that I cannot find a word in standard or Trengganuspeak that can be directly translated as melancholy. The Welsh have it with *hiraeth* and the Turks have it with *hüzün*, but the nearest to it I can think of in Trengganuspeak is *kkenang*, which is from the standardspeak *terkenang*, a longing for the past that is tinged with sadness and loss. A feeling that is embellished with *sayu*. Now, *sayu* is a very Malay sentiment that grabs longing by the throat. It comes a-dancing with that most traditional of Malay songs,

Tudung Periuk. Many understand it nowadays as 'nostalgia' but it is much stronger than that.

Again, *kkenang* is an ambiguous word in Trengganu. On seeing someone one can say, *'Kkenang pulök pada tok dia'* ('Reminds me of his/her grandfather/mother'), perhaps because of a facial resemblance. Or, to lament a fate or death, *'Döh nök wak guane, dok kkenang je lah ...'* ('What's there left but memories ...'). Those are melancholic moments writ large. *Kkenang* can also be an affliction. *Kkenang beruk* is someone—a child normally—who takes after a baboon. How so? By the mother being unkind to the animal when she was pregnant, perhaps, or by some other method of transference that cannot be explained in a normal, rational way. But even this *kkenang* has an element of memory in it, a memory that's become embedded in a physical being, that's to be avoided.

But why, for a people so overcome by a sense of loss and longing, do we sometimes do acts that surprise even ourselves? It always surprises me whenever I see public acts that bring about nothing more than destruction, not just in Trengganu but in other places too. Who, for instance, thought up the idea of building a hideous LRT station to obscure perhaps the most iconic landmark in Kuala Lumpur, the Masjid Jame? Who in Kuala Trengganu thought to build a hotel on a bank to obscure the view over the historic Trengganu that is probably one of the most beautiful views of the river?

Perhaps these are deliberate acts of disassociation with the past, expressions of some wish to break free and redesign anew in whatever image is deemed appropriate on the day. An easy leap from the ancient to the modern, and to be reborn like Si Tenggang who disowned—or broke free—from his own *Orang Asli* mother for the life of a successful seafaring gentleman-about-the-sea. If that is so, then it is patently misguided. To *kkenang* means not to go back, but to remember and learn and be blessed, then to look ahead and be guided.

I was reminded of Si Tenggang when a kind visitor recently mentioned his name in connection with Batu Belah, meaning the cleft stone, of Kuala Brang. Batu Belah may or may not have connections with Si Tenggang, but hearken unto him I say. He does not just exist in folklore from the past, he is a parable for our day.

235

So Long, Long Ladang!

AS A BLOGGER I've been privileged to have a handful of people who leave snippets of themselves here, a query there, a correction occasionally and further thoughts to illuminate what I've already said or to put what I've said in a better perspective. I welcome them all—no contribution is ever small, no comment unnoted. Many prefer to hide under an anonymous cover; some are names that I instantly recognise and welcome: Abidin, Adzakael, Atok, Bergen, Cek Long, d'Arkampo, Derumo, Honeytar, Lion3ss, Maya, Mek Jarroh, Nazrah, OOD, Pak Idrus, Penyu Mutasi, Pök Ku, Ubisetela, Wok. (If I've missed anyone out, forgive me).

And then there was Long Ladang.

Long Ladang first made his appearance on my blog 'comments' page on 9 May 2005, and continued with his delightful contributions until 8 September. I suspect that he may have made his appearance earlier, as Anonymous on 10 April 2005, and as simply as Long twelve days later. In his contributions he was informative, amusing and always wore that blanket of nostalgia that one often wears when living away from one's 'home'. On 14 June he made the following comment that made me feel the gusts of the north-east winds blowing on our Trengganu shores:

'Upon reading your blog, I closed my eyes and imagined myself on a tèksi *in the evenings of the days before the monsoon. With strong wind blowing the banana leaves to shreds; with the coconut trees swaying low to the ground; with the flappings of the atap* nipah *of the houses on Jalan Tanjong. Past Padang Malaya, Pasar Tanjong, Kelab Pantai, Surau Besar, Tanjong Che Mat Tokei, Jambang Ijau, Tanjong Kapor, Tanjung Batu 1, Tanjung Ladang, Ladang Sekolah Arab and finally to the Kubur Tok Pelam. I always enjoyed these rides when the wind was blowing strongly, as the hood of the* tèksi *kept on flapping, flap flap flap and the* tukang gohek *pedalled hard to maintain balance. Do you remember Che Kaleh? Wow, I am down in memory lane.'*

He then added: *'After Tanjong Batu 1, I would pass by Tanjong Mengabang. Ahhh ... the air smells of* belacang *and* budu*. How aromatic.'*

Then he became a regular contributor, adding in details to the vistas that I'd drawn, giving personal impressions to the nooks and corners that I too travelled once. Though not myself from Ladang, I began to 'know' Long as a Ladang man through and through. I once wondered about a big white house in Ladang, and Long came back to give me the name of its owner, and the name of the boy I remembered living there and where he is now. I went to my first school in Ladang and was familiar with the terrain, and this painted idyll by Long (28 July) brought me close to tears:

'Buöh-buöh kerekuk, ppisang, setor, setiar, jambu golok, jambu arang, jambu air, jambu butir banyak, mminjar *and* terajang *were indigenous to my* kampung, *Ladang. Come to think of it, it must have been a jungle to me in my youth, to have such an array of trees; seemed to be endless in terms of its border. There used to be a* bendang padi, *a* paya *where* biawaks *roamed, a* gambut *where birds flocked, even a small stretch of rubber trees before P. Jalil's house, and not to mention bushes and shrubs where we played cops and robbers, or went bush trekking. Today it takes just a mere five minutes to drive through the entire Ladang. Or maybe I imagined it to be so vast an area. As they say, the mind of a child is vast and wide.'*

I was beginning to form a mental picture of Long, a born and bred Kuala Trengganu boy who went fishing on the *benteng,* crossed over to Seberang Takir to dig his bait, who played football in the field near the Arabic School in Ladang, then borrowed a *kain ssahang* from the local *surau* to bathe at the well. Long, as a boy was, of course, not averse to mischief. He enjoyed the occasional *tagor,* the Trengganu art of stone hurling, but it was all, he added, in good humour. Long of Ladang Padang Cicor.

Following his comment on 8 September, I invited him when I was in Malaysia to make contact so we could meet for tea. I never heard from him again and, sadly, that was the last comment he ever made.

Then, on 4 October a person signing in as Anonymous entered a comment that I reproduce here:

'[D]uring the recent umrah *a middle-aged man was talking of his time on the Net, and participating in some. He mentioned your* Kecek-Kecek *as a site that he liked a lot. We had just a short encounter with him as he passed away just after the* umrah. *We called him Pak Long, from Sedili, Johore. Do you know him?*'

I asked Anonymous to come back to tell me about the encounter. There are questions I'd like to ask him to give me a better picture of Long Ladang but alas, he never answered my call. I am, however, convinced now that the man he described meeting in Makkah was indeed our dear Long Ladang. I can't help thinking that his telling Anonymous about his visits to my blog page was his way of saying goodbye to us, so news of his passing could be passed on. I've read 'al-Fatihah' for him and I urge you, if you can, to do the same.

I know now that you can shed tears for someone you've never met, because I have done just that. I miss Long Ladang for the special qualities that came through in his writings, and for the good person that he was. So long, Long Ladang, I pray that your *umrah* was fulfilled, and that you've found your abode in Jannah!

Picking Up the Pong

IN TRENGGANU, sometimes the world turned upside down, inside out and front to back. Sometimes a friend would say, '*Gi teki kangma sikna kkeda yangpa.*' It would have taken you some time if you were not taken aback, but soon you'd have latched onto the mode and said, 'Ok,' and off you'd go for a *nasi hapör* or *nasi dagang*. It was quite simple really to crack the code that was Trengganuspeak uttered backwards. '*Gi kita makang nasi Kkeda Payang,*' ('Let's go eat rice in Kedai Payang.')—that's what the friend would say. This was a popular way of speaking in code, but the code would be cracked quite easily by someone in the vicinity who cared to *bang dengör*. *Bang dengör* was pricking up one's ear to listen very closely.

There was also something akin to the Cockney rhyming slang in Trengganu. Cockney rhyming slang works on a very simple principle:

that what you intend to say rhymes with what you're saying. So, Barnet Fair is hair. Trouble and strife, wife. In Trengganu, sometimes a person was looked at disapprovingly, perhaps with a shake of the head if not the sucking of air through the teeth. *'Dia ni Di Muhammad.'* *Di Muhammad* (pronounced *Muhamma'*) had in it both description and a moral note because what you echoed back in your head on hearing that was, *'Orang jjudi dök selama.'* ('A gambler is always trouble prone.') So the man was a gambler, tut-tut. Now, in our family there was another phrase which was used to indicate that someone (usually a little child) had done the dirty in his or her nappy. It sounded very arcane, for the phrase was *'Long, lek long.'* But a knowledge of Trengganu lore would've easily solved that. This was based on a very old, cryptic children's rhyme, which went:

'Long lek long,
Buöh labu buöh le'ik,
Jamoh j**o Sulong, Berasa ta*ik.'

This had a whole host of information: childish prank, unhygienic behaviour, Sulong's loose bowel, and a local vegetable-fruit. And, of course, expletives sanitised. For a long time I was puzzled by the *buöh le'ik,* but I'm more than convinced now that it was a nonce word. There must've been some bad food in Trengganu in those days when those rhymes evolved, or at least poor storage because I'm reminded of another, much recited by children at play, which also had an unsanitary end. It went:

'Pik Pöng,
Motoka Haji Salleh,
Ketut belepong,
Ta*ik nèllèh.'

'The klaxon's a-sounding
from Haji Salleh's motor
The fart's a-blasting
And the sh*ts aflow.'

Now, as in most nursery rhymes throughout the world there's humour there, a slight misfortune maybe, but also social commentary. Haji Salleh, I have it on good authority, was Haji Salleh Sekateh, a tall, lean man who wrote copiously on the history of Trengganu. He had the pen name of Misbaha, which was an acronym created from the Jawi initials of his full name, Muhammad Salleh bin Haji Awang. And it was a clever one too at that, because *misbah* in Arabic, means 'lamp' or 'light'. And *sekatèh*, the name given to him by Trengganu folk, is synonymous with *lönjöng*, a tall person. *Katèh*, I suspect, came from the long legs of the *belalang*, the grasshopper.

To be fair to the late Haji Salleh, Allah yarham, his role was just in the *pembayang maksud*, as is commonly the case in the *pantun* form, where the first two lines have no connection with the last two, except as an hors d'oeuvres. Haji Salleh was one of the early car owners in Kuala

Characters in front of the Grand Hotel, KT. [3rd from left], the Mufti Syed al-Zawawi; [4th left], Tuan Hj Salleh; [4th from right] Father; [extreme right] Ku Haji Ambak.

Trengganu, and he must've used his car horn sometimes to disperse those Trengganu goats sleeping on roads; so another example of the onomatopoeic word, *pik pöng*. To sidetrack, there were goats and goats in Trengganu; and the ones with the strongest BO, or most *hamis*, were the *kambing nerok*.

Songs in my Head

FOR MANY YEARS a song had been singing in my head in words that I couldn't fathom. It reminded me of the Tamil shopkeepers of Kuala Trengganu who put the words there in the first place, by their early closing and their congregating in our *surau* to sing to their hearts' content. They cooked a special meal of *ghee* rice in a huge brass pot, portions of which were scooped into newspaper pages lined with plastic sheets, then wrapped up and piled into neat stacks. They then brought out the sweets: whorls of syrup-filled thin *jelebi* tubes and balls of *ladoo* that got me hooked for life.

After the dusk prayer was over and the supplications said, our Imam Pök Lèh would withdraw to a corner on this one occasion of the year to make room for these keepers of our grocery shops, our spice retailers and our cloth merchants in their freshly ironed shirts and sarongs of pure white, of the type found in Pulicat, woven in their native Madras. They wore woollen Afghan hats, or simply wrapped kerchiefs around their heads, then they sang the song the way that I hear it now:

'*Maula ya salli wasal*
lim daiman nabada,
Ala habibika khair
ril khalqi kullihimi'

It was a tune that haunted me and spun endlessly in my head, and I've carried it with me all my life. I didn't know what it meant except that it was sung by our Tamil neighbours during the celebration of *mawlid,* the birthday of the Prophet.

It was a joyous occasion for us, as the Tamils were big on the *mawlid* and lavish with their feasts. And they did this not once but twice a year, the second one developing over a week, which they devoted to a saint from their native land named Meeran Sahib Abdul Qadir Shahul Hamid Badshah of Nagore, born more than five hundred years ago. For this they decorated our *surau* with buntings and gonfalons of bright colours, and for us in that corner of town who'd never ventured further than Kampung China, Nagore in Tamil Nadu had come to us.

During quiet periods before the annual *mawlid*s, when the Indian Tamil members of our community were back in their trades, our *imam*, Pök Lèh led the young girls of our *surau* in their lyrical turn, their voices trilling behind the deep bass of our Pök Lèh, drifted up to our house, through the window of our dining room that looked down on the *surau*—voices that haunt me still:

> '*Ingat, ingat serta fikir,*
> *sehari, hari,*
> *Kamu duduk, dalam kubur*
> *Seorang diri ...*'

Those are the soundtracks of my Kuala Trengganu when I look back to those years: songs of the Tamil *mawlid*eers and Pök Lèh leading the girls with his *nashid* while men, being men, were all gathered in the open verandah of the *surau*, hoicking it out or smoking thin cigarettes of black tobacco threads wrapped in thin dried leaves.

Many years later, last week in fact, I travelled to Oxford to the house of an erudite Malaysian living there so I could share his learning and also to seek his counsel on something that I've been interested in of late: the Moroccan Arabic script. We chatted and looked at his collection of medieval Moroccan manuscripts, then rose for the mid-afternoon prayer which he led. As soon as we finished he broke into a chant that found me holding back my tears. I saw again those shopkeepers and their kerchiefed heads, the *ladoo*s and the rice, and Pök Lèh; and I heard again those words (as my learned friend sang it to us):

> '*Maula ya salli wasallim daiman abada,*
> *Ala habibika khairil khalqi kullihimi*'

The song that'd been singing in my head all these years, I was told by our Malaysian scholar, was the *qasida* of the Prophet's mantle, the *Qasida Burda*, composed by Imam Sharafuddin Muhammad Al-Busiri more than seven hundred years ago after he dreamt that the Prophet had placed his mantle around him in his sleep. Al-Busiri was then suffering from paralysis and had prayed to God for recovery before nodding off to sleep. When he awoke he was fully recovered, so he wrote the 160-verse *qasida* in the Prophet's honour and to give thanks to God.

On the bus with the *Qasida Burda* playing again and again in refrain in my head, I thought of Pök Lèh and his song of darkness and loneliness that held me with an even greater grip in this almost empty bus heading home. And I realised again with an intensity that nearly hurt that, in a sense, we're all going there, journeying on, ever homeward.

* * *

Since writing about Trengganu's *pinas* or *perahu besar* and Bachök, the coconut tree feller, I've had repsonses from people who know more about Pulau Duyong than I do, and who knew Bachök even better. As I've mentioned before, there are many similarities between Trengganuspeak and some dialects spoken in or around the Sulawesi area in the Nusantara. Once, while discussing this with an academic at the School of Oriental and African Studies (SOAS) in London, I was told that Trengganuspeak shared its penchant for replacing the 'an' ending with the nasal 'ng' sound—for example, *bulang* for the standardspeak *bulan*—with people from a place called Tukul Besi in Sulawesi.

I'm told now by a correspondent that the Bugis went to Trengganu in force during the time of Daing Perani and Daing Merewah, when Trengganu had strong links with Riau. The Bugis, of course, settled in great numbers in Riau-Lingga and the Malay peninsula in their diaspora, soon after the arrival of the Dutch to the Nusantara. In Selangor they played a pivotal role in the sultanate, as they did in many other places too in Peninsular Malaysia. Sultan Mahmud, the second sultan of Selangor of Bugis descent in fact led the fiercest resistance against the Dutch after their capture of Melaka. The Dutch made inroads into Selangor and set up a near-impregnable fortress on Bukit Melawati in Kuala Selangor, but Sultan Mahmud and his men (some from Pahang) scaled the hill one night and engaged them in a fierce battle which came to be known as Perang Satu Malam, the Overnight Battle, that continued till dawn when the Dutch were finally driven back to Melaka.

I've also been told that Bachök, contrary to what I'd heard, never made it back to the Ujung Panjang of his birth. Towards the end of his life he expressed his desire to return many times, to see once again the land of his origin, but his body belonged to Kuala Trengganu where he was buried, his wish unfulfilled.

Pak Leh Perancis is another name I have been given that may also have connections with Martin Perrot, the man who made the *pinas* synonymous with Trengganu and famous in the archipelago. Duyong boatmakers are still today making boats without resorting to nails. I remember that what they used to caulk the boats was a sticky, putty-like substance called, in typical Trengganuspeak fashion, *ggala*. If you find that difficult to pronounce, then try it in the original Sanskrit, *gala* or the standardspeak version, *gegala,* or *gala-gala.* I don't remember all of the things that went into it but I do remember one of the key ingredients as it bubbled in the pot were pieces of jute strings. These probably gave it the resilience and fibre it needed. Which still leaves me with one question: why did M. Perrot journey out to Trengganu in the 1840s?

When I wrote *Songs in my Head* in which I recounted my early meeting with the *Qasida Burda* and how it came back to me in Oxford two weeks ago, I received some of the most moving responses from many unexpected quarters. I never expected Kecek-Kecek to be read by more than a handful of people who were born in or have been to Trengganu, so I left our Imam Pak Leh's ditty as it was, and it brought a few emails asking for a translation.

I mentioned the *nasyid* before in an earlier section and I give it here now, the full version as I remember it, and the translation:

'Ingat, ingat, serta fikir sehari-hari,
Kamu duduk dalam kubur seorang diri;
Rumah besar, kampung luas, itu ia,
Semua itu, tinggal juga akan dia ...'

'Remember and think you of this daily,
That in your grave you will be so lonely,
Your house and estates all so widely laid,
Will all be behind you once you're dead.'

My Cousin Chén

I LEARNT WITH GREAT SADNESS today of the passing of my cousin Chén after a long illness.

Chén left Malaysia before I was born, but he was always in my mind during my childhood years in Trengganu as he was always sending us figs, *zabib*s and apricot paste folded into a mat (Qamr al-din) from Egypt. But what stuck to my mind most, before I even met him, was a picture we received of him on a camel standing before a pyramid in Giza.

My cousin Chén (standing) in Saad Zaghlul Square in Cairo, circa 1950s.

245

When I myself was in Giza many, many years later, I gave the camel a miss; one man in the family on a camel was enough, I thought.

I admired Chén greatly for his courage, venturing out to Egypt when sea travel was a hazard and the pyramids, in another world, another place. He went with a group of brave Trengganu lads, one of whom later became a minister in the federal government. Chén was a product of the Sultan Zainal Abidin Arabic School, and his venturing out to Egypt was to continue our family tradition of Arabic learning, an area in which I am sadly wanting.

When Chén came back to Trengganu after many years abroad, I remember I had a towel wrapped around my waist as I was about to have a bath at the family well. Undaunted, I went out to his car to meet him for the first time, and thereby established a Trengganu tradition in the eyes of his Egyptian fiancée of Trengganu folk wandering out in a towel wrap-around when first meeting foreign visitors. That was the first time I saw Chén too, and I was greatly moved and impressed.

Chén took a little interest in politics, but mostly he was an academician. He taught briefly at the Sultan Zainal Abidin, then moved on to a university in Kuala Lumpur. Then, on his retirement, he left for Brunei where he taught for a few years. While there he was so badly

My cousin Chén on his wedding day. To his right is his sister Chöh. Looking at him from his left is Mother.

jolted in a serious road accident that he lost the bulk of his memory. He was still a humorous man when I saw him last July, making jokes—as he was fond of—by word association. He was a learned man with a doctorate from al-Azhar University; he wore his knowledge lightly and was always good company.

When Chén got married to his Egyptian wife, a man who did odd jobs for us asked me, *'Bini dia Hindustan?'* ('Is his wife Hindustani?') I didn't know whether to sing or dance. But something else was yet to come. His wife learnt to speak Malay, and it was Trengganuspeak that she chose. When I met her last July, while Chén was ambling between remembrance and forgetfulness, his wife continued the conversation in Trengganuspeak. I was much assured by that because a part of Trengganu had spread its vines into the mind of a daughter of Misr.

I shall miss Chén very much for his learning, his humour and his easy-going style that I valued.

May Allah rest him in peace and make his abode in Jannah.

Budu Spell

BEFORE WE MOVE into *budu* proper and dip our fingers into the sauce, let's first dispel a few myths about *budu*. *Budu* does not come from *berudu,* or, as we call it in Trengganu *anak bbudu,* which has the *shaddah* or the *sabdu* in it. That's the double consonanted beginning which, in Trengganuspeak, normally indicates a shortened word. *Budu* detractors have always judged *budu* by sight, and are quick to make the accusation that it's made from wiggly tadpoles; but it's *budu* we're talking about, not *bbudu,* for in the market if you ask for the latter they'll probably ask you to get them yourself from the pond, or go take a long jump in the *paya.*

A *budu* does not swim about or see the light of day when it's growing up, but stays in a deep *tempayan* claypot beneath a house. I know this for a fact because many times I stumbled on a *tempayan* or two of *budu* when hiding under the house of our neighbour, Wang Mamak. Wang Mamak was not a *mamak* in the true sense of the word, but was born Wan Muhammad. He became Wang Mamak in Trengganuspeak, or

Ayöh Wang as he was known to us. During the day Wang Mamak made *keropok* in bubbly cauldrons in his front yard, but quietly he was a *budu* practitioner in the deep, dark quiet underneath his house. There, unknown to most of us, he placed his *tempayans* and filled them up with glittering slivers of *ikan bilis,* or the whitebait of the Stolephorus family. Then he filled it up with salt water, twice the amount of the fish inside, then maybe he'd hum to them a lullaby as he put them all to sleep.

In this dark space beneath his house which sat on stilts taller than an adult and a bit more, the *budu* tossed and turned in their *tempayans,* fermenting in their sleep for maybe six months or so, unless they were stumbled upon by people like me, who hid underneath Ayöh Wang's house when playing the game of *to nnusuk* or hide-and-seek. If such an event occured, the slumbering *budu* would just heave a little sigh and then go back to sleep once more.

When a *budu* is mature it gives out a brownish liqueur at the top of its body. Just when it was so, Ayöh Wang Mamak would pour it into a pot then boil it up before sending it to his *budu* seller. Good *budu* has a colour of its own, not the reddish stuff that's benefited from artificial aid that you see nowadays in the shops. It has the whiff of something long forgotten, maybe an animal that's long been dead. There are fish aroma indices for all this, you know, and someone has even come up with the startling fact that *budu* has a pH of 5.97, but I shan't worry you with such trivia.

There's lactic acid bacteria aplenty lurking in *budu* and microorganisms incognito. The salt in *budu* is high (8.66 per cent compared to 5.82 per cent in *kicap*) but as you're not going to drink it in a cup or use it to clean your car, I think you can safely put that to rest in the back of your mind as you take your own choice of *budu.* Some makers, hoping to liven-up the stuff, put tamarind sauce into their pot. Others sweeten it with coconut sugar. But robust unadulterated *budu* gave Megat Panji Alam the spirit he needed to meet a Malaccan interloper in Pahang who wanted to take his fair lady Tun Teja.

The spirit of *budu* didn't die with our Megat but still lives on to this day. When *bubor lambok* is bubbling in the pot towards the end of the *puasa* day of Ramadan, a dollop of *budu* is added to give it a fine body. My grandfather, if he knew that *budu* was on the table, would give orders to pluck the shoots of the cashew. Freshly grilled fish and cashew shoots go well with *budu* that's been garnished with shallots. It's served with a squeeze of lemon, and red chillies crushed into the *budu* until it takes on a pungent flavour.

Nobody quite knows how the *budu* originated or how it came to be, except that it's been with us from a long time ago. The microbes that make the *budu* may have been passed on in the secret handshake of *budu* makers, in a long lineage of Budumasonry. But one thing we're certain of, though, is that the *budu* wasn't carved in the Trengganu Stone, nor mentioned in the annals of old Melaka. And all that's left for me to say is that in Turkey they have something on their table called *kadin budu* which is translated as 'lady's thigh meatballs'; and that's unlike *budu* that you or I know.

Empire of Sauce

'IF YOU GROPE into the *pekasam*,' so goes a Malay saying, 'you must dip your entire arm's length.' What is *pekasam*? Winstedt says it's fish, shellfish or meat pickled in brine along with bamboo shoots; whilst my friend Hj Zainal Abidin Safarwan says, without bothering to explain, it's *tetungap, tempoyak, kenas*. I know that *tempoyak* is fermented durian, which isn't my favourite dip, but I had to go back to Winstedt to find that *tetungap* is fish preserved in salt, and *kenas*, a pickle of shellfish. Then I had to go back to them both again because I remembered something in Trengganu called *ikang belara*, which seemed to me to be fish, either smoked or wet-salted. And there my trail ended as both my sources were silent on that subject.

If you're a regular visitor to this place you'll know that I'm referring to Winstedt's handy little volume, *An Unabridged Malay-English Dictionary*, and to Haji Zainal Abidin's voluminous *Kamus Besar Bahasa Melayu*. Of the two Winstedt's is the more scholarly work, with etymology thrown into it, though not always hitting its target.

When I looked into the deep, dark mysteries of *budu* I didn't realise that I was dipping into murkier depths. The comments of one correspondent, Anasalwa, seem to suggest that *budu* may have originated in Vietnam; while another, Atok, has helped by sending in the Malaysian *budu* regulations should I plan to set up a factory in my back yard.

Well, it's difficult to speculate on food origins without starting a fight. I am aware that fish sauce is found throughout Southeast Asia under various names: *budu* in Trengganu and Kelantan, *nampla* in Thailand and *nuoc mam* in Vietnam. Fish, in fact, has been sauced worldwide, dating back to ancient times when a Roman, Apicius, recommended that *garum* or *garon* or *liquamen* be used in his recipes, and these sauces were fish-based. It's only in Southeast Asia that the fermenting of fish has survived with such gusto and aroma, so we're back to where we started: where did it all begin for us?

In Vietnam, layers of anchovies and salt are placed in a wooden vat till it is filled to the top. Then it is sealed under pressure and left to ferment for about the same period of time as the *budu* was left to mature under the house of Wang Mamat. But in Vietnam, the brownish liquid is released from a spigot at the base of the vat then poured in again until the whole thing is properly matured. *Nampla* is done in much the same way, but *budu* is a thicker and darker substance. In Thailand, *budu* is found in the Muslim south, while in Vietnam I'm surprised it's there at all, living side by side with *nuoc mam* sauce.

Now that it has come to this, maybe I'll have to resort to looking further back and consider that Patani in southern Thailand, Kelantan and Trengganu were all once part of the vastness of Langkasuka, and so the similarity in food could've been one outcome of this union. Vietnam, of course, was once ruled by the Chams, people of Nusantara origin who ruled them for a thousand years. In the fourteenth century they had a king named Che Man (Jaya Simhavarman), and I knew many Che Mans in Trengganu when I was there, but I doubt if they were descended from those brave sailors who built a kingdom in central Vietnam.

Now that, I guess, is how history connects with *budu* sauce. It's up to you to question whether it moved upwards with the Chams when they sailed north and stayed a thousand years, or came down with them when the Vietnamese bested the Chams in war circa 1470 and sent them scrambling back down south to Cambodia and homeward to Patani, Malaysia and Indonesia.

Words by Association

IN OUR HOUSE we kept clarified butter—*minyök sapi* to you and me—in a *mölör*. I don't know how they made *minyök sapi* in Trengganu, but it arrived at the market in clear bottles, bunged with bits of old newspaper. It smelt heavenly and was nothing like the *ghee* that you get nowadays in that fat green can that has the initials QBB. *Ghee* is a Hindi word, as you know, which is said to have come, in turn, from the Sanskrit *ghri,* meaning to sprinkle.

But where do you sprinkle *ghee?* In Trengganu our *ghee* wasn't as thick as QBB's but finer, with a more delicate texture; and paler too. During the monsoon months the *ghee* hibernated in a bottle—'*Minyök sapi doh tido,*' as Mother said. It had to be coaxed back to life by placing the bottle near the kitchen fire. Then we sprinkled the *ghee* on steaming rice fresh from the pot and mixed and mixed it thoroughly with our fingers before mixing in *garam lada. Garam lada* was a simple concoction of fresh red chillies pounded to bits with perhaps a spoonful of sea-salt crystals. You didn't need an accompaniment because the salt from the sea, the hotness of the chilli and the rich creaminess of the *ghee* all acted in unison to rouse your taste buds into a celebratory awakening after a dull day at school. But a good accompaniment, if one was needed, would have been *ikang kembong,* the local mackerel brought in fresh from the market and still dripping with briny sea water. It was grilled slowly over the glowing embers of a coconut-husk fire.

It was the *mölör* that brought me to this point, but I got waylaid as it reminded me of *minyök sapi.* A *mölör* was a round porcelain jar the size of a small cooking pot, and it had straight ears sticking out from opposite sides at the top. They jutted out only slightly so you held them daintily when carrying the *mölör* from one place to another. Its lid had a low ridged handle which stick out from the centre top. You held it firmly between your thumb and index finger. It was white with blue floral patterns, and probably came from Japan or China. I was curious about this *mölör,* about which Winstedt is silent and which no other dictionaries seem to know of. So I Googled it once hoping for a trip to some auction house or factory outlet in present day China but no, the only credible answer I got was Mölör, the tyrant ruler in *Star Trek* who ruled Qo'noS 1,500 years ago in Klingon traditional history. 'Surely not that,' I said, putting the lid back on the *minyök sapi*.

Our *mölör* had a chip in its lid anyhow, the result, probably, of an act that rhymes with it: *selör bölör*. This refers to awkward behaviour that results in breakages, unhappiness, toes being trod on and accidents here and there. In Kuala Lumpur, you see, there are those irritating rhymes in china shops that say, 'Nice to handle, nice to hold. If you break it, consider it sold.' In Trengganu, I think, we can put it better: '*Kalu mung selör bölör, mung pakse kena bayör.*'

But where does that take us with the *bekwöh* of yesterday? Nowhere, I regret to say. A correspondent, Penyu Mutasi, thinks its origin was in the massive pot that we brought out during times of feasts. Another, Atok, thinks it came from the English words 'big work' and ended in *bekwöh*, while my *kamus* thinks it's from *kenduri arwah*. I myself am inclined towards the following *kawöh* explanation. Just imagine two men talking about a big feast.

'How many guests?' one asks.

'Oh,' replies the other, 'maybe forty, maybe fifty people.'

'Ah,' comes back the other man, '*ni kena bekawöh ni.*' ('You'll need a massive pot for this.') This would have been repeated again and again, whenever a feast was mentioned. '*Ni kena bekawöh ni!*' And so the birth of another word, *bekawöh*, to feast in a big way.

Can that be so? Well, that's the majority opinion now, never mind if it's only Penyu Mutasi and me. That's how issues are resolved in the *kampung* at least. Wider opinion is always respected, always used to dispel the Doubting Dianas.

Scene: Marketplace. Enter two ladies.
First lady is eating a *pisang kembar*, two bananas stuck together like conjoined twins.
First Lady: '*Eh, Semek, mung dök léh wak ggitu, nati beranök kembör kang!*'
Second Lady: '*Hisy, sape kata?*'
First Lady: '*Betol tu, orang kate ggitu belaka!*'

('You can't eat that,' the First Lady says, 'you'll end up having twins.'

'Sez who?' asks the Doubting Diana.

'Everyone says so,' comes the authoritative reply.)

So there you are, *kampung* life in a nutshell, where consensus is always the order of the day. Nobody goes against received wisdom is the commonly held view. When it's so blindingly obvious, even the parrot knows: *'Pitis sekupang genap, hendak membeli kancah berkerawang, nuri pandai berkata.'* This is a standardspeak description of someone who lives beyond his means, with one word that still survives probably only in Trengganuspeak, *pitis*. Even a parrot knows that he who has only a penny to spend cannot afford a life of luxury. Go read that again: isn't that just beautiful?

From Ptolemy to Here

IT'S NO EASY TASK peering back into the mists of time for the many uncertainties that lie there: A figure lurks there but who is she or he? What is that shape behind the haze? What areas are we looking at?

But the marvel is that we can look there at all. There are mysteries galore in the past where we came from, there are remnants today of what happened long ago. Looking back into the history of Trengganu, Taring Anu, Terang Ganu or Terangan Nu, there's certainly a wide gap between knowledge, history and mystery. The last name mentioned is interesting as it actually indicates the spot on the river where Trengganu actually originated, where the rivers Terengan and Kerbat met. The villagers, soon tiring of this distinction between Terengan and Kerbat, began to indicate them by just saying Terengan *ni* (this Terengan) or Terengan *nu* (that Terengan), the latter developing, in its own right, into the Trengganu that we've come to know.

But if we need to go further back in time, there's always the Alexandrian called Ptolemy, who lived between AD 87–150. He included in his map of the world the ports of Primula and Kole, believed to be the river mouth of the Trengganu River and Kuala Kemaman respectively. That certainly does go way back in time. In fact, from archaeological evidence found in Bewah Cave in Ulu Trengganu, there was habitation there 4,000 years ago.

In 1225 the Chinese trader Chao Ju Kua recorded in *Chu Fan Chi* that Trengganu (Tong Ya Nong) was part of Palembang. Trengganu was conquered by the rulers of Majapahit, according to the Javanese epic poem *Negarakartagama*, written by Mpu Prapanca in 1365. Interestingly, the *Negarakartagama* also mentioned Paka and Dungun, also under Majapahit rule.

From responses to questions I've raised about Megat Panji Alam, I'm pleased to know that there are many out there also asking the same questions. The Batu Bersurat bore the inscription AD 1303 / 702 AH, stating the rules of Shariah and also mentioning the name of Raja Mandalika. He must be the earliest ruler of Trengganu that we know of. From later sources we discover two other names: Megat Panji Alam and Tun Telanai. I'm inclined now to believe that our Megat had control over Trengganu in the earlier part of the sixteenth century. As for Tun Telanai, well, maybe someone may be able to help me there.

After these rulers Trengganu came under the influence of Johor, two of whose men—Laksamana and Paduka Megat Seri Rama—were sent to rule. Of the names that followed were Bendahara Hassan and Tun Zain Indera. Of Tun Zain's children, Tun Sulaiman became sultan (based in Balik Bukit), while Tun Yuan became a bendahara and Tun Ismail, minister in Tersat.

The first sultan of Trengganu was the son of Tuan Habib Abdul Majid, the bendahara of Johor. He became Sultan Zainal Abidin in Kampung Tanjong Baru in Ulu Trengganu in 1725 before moving to Kampung Langgar (in Pulau Manis) and then finally to Kuala Trengganu in Kota Lama (Old Fort).

The origin of Batu Bersurat is still shrouded in great mystery. It was found in Padang Tara, Kuala Brang where it was used as a stepping stone to the Tok Abdul Rashid mosque. In 1887 a trader named Syed Husin bin Ghulam al-Bukhari (probably originally from Bokhara) realised that it bore interesting inscriptions. The jury is still out as to the origin of the stone or who carved the writings into it, but the words were Malay written in the Arabic script, and they mentioned the name Trenkanu (the Arabic alphabet has no hard 'g').

Stories I've heard claim that the Trengganu Stone was inscribed at the behest of a Hadhrami Yemeni preacher, one of many who came to the archipelago. One version attributed mystical powers to this man, who is thought to have inscribed the dictates of Islamic Shariah onto the stone with the strokes of his finger. Unfortunately I've forgotten his name but I'm inclined to believe that it was the Yemenis who brought Islam to Trengganu, and they did come in great numbers, through India, Champa, then Patani and Malaysia down to the Indonesian isles.

These preachers-cum-traders-cum-travellers mingled with the elite in each port of call, marrying and staying for a generation maybe before moving on to another place. Many became members of ruling houses, as they did in Champa, in parts of India, Brunei, Indonesia and Malaysia. The famous Wali Songo (Nine Saints) of Java were descendants of Yemenis, and it's rare not to find Hadhrami blood in the genealogy of prominent families in Indonesia, Singapura or Malaysia. In Trengganu, the Tok Kus were men of Yemeni origin. Tok Ku Paloh, Tok Ku Syed Sagar (al-Saqqaf) and so on were from there too. These were remarkable men of great learning and power.

In the sixteenth century there was a Sharif Muhammad al-Baghdadi (probably originally from Baghdad as his family name implies) in Kuala Brang whose grave is now in a place called Batu Belah. His descendant, Abdul Malik bin Abdullah, was better known as Tok Pulau Manis, Waliullah, (d. 1736), a man of learning who returned to Kuala Brang circa 1690 after years of sojourn in Makkah and Madinah.

Hard Kör Player

TO HAVE STREET-CRED you had to have a *kör*. A *kör* was a throwing object which was used in a game. Name a game. Well, someone suggested *ggéng*. There's no mystery to *ggéng* actually, as it features prominently in the children's calendar of many cultures. It's hopscotch. To hop, like a Scotch (presumably). To play *ggéng* you needed a *kör* to throw into the squares. So you looked around for the most balanced piece of discarded porcelain you could find, a chip off an old Ming if you were lucky. You trimmed its corners till it was nicely rounded to take the sharpness off its edges so that when you kept the *kör* in your pocket it wouldn't cut into your delicate areas.

Kör could've come from the sea, or from the land where the *kör* trees grew. In its sodden, unpolished, tangled-in-seaweed state it was called *buöh ipir* or *buöh gömök*. They came drifting in from the sea as ebony-coloured flat seeds the size of a newborn's palm. The seed had a tough, white kernel, and a lot needed to be done before it became a *kör*. From the sea a good many things came drifting to us in Trengganu: the spaghetti-shaped *rumput jjuluk* that I've written about before, the tune of the *nobat* and our *kör*. All—with the exception of the lilt of the *nobat*—came drifting to us in the months of the *musim gelora,* when the waves rolled up in turbulent shapes and the sea spirits spoke with a deafening roar. Folk didn't venture out to sea during those monsoon months. Instead the sea came to us and washed things ashore.

Buöh gömök was taken home and polished with spit and Kiwi. Its kernel was sometimes left intact to give weight to the *kör* but often it was picked out bit by bit with a sharp stick, or cleared out in devious ways.

The game of *wök* was indeed *to* or *tol,* which is basically hide-and-seek. *Wök* had the added ingredient of a *kör* made from a milk can that had been filled with pebbles, then sealed by flattening its open mouth into a wedge with a fist-sized stone. This was done with great childish effort so as to make the *bibir jjuèh,* lips pursed in concentrated intensity. This *kör* was the object that was thrown as far as possible when the game was played. A person on the search team then went to retrieve it—maybe from behind a *rök* or a bush—then placed it within a circle that had been drawn in the game area. The object of the game for this player was to go and catch all the players from the other team by a *cot* or by naming him or her on sight. For the other side, the object of the game was to creep back quietly to the circle, get hold of the *kör* and rattle it furiously in the air. Then the game was played again, hiders and catchers taking their positions as per *status quo ante.*

Playing the game was an arduous business and it normally took place after school, near *ggarék* time and the first *solat* of the evening that came soon after sunset. The object was to finish the game before bath time at the well, then go home for prayers before sitting down for dinner. It was always better to be a hider than a searcher, needless to say, but some players were born to be searchers, never managing to be in the advantageous position, much against their natural desire. Some just gave up, returning home instead of going to retrieve the *kör,* leaving their tormentors hiding forever in the *rök* or in the back of the *jambang.* Sometimes the hiders themselves colluded to play a dirty trick on the searchers and went home instead of into hiding, leaving the *kör* carrier in the lurch.

A person or team that couldn't better their position time and again was called a *lepèk.* To be a *lepèk* was an onerous and a shameful thing, for the name stuck even beyond play. Even at school, at recess time, you were taunted for being a *lepèk,* carrying the wimpish flag of defeat, stuck in a rut as a playground non-performer. Hence the taunting note in the verse that d'Arkampo and a few other people have brought back to me:

'Pèk pèk li
watakök lang
Lepèk sekali
berbulang-bulang.'

In other words, once a *lepèk* always a *lepèk.* The opening lines to the verse are, I think, mock Arabic. We were influenced in those days by what we learned in Qur'an classes and religious instruction, and Arabic permeated much of our lives, even if we only spoke a little of the language. The way we used to sing it was: *Pèk li/Wataköllang* ... The ellision between the nonsense words *watakök* and *lang* (*wataköllang*) gave it an Arabic flavour, as did *pèk li* which sounds to me like the Arabic *fe'li*—which means 'actual', 'de facto', 'real'—from the word *fi'il,* meaning 'activity' or 'behaviour'. We use *pe'el* in Trengganuspeak to describe someone's behaviour, as in *'Isy, pè'él budök ning hudoh ssunggoh!'* ('This kid's behaviour is, oh my goodness!').

I don't know where *kör* came from, but I suspect it came from Yemeni shores, with the Sayyids on those dhows. We had many in Trengganu of such pedigree, and I can just imagine their little kids playing their little games with the locals and producing their little *kör.* Except that it wouldn't have been the *kör* that we know today, but a *kurah,* Arabic for 'globe', 'a little ball'.

'*Apa tu?*' ('What's that?')

'*Ini kurah ana,*' ('That's my *kurah,*') the little Yemeni would say.

Back came the reply, '*Oh, kör!*'

It may not be as fanciful as you may think. Some Trengganuers probably remember *bola sekalad* which was our name for the tennis ball. What's *sekalad*? Why, from *sakhlat,* of course, which in both Arabic and Persian means a woollen cloth, which was the texture of the tennis ball.

Then there was *sakhlat ainul bana* but that's another story ...

I can't thank you enough for all your wonderful comments, bringing back all those fun games, some I'd forgotten, some I'm delighted to have rekindled. Those kids' verses especially are a gem. Thanks all you wonderful people!

How to Wök

THE PAST MAY BE ANOTHER COUNTRY, but there you know many people. The comfort of sharing makes pals of perfect strangers; you meet someone unknown to you in a strange place, then you begin to talk, and you know such and such and so-and-so. You feel part of a camaraderie based on shared experience. This is how I felt when you wrote in about your fun and games, and familiarity with places and people that I've written about. We're not strangers but friends from a familiar shore.

So thank you for all your comments that jogged my memory. For example *wök*, a game that was played by hurling a stone-filled milk can that was sealed flat at its opening so it was shaped like a wedge. The person doing the *wök* ran after the clanking can, put it in a designated place then looked for people to catch among the players. But everyone would have gone into hiding already. I think you would stealthily come back to jangle the *wök* can in the air to proclaim victory as that other ·person went about looking for you.

This tin of condensed milk played quite a big role in our lives, considering it was just a small can. When I first set foot on the shores of Blighty, the people there were quite amused to discover the extent that a condensed milk sustained our daily lives. In Blighty it's only thought about when going out on a picnic, or when Boy Scouts and the girls that guide them go on a jamboree into the wild. But in Trengganu, as elsewhere in the peninsula, condensed milk put the cream in our *tèh tarik,* so to speak, and you could judge the role played by an item from the different names given to it. The round can that stood just over three inches tall was called a *po'* (one of many Trengganu words that end in a glottal stop.) *'Pegi Awang tulong beli susu se po'?'* ('Son, could you please go and buy me a can of milk?')

Once the can was emptied, the *po'* became a *cètöng* which could be used for bailing out a leaky boat, for scooping water from the *ppayang* (Ok-*lah,* you posh people, *tempayan*), as an earthen jar at the foot of the steps of a *kampung* house or recycled as a container for take-away *teh tarik* from a *mamak* stall. The lore among *teh tarik*ers was to open the can by cutting around its top but leaving about an inch of it uncut so that the lid would stay as a flap on the cylinder. The cutting was done with an opener that punched a hole in the middle of the can's top, from where the opener swivelled to cut the can open around its rim. When the can was refilled with *teh tarik,* a string was pushed through the bottom of the hole so its un-knotted end popped out on the other side. The flap was closed, and the happy customers walked away with the piping hot *teh tarik,* dangling it in the milk can that was held daintily by its string between the thumb and index finger.

Nowadays, of course, this is no longer de rigueur, as *tèh tarik* is taken away in a plastic bag that's knotted at the top with a rubber band with a ridiculous straw sticking out of its ruched centre. You see these bags dangling from some odd places: tree branches, bike handlebars and rear view mirrors. If you want to know where the rot started in our lives, it started from here.

Song and Games

WE PLAYED GALÖH PANJANG, *to nnusuk* and *petik mata* on sunny days. On rainy days we played *enjut, enjut semut,* made mud pies or sat under the house darkening sheets of glass with a candle flame, then drawing figures or writing titles in the layers of soot. These we then projected onto a white sheet with a battery-powered torch in a 'theatre' built from

Mother's sarongs wrapped around the legs of a table.

We lived in a tall house that stored many surplus pieces of furniture, battered pieces of luggage and a myriad of articles of unknown provenance. When Father retired from work in Kuala Lumpur, he returned with Mother to the house and also gave shelter to a man who'd worked as a labourer at his former place of work in Kuala Trengganu. I remember the man as Retnam. He made a cosy corner for himself in the space beneath our house and, when the mood took him, he'd make out-of-this-world lime pickle from a recipe he carried in his head from South India.

When I went back to the house recently, I could still see the debris of our past, down to the broken shards of glass from which we projected our home-made stills. There was an old oil lamp that came from the *surau* with which our house lived cheek by jowl, and the old henna tree still stood there. Also still there were remnants of *chengal* wood left over from when the house was built by workmen from Besut around the turn of the century.

The voices of those old games that we played came back to me when I saw children rolling metal wheels they'd detached from some old bicycles, guiding them with sticks and cursing as they rolled out of steer. The kids were still playing *galöh panjang,* though, a game much like the Indian *kabbadi,* with two teams trying to break into each other's hold at opposite ends of lines drawn in the sand. *Petik mata* was perhaps by then a dying art, as it involved the skill of flicking up a stick from the ground then hitting it in mid-air as far as it could fly. Those were skills acquired from years of practise, and kids were beginning to lose patience for that when there was a TV set flickering in the corner. So, needless to say, that was also the end of hand-drawn pictures projected from soot-stained sheets of glass in the darkened space under a table.

In my day we stopped play by announcing *cot-ko,* a word whose origin puzzles me but we understood it to mean 'let's rest awhile'. Thinking of the games that we knew, it appeared to me when I visited that the kids had stopped play forever.

As I looked out from the wooden staircase of our house into what used to be the old market, I saw again in my mind's eye a group of children behind a makeshift *batik lepas* banner, singing a raucous song as they wove their way between the shops. These were kids known to us as *budök pasör,* rough and tough market boys who spent their mornings and afternoons among the fish, and the in-between hours devising as much jollity as they could muster. The song they sang came distinctly back to my ears:

> *'Anöklah ikang lah ikang*
> *di makang ikang*
> *Di mana tuang lah tuang*
> *Di celöh gigi.'*

('Little fish, o little fish
devoured by the bigger
where are now o little one
caught in the gnasher.')

It was the universal story of a small fish eaten by a big fish, but I remember that as I watched them from the *surung* of our house all those years before, I was enthralled by the way they were repeating the verse with a spiritedness that was almost hypnotic.

Songs and poetry are a major part of growing up because children abide by what makes sense to them. In language, rhythm comes before logic or grammar, and singing makes words last forever. A lot of what we sang as children in Trengganu were nonce words heaped upon the nonsensical. It was the rhythm and the peculiarity of the words that made them special, and I remember them even now. Take this one for instance, as baffling as can be even for Trengganuspeakers:

> *'Patendu patendéng*
> *lalak kumang béng*
> *bulu ketang maséng*
> *malikéng ccöngak.'*

This may have been part of a longer recitation in a game, but even now the only words that make sense to me in a sentence are *bulu ketang masèng,* meaning 'the salty hair of a crab'. What kind of fly is *lalak kumang bèng*? And what manner of pose is *malikèng ccongak?*

And what manner of man was Mak Ming (Trengganuspeak for Muhammad Amin)? Was he born *in vitro*? Read this to yourself aloud:

> '*Mak Ming ttönjö*
> *beranök ddalang bötö*
> *timbol tenggelang*
> *terus masok go.*'

> 'In the bottle he was born in
> Afloat he is and then a sinkin'
> into the goal he did go in.'

Thanks also to the person behind the veil of Anonymous who sent me this doggerel:

> *Jook-mak-jook Jjalang tepi pata;*
> *Ttemung P Ramlee muka kerutuk,*
> *Boh öbak pinang gatal.*

This amused me greatly, not least because I knew and have referred to *pinang gatal* in my blogs a couple of times. It's the little red fruit of a palm tree that gives an itch when smeared on the skin. Then, of course, the image of Gog and Magog (*Jook-mak-jook*) walking along the beach and the cruel children's humour about a famous film star made this evocative and memorable.

Banana Fritters

A LADY FROM FATHER'S CHILDHOOD DAYS—Mök Cik Yöh, I think she was called—once reached into her rice storage jar in the semi-darkness of a Besut night. She wanted to feel how her bananas, which she'd placed in there to ripen quietly, were faring. When she squeezed the fruit a little and got back a sound, she knew there was something untoward coiled up in there for fruits did not normally hiss, especially not Trengganu bananas.

That was Father's favourite banana story and it raised a chill in us and probably a bit of the Freudian in some of you. There were snakes in the grass in those days, and pythons (*ular sawo* as they were called in Besut) thought nothing of coming into the house to look for places to recoil after having uncoiled themselves for most of the day. You don't see snakes seeking warmth in pots of rice in these days of high rises, and as for bananas, I have to say, some names we used to know are no longer around for us to peel.

For a long time I was corresponding with my friend Kura-Kura about the state of Trengganu bananas. Was there still the *pisang Raja Embong?* I would ask. So on his next trip to Trengganu he'd pose the relevant question to the state agricultural officer (he's a very well-connected man, you see) and come back with the assurance that there were still seeds of that type languishing in some dark drawer in some Trengganu repository. I'm using 'seeds' in a loose way here, you understand, as I do not know how bananas are kept and saved for posterity. For a while I was debating intensely with another friend in some outpost in Brazil also on the subject of bananas, wondering if they came from a shrub or a tree.

I remember from my Trengganu days the many bananas that came our way. When one of us was down with the ague, Mother would throw a *pisang bakaran* or three into the wood fire that was burning underneath her pot of gruel. *Pisang bakaran,* which was green if I remember correctly, was food for the ailing, it being neither heaty nor cold. This was the way she saw it, applying the accepted wisdom from nature's pharmacopoeia. Foods were divided into three types in those days: heaty, cold and neutral. Heaty foods were to be taken in moderation, neutral taken whenever possible and cold foods to be taken sparingly, if at all, especially when you were ill. The prickly durian would've been categorised as a heaty fruit, hence its sarong-raising proclivities; the cucumber, in turn, a cold vegetable. Peanuts, rice and *roti canai* are, as I understand it, all safely neutral.

But our *pisang* remained a mixed-bag of 'temperatures'. *Bakaran,* as Mother believed, was in the class of neutrals but it was a cooking banana, delicious when cooked but unfriendly when plucked from the tree. Another one that she served with relish, piping hot from a pot of boiling water or with skin charred as she pulled it from the wood fire, was the *Raja Embong.* Embong was a popular Trengganu name, and was *sans culotte,* if you ask me, so I can't explain how 'he' became a Raja. But the taste of the fruit would've clinched it for him, a tribute to the cultivator of this variety for all, a *pisang* neither hot nor cold.

There were bananas for a quick bite too, for someone in a hurry anxious for a quick fix of energy. I would put on top of this the *lemak manis,* a puny fruit with a burst of many colours. It had a sweetness and *lemak,* which cannot be expressed in English satisfactorily. It also had the wonderful taste of happy hours and birds singing in the trees. There was the *pisang bunga* and the *berangan,* and the *kelat jambi,* bananas all. Of the *kelat jambi* I must tell you. It was not *kelat*—a taste that you'd generally associate with unripe fruit—and, as far as I know, not connected to Jambi in faraway Indonesia. It was another one of my favourites; an eating banana with seeds the size of a peppercorn and a taste that lingered more than awhile.

There was also the *pisang berangan,* of which I know very little, and the *pisang bunga* which retained its greenness even when ripe and was a delightful fruit to have after a meal. *Pisang jelai* was one Mother avoided for its unmentionable qualities. We never had it in the house and never gave it the time of day. These are the bananas of old Trengganu. I wonder where they all are now.

At the time of writing there is a world banana revival. It's the fastest selling fruit in British supermarkets, and the Japanese have a yen for it aplenty, except that they've broken all banana lore and made strenuous demands of our Malaysian growers to grow their bananas straight, not curved, and to make them all blemish free. And I wish them all hissing snakes for their lack of banana savvy because, as you know, bananas don't just grow like that from trees.

In those days before the Telanais and the Megats, when the carvers were still debating the spelling of 'Mandalika' on the Batu Bersurat of the *ulu,* I imagine the bananas to be there, with *ubi kayu* and *kerepok lekor* in the food pantry of Taring Anu. There were bananas then of many types, dangling from their many broad-leaved trees, flapping and waving in the breeze like some demented, multi-armed ladies. They were burnt, boiled, mashed, fried, dried and cut into thin slices. A green species called *pisang benggala* was pickled in jars and served to discerning guests as a meal on the verandah on a sunny day.

Thought for Food

THERE'S PRECIOUS LITTLE in old texts about food, beyond the occasional mention of *pekasam* and *jeruk,* two kinds of preserves. Malays seem to me to have been far too busy with other business in their *hikayat*s to make a big fuss about what they ate, which strikes me as odd, seeing as how dedicated we are now to our dining table. The *Hikayat Awang Sulung Merah Muda*—which, according to Pawang Ana of Perak, was written about the land of Pati Talak Trengganu—described the *kenduri* as full of form and function, but only with regards to the preparatory bustle: those itching from skin diseases carrying bamboos on their backs, the blind blowing into the mortar and the deaf dealing with celebratory cannon fire. But not so much as a hint as to what was on the table, whether it was *singgang* or *rendang, sambal* or *pulok lepa.*

Flipping through the *Sejarah Melayu* in search of its mouth-watering parts, I found only an oblique reference to *ayam suapan* and *nasi kunyit. Nasi kunyit* is, of course, glutinous rice coloured with turmeric, but there isn't so much as a hint as to what *ayam suapan* was—perhaps they were bite-sized chicken morsels. Even the sultan, when he was pleased with someone, only deigned to send *sirih* leaves from his *puan*. No, not from his missus but out of his silver caddy royal.

Sayur kangkung was the nearest the *Sejarah* got to a recipe, but that was only as a ruse by Tun Perpateh Putih to take a peek at the forbidden face of the Chinese Emperor. Brought before the Emperor, who was presumably sitting on a very high pedestal, the delegation threw their heads back and raised the full-length *kangkung* to drop down their gullets, while also keeping their eyes wide open for the monarch on high. An old Melakan custom, they explained to court officials. The Chinese people became great *kangkung* eaters after that, said the *Sejarah Melayu* (*The Malay Annals*) magisterially.

All this talk about foods of yore came about when a friend wondered how Megat Panji Alam would've munched his time away on his long walks to Pahang to claim his belle, Tun Teja. And that was what brought on this lament: how deficient was our old literature on the subject of comestibles. The *Hikayat Petani* had much about genealogy, court women and their magic spells but little about what was served to all those hungry players once they were seated around the *tikar*. Why, even when there was any mention of food at all it didn't prove very useful, I ventured to tell my friend, drawing on my attempt once in the British Library to study an ancient tract. Take this instruction, I said, from an old recipe: *'Sepuluh sen daun kesum.'* ('Ten cents' worth of *daun kesum'*). Now, how much *daun kesum* is that in today's measure? And that's from something written in the 1950s.

But coming back to the dining *tikar* of the Megat, or even the Telanai for that matter. What *did* they eat? I imagine it would've been foods that were really rooted in the peninsula, if not just Trengganu. The Megat would have munched on *ssagöng* en route to the Kijal ferry, though his coconut shreds wouldn't have been packed in a thin tube of old newspaper with frivolous strips of coloured paper attached to it. Maybe his would've been in a *mengkuang* container, or in a henchman's *kelepèr*. At home he'd have eaten all the foods of old Trengganu: the *ulam* dish of *daun bola, pucuk ubi, cekor manis* and *jering* or *petai* maybe. There most certanly would have been fish from the river or sea, baked in a packet of banana leaf and stuffed maybe with coconut, turmeric and *lengkuas* or ginger. There would probably have been *pelanduk* or *ayam hutan,* or the battle-hardened meat of the water buffalo, grilled in the *panggang* over a wood fire, and maybe a dip or two of *belara* or *budu*. And *sayur* from the clay pot of *ubi setela* with shoots, turmeric and ginger thrown in and boiled in the *santan* of *nyiur* (coconut milk).

'And maybe,' my friend said now getting into the mood and a little whimsical, 'they had dessert of *buöh ulu,* baked appropriately by the *ulu* people.'

'No,' I said, quite confident that the *buöh* didn't come from the *ulu* but from the hands of another. For you see, soon after Melaka fell and they'd plundered stones from the graves and the mosques of the city to build the Famosa, the time was right for a fiesta. So they cooked and baked the *bolo* which was Portuguese for 'cake', and which most certainly travelled a linguistic distance to give us first *bolu*, then the *baulu* of standardspeak, then the *buöh ulu* of Trengganu people.

The Spaghetti Tree

ON SUPPLY DAYS Ayöh Wang had bulging sacks delivered to his door. These were special sacks, woven from *mengkuang* leaves. In the sacks was a starch-like, off-white powder.

In 1298 Marco Polo, imprisoned in Genoa, dictated his 'travels' to a fellow prisoner, one Rusticello from the town of Pisa. To him he narrated tales of his epic travels to the East, and finally his stay with the Great Khan of China. What's of interest to me—especially in light of all those bags of white powder delivered to our Trengganu neighbour—was Marco Polo's stop at 'Fanfur' where he saw a tree 'from which, by a singular process, they obtain a kind of meal.' I'm referring now to the translation by Marsden, where the great Polo also said that the meal was used to make cakes and various kinds of pastry 'which resembles barley bread in appearance and taste,' some of which Polo took back to Genoa.

The original version of his Travels has been lost, but there are translations extant, said to total more than a hundred and thirty, in Latin, French, Tuscan, Venetian and more with varying degrees of reliability. The Tuscan version is said to be the most faithful to the original, where the tree mentioned above was described as having a thin bark inside of which was a kind of flour. It was this flour that gave birth to the myth of spaghetti as a food of Chinese origin. But of that, more later.

I could not find this in the Marsden version of *The Travels* that I have, but I have it on the good authority of Australian writer Peter Robb (whose book, *Midnight in Sicily* I commend heartily) that in the Tuscan version the land where the powder trees grew was the Kingdom of Fanfur in Baros. Baros, on the west coast of Sumatra, is a place well known in the Malay world, especially by those who are enamoured of its Sufi literature for it was the home of Hamzah Fansuri, the Sufi poet credited with having written the first Malay form of the *syair*. Fanfur or Fansur was, of course, Pancur, which was Arabised into Fansur, hence Fansuri, man of Fansur.

I recognise now that the white powder that so intrigued Marco Polo and which, according to Robb, made the Italians drool so ecstatically over lasagna and other delights of pasta, was indeed our *sagu* or, as the world calls it now, sago. *Sagu* was what Ayöh Wang received in those fat *mengkuang* bags that we in Trengganu called *karong*, and which he despatched hastily to the semi-darkness of the storeroom beneath his house. On sunny days when the fishermen landed ashore with baskets of fish—*tambang*, *pparang* and *butir nangka*—his wife, Mak Som (Mök Söng, if you're from Trengganu), would sit on her haunches, as would the other girls, near the place where the water flowed. There they'd clean the fish, lopping off their heads and tails and occasionally throwing these bits to the cats who were miaowing a chorus of 'Gimme that, now.'

In the meantime Ayöh Wang, his lower half draped in a *batik sarung*, his headgear a coil of *kaing ssahang* material, would be stooped in a corner measuring out the correct proportion of *sagu* which was then turned into a mush of fish pounded in a wooden mortar with a long, round, wooden pestle. There'd be two workers: the stronger of his daughters would be pounding one mortar in time with another, making thump-tee-thump sounds that made passers-by walk with a distinct sway, enraptured by these rhythmic beats of pounded fish. Next door Mök Nab and her children would be doing much the same in their own doorstep manufactory. And the rhythms beat on till the braziers were hot and the cauldrons brimming with coiled-up, protein-rich, sago-reinforced *kerepok lèkör*.

As I said, it was the *sagu* that gave Europeans a false picture of spaghetti. Marco Polo, as some contend, never did go to China. (*Did Marco Polo Go To China?* by Frances Wood, Secker & Warburg, London, 1995) And spaghetti never actually came from there. It was the Arabs, in fact, who shaped the first Italian spaghetti when they ruled the isle of Sicily, bringing with them not only their skills in food technology but also the necessary durum wheat for its manufacture.

But besides sago, our interest in Baros also lies in another: in the substance called camphor which is a form of *kapur* to the Malays. *Kapur* that came from there is none other than our *kapur barus,* a funerary material and a medicinal.

Sago, by the the way, is not a palm but a cycad, one of the oldest plants on earth and unchanged for many millions of years.

The Art of Ssahang

SSAHANG, WHICH COMES FROM the standardspeak *basahan,* is an everyday wear and word.

'*Nök gi duane ni paka lawör sangak tu?*' ('Where are you going in such beautiful attire?') a person would ask of another.

'*Lawör guane,*' the person would reply dismissively, '*ni baju paka wak ssahang je!*'('Not really, this is just my everyday wear.')

And so the word is transformed—from the piece of cloth wrapped around your waist (if you're male), or wrapped at armpit level to cover the body with arms and shoulders laid bare (if you're female)—into an everyday word to denote rough wear, something that is worn at play for everyday use not for any particular ceremony.

The word *ssahang* or *basahan* comes from *basah,* meaning wet. It is the cloth that protects you as you pour water from the well over your body. Protect? From what? Why, prying eyes, most definitely.

The female style of wrapping the *ssahang* is also known as *kkembang.* Some do it all day at home, as some people nowadays strut around in their pyjamas. And some men wore the *ssahang* all day long as they went about their daily work. I knew many men in Tanjong who wore nothing but the *ssahang*; and then, on a Friday, you'd see them in a new *söngkök* and *kaing pelikat,* topped in a freshly laundered *baju,* and you'd bless your luck to see them so. So you'd rush to them to do the *salang,* which was the Trengganu form of the handshake and had something Masonic in quality.

Women had little choice when it came to their *ssahang* material, just any faded sarong would do. But for men, the world was really their sarongster.

When I saw those dastardly Khmer Rouge emerge from the wild in the days of Pol Pot, I noted that they carried with them a length of chequered material. The world called it the Khmer Rouge scarf, but that was the *ssahang,* for sure, given an ideological world view. The Chams—who were originally Nusantara people—also carried *ssahang* cloth, and with it they ruled Cambodia for more than a thousand years.

The male *ssahang* came in many shapes and in as many colours. As d'Arkampo has pointed out, it's a rare and expensive material now. In my day we had mini *ssahangs* for little people, and light blue was our favourite colour. Our mini *ssahang* had black stripes, and was about a yard and a bit in length and perhaps a yard again from waist to ankle. The *ssahang* mentioned by d'Arkampo was red with black stripes, and would have attracted wild buffaloes. But I believe our d'Arkampo was a town child who bathed at the community well of his *surau*, and not in some bucolic surroundings where water buffaloes lowed and grew.

In the early days of the stock market, when share prices were quoted on the radio, Trengganu folk were delighted to know that their *ssahang* floated daily on the ether. When it was time for *sahang jatuh* *, they rushed home very quickly so as not to be caught unawares.

In old prints drawn by the Dutch of *Orang Malayo*, many wore nothing but waist cloths to while away the day. That was, no doubt, the heyday of the *ssahang* in our history.

When fashion took over and the sultans made a habit of giving away *persalinan* (a change of attire) to the favoured few, the *ssahang* still remained but as a band of cloth worn as a sash or cummerbund around the waist. You will still see the practise of this art in cultural dances put on by the Culture Ministry. Young people prance about in their *baju*, loose trousers and *selimpang* (a glorified *ssahang*) across their chest or waist.

The *ssahang* was a useful cloth which should be revived for our glory. Let's use the *ssahang* for all purposes, and not just for the *mandi*.

* * *

Sahang is Trengganuspeak for the standardspeak *saham* meaning 'shares'. *Jatuh* means 'fall'.

Manner Maketh the Mang*

NEVER LET IT BE SAID that your childhood is lacking in *cakne*, though many will contend that it is merely a growing-up pain. In *Hikayat Awang Sulong Merah Muda*—a tale that purportedly took place in Pati Talak Trengganu, even if the territory came mostly from the splendid mind of that Perak folklorist, Pawang Ana—the wastrel came home when the cockerels were crowing and dewdrops were beginning to glisten like pearls on blades of grass before taking on the pomegranate red of dawn. This was youth with gay abandon when gayness was an expression of the heart, not connected to sexual matters.

This is wayward behaviour born of *dök cakne*, and *cakne* is something I've been hunting for like the snark and yet am still nowhere near the door of its birthplace. I hear, though, the mother's words, *'Döh nök wak guane, dia dök cakne setabok döh le ning!'* So without corroboration I can only say that one who is without *cakne* is one who disregards the words of other people, especially those of elders. *'Döh nök wak guane, dia dök cakne setabok döh le ning!'* ('What can I do, he doesn't listen to me any more these days!')

This is the *tekök* boys brigade of the *babé* (pronounced *bah-bay*), two words to describe anyone lacking in *cakne*. It is from little *dök cakne* that big *waballaghö* lads do grow. And a *waballaghö* person is a goner, neglectful of his duties, uncaring of his behaviour and probably also possesses a loose tongue and looser morals. *Waballaghö* and *lèrè* are two Trengganuspeak words that metamorphosed from one Arabic mother, *lagha,* meaning to make null or void. Children may start by being a little *naka* though some may take it a little further and become *söngö*. As to when *söngö* becomes *bedö'öh* may hang on the tolerance level of the adult beholder. But the unnecessarily showy behaviour of *göng* may cling on till later life to win, by popular denunciation, an act that is over the top, *ddö'öh lalu*. What's fascinating here is how one word that starts with one meaning in its source language ends up on a harsher note in another. *Lèrè* and *laghö* (from the Arabic 'invalid') find their apotheosis in *waballaghö,* a word that now mocks its origin to describe someone probably beyond a glimmer of hope. While *bid'ah*—a word that is widely used by Muslim scholars to describe an innovative behaviour that leaves the norm—becomes aggravated in Trengganuspeak into *bedö'öh* or *ddö'öh,* something excessive and therefore of unsound behaviour.

Hisy, lekak pah ttua (carry to adulthood) *kö'ör!* adults would sometimes say of certain types of childish behaviour. This is the type of speech that makes Trengganuspeak so difficult for outsiders to grasp and so foreboding to its youth. *Lekak*, *pah*, *ttua* but *kö'ör*? Well, *kö'ör* is an expression of anxiety or concern over the eventual outcome of a thing or act.

The essence of this is that every Trengganu parent wants his or her child to grow up *tertib terning*—from another Arabic word, *tartib*, but one that hasn't strayed too far from its original meaning of 'order' or 'sequence'. *Tertib-terning* is a form in Malay that I call ding-dong word making, or giving a word an alliterative or rhyming companion to strengthen its meaning and to embrace everything connected with it. So *tertib-terning* would not just mean doing something in an orderly manner, but the word also embraces everything connected with it. In Trengganuspeak we have many other ding-dong words, like *ggura-selöröh*, *perösa-er* and *semayang-bang* to name but three.

There's a catalogue of things that a child should not be when he or she is growing up. He must not be *dök jjuruh*, a mild admonition that is far removed from the standardspeak *kurang ajar*, which is a serious charge. *Dök jjuruh* is a minor peccadillo, a mere lapse in good manners; a *kurang ajar* person lacks good breeding, speaks out of turn and eats the *akök* before the *imam* at a wedding (where he isn't even invited). This is many grades above *göng* and miles ahead of *tebölah* which, by the way, ends on a nasal note. Well, a *tebölah* is an awkward kid who eats his *nèkbak* with his soup, wears his *söngkök* with the sharp ends to his sides and has a finger in every *akök* pie. This is *nanör* without a Master's degree, but *nanör* can be carried into adulthood. *Nanör* is around you, everywhere.

* * *

*Mang is the Trengganuspeak short version of Osman, a male name.

Game of the Name

ONE DAY, while entangling my mind in knots trying to remember the name of our second cousin, I finally remembered that we called him Ssipo. He had a brother called Mat Yéh who has since departed this mortal coil. The news that brought this on is that their father, Abang Wè, has just departed to the realm of souls.

The embellishment of names and the foreshortening of some is a way of remembering in Trengganu.

There was Tuan Bèng, an Englishman who, I believe, was a banker (hence the name); there was a Pök Héng, a tropicalised lobster-red man who drove an open-top sedan from one end of town to another. I believe he was in money, counting it in an imposing building at the foot of Bukit Putri that was the Chartered Bank in my day. 'Nök gi duane Pök Héng?' kids would ask him whenever he appeared in Trengganu light, and sometimes he'd toss them a few coins for their trouble. But I must add here that those where-are-you-off-to words did not make us busybodies—it was just our way of saying hello. And then there was Mr Preedy who wheezed past us on his motorbike and surrounded himself with many boys in his Batu Burok bungalow.

At school, behind the sales desk of our canteen, was Pök Awang and his earth mother wife, Mök Mèk. They were from good old Chinese stock on the riverside of Kuala Trengganu. There was Köhéng, our coffee-shop man; Tökeh Jing and Tökeh Luga, two opposite characters in opposite shops in Tanjong who dealt in spokes, wheels, bikes and the tracing and patching of our punctures. Luga is, of course, a Trengganu word that describes nauseous feelings and stomach acids when you've not had a bite come midday. Its close cousin is löya that surges up once the nausea has taken over. By association, luga is a down-and-out word for someone who probably had one sen but not another to rub together. Our Luga was a prosperous man who was touched by the inverse effect of his misnomer. Looking back across the road you'd expect to see an enormous man among his bikes, but our Jing was an average-sized guy who was nothing like the jing of Trengganuspeak, a word that describes the djinn of Arabian Nights that sometimes came fizzing out of a bottle. I suspect Jing, like Köheng, got his name entangled in our Trengganu tongues and became, like Wè (Ismail) and Ding (Din), more Trengganuised by the day.

I came to learn that Ssipo, our second cousin, was not named to describe his mien, all entangled and knotted up like the Trengganuspeak ssipo. Rather he was just an ordinary person with the sharp-edged name of the Arabic saif, meaning 'sword', and so Saiful. Now this puts him in the same class as Zainal, another popular Trengganu name, and indeed a Malaysian one too, that is left a-hanging in the air. *Saif* is 'sword' as *zain* is 'jewel' but from whence come the *al* or *ul* in their tails? The answer lies in the Arabic definite article that latches the character to the noun that came with it. Saif al-Din (pronounced Saifuddin), for instance, is a name given to warriors of the faith or *din*. Zain al-Abidin is for someone who's the jewel of worshippers or *'abideen*. But Malay and Trengganuspeak, being foreshortening tongues, they slip off the latter more easily as Saiful (Sword of the) or Zainal (Jewel of the). The way we looked at it in Trengganu, Saiful became shorter still and popped off our palates as Ssipo. I am not too sure, though, of Mat Yéh but he was probably our Muhammad Idris walking about in mufti.

That's not the long and short of it, though, for we have another way with the monicker. We simplify names and make them short for ease of grasp and to make them easy to remember, just as people do all over the world. My cousin Ding (Dziauddin) is one such, and there's Mat Ming (Muhammad Amin), Mbong (Embong), Sop (Yusuf), Munöh (Maimunah), Ttimöh or Möh (Fatimah). Then there's Ping (Ariffin), Yik (Taib), Yang (Mariam), Song (Kalsom) and Nab (Zainab).

Sometimes the job became the name, as in Pök Mat Bbiang who was Muhammad of the Customs Department (*bbiang* from standardspeak *pebean*), or Ddölöh Tèksi (Abdullah the rickshaw man). Or the character became the name: Mak Jéng Tönjèng (Muhammad Zain the clubfoot), or Lèh Birat (Salleh with the scar in the corner of his mouth), or Mang Göng (Abdulrahman the show-off) or Minöh Janda (Aminah the widow).

But of the names that I can remember there's one that I treasure most for prosody, and she was the lady that we only knew as our Mök Döh Pök Mat Kupi.

Ghosts in their Posts

'GO ON, WRITE ABOUT THE OLD MAGIC *of Trengganu*,' wrote Mr Chung Chee Min, a teacher from the Victoria Institution where I was banished to after a few years at the Sultang Sulaimang Secondary. He himself, he said, had been charmed when he ventured out to Kuala Trengganu with his classmate after their sixth form exams in the Sixties. He saw darkness and then, from afar, ghostly lights:

'My classmate Amlir had warned me about those east coast people who indulged in charms and magic more avidly than the west coasters. And their charms were many times worse than those in the west coast. I guess my ignorance of such matters at that time saved me from indulging in too much worry about it. But Amlir had evidently worked himself up well before the trip with dark fears, real or imagined.

That evening, as we were walking back to the government rest house after our dinner in KT (I cannot remember where the rest house was but I think it was outside KT town, maybe to the south), we passed a kampong of sorts. Free of the glare of the town lights, I noticed that the sky was filled with stars, a sort of celestial display that I, a city slicker from KL, had never witnessed before. Mesmerised, I gazed skyward to drink in the scene as I walked, meandering left and right. The sight of me walking as if in a trance caused Amlir to freak out, thinking I had been truly hit by some Trengganuan charm, slipped doubtless into the food I had partaken of earlier. He gave me a severe reprimand for frightening him, saying that I was never ever to gaze at stars again.'

Spiritual things are very difficult to grapple with, not least because you can't see what you're thinking about. Sometimes you tend to see too much in your head. But in the years that I was in Kuala Trengganu (or on those occasions when I was with my grandparents in Besut), I never saw any ghosts nor had to seek the permission of one when treading an unfamiliar path. I remember, though, the salutation that people used to give when they were about to fell a massive tree in the forest, or when entering a path untrod: *'Assalamu alaikum! Anak cucu nak lalu!'* ('Peace be on you, please allow your kith and kin to pass!') Why do we claim kinship with ghosts?

I remember, though, ghosts that stalked in quiet places. A teacher once said, perhaps in jest, that it was inadvisable to stop your car in the stillness of Jalan Wireless (now Jalan Pusara) in the middle of the night as the chances of your car not moving again were very great. This, if anything, showed up Trengganu's car mechanics and the quality of their work. Then, as I've said elsewhere, Trengganu ghosts were more silly than scary (like the ghost who stretched his legs wide at the gate of Istana Maziah at midnight), or they were of the sulking type, like the spirit princess of Bukit Putri who went away when promises to her were not kept.

But then there's magic, just as there are ghosts. Ghosts are in distant places and on uninhabited isles like Pulau Kapas where, I was told, two teachers from our school walked in circles for hours, disorientated under the spell of malign spirits. This was part of the hazard of venturing out, especially if you were young, to lose sight of your direction and your self and be transported to a virtual place. *Susuk dihantu,* which referred to being hidden by ghosts, was an alarming plight—children going missing and then found in the branches of trees happily eating noodles, oblivious to the precariousness of their situation. And, of course, the noodles turned out to be worms served up by you know who, or what.

I remember also the first time I went to Langkawi (before it became the haunt of urban dwellers intoxicated in their own spirits). I was going out for a walk at dusk and was warned not to accept the hospitality of strangers, especially if their feet hovered some few inches above the earth. Langkawi was a spooky isle, with burnt rice and barren earth, cursed for generations by a woman wronged. There were islands whose silhouettes formed a pregnant handmaiden, lying supine in the waterways.

Meanwhile in Kuala Trengganu, a goalkeeper jumped at a football only to find another slipping into the goal. And attackers found defenders crowding around the posts, some of them phantom figures, no doubt. This was when the crowd on the sidelines livened up the match with accusative cries of *'Bomoh! bomoh!' Bomoh* was the man with a sarong wrapped over his trousers and a band of cloth around his head, hovering furtively behind the net. *Bomoh*s cast a goodly kind of magic in those days, making champions of our mediocre eleven and hurling balls that suddenly vanished from the rival goalkeeper's sight. Trengganu slipped in the national league when *bomoh*s were decommissioned from behind goalposts.

It's a funny thing this ghostly world, like the germ across the river and the elephant before your eyes. Soon as I arrived at the school in Kuala Lumpur where Mr Chung was a pupil and where he taught, I was told by my classmates not to look up to a classroom just above the bicycle park on a moonless night, for in the window up there many had seen an expressionless, headless ghost. The classroom was reputedly the torture chamber of Japanese soldiers when, many claim, they'd used the school as their base.

Rack and Ruin

THE ROAD TO HELL is paved with good intonations.

In the neighbouring state of deer rampant and Taman Sekebun, a person is said to be *jahannè* if he or she has gone wayward, but in Trengganuspeak s/he is just *rösök*. *Jahannè* has its origin in the fire and brimstone of Jahannam, and is familiar to Western readers as Gehanna, but in effect its meaning has been toned down to just the Trengganu sense of being spoilt or broke. A Kelantanese may sing or rant, *'Habih kerano mu mèk oh, jahannè ...'* to lament the fate of someone torn to bits by the sight of a comely lass. But this is their equivalent—wrapped in their *semutar* of hyperbole—of their Trengganu neighbour's *'Rösök döh, rösök döh!'* We know of *jahanang* too in Trengganu, but normally of things rather than people. *'Habih jahanang basika mung, Mat!'* are appropriate words of commiseration to someone whose bicycle has just been run over by a juggernaut.

But bicycles, as do cars, go *rösök*. Broken down like people who're not just spoilt but damaged. Hair tinted red, cigarette hanging from pouting lips, trousers oh-so tight, eyes darting round like a regular coquette. *'Rösök! Rösök, budök tu!'* The male equivalent has bouffant hair, Craven-A cigarettes in a bulge in his back pocket and eyes wilting from a whole night's work. *Rösök.*

'Parök!' cries another. *Parök* is beyond the pale, extreme damage.

Yet it all started so innocently, as an act of *söngör* maybe, and *söngör*, bless its heart, is a mirthful word. It's just hovering there in jest but not quite over the top, just a wee bit rude, perhaps. A little cheeky chappie lad.

Then he becomes *haru biru* and she becomes *dök jjuruh* or, worse, *dök jjuruh aröh*, as it is sometimes said. As *aröh* is a direction word, it aggravates the movement of the *jjuruh* which is *jurus* in standardspeak for 'straight' or 'moving in one clear direction'. *Dök jjuruh aröh* is the path of the wayward, which is much like the *haru biru* chap, a jumbled up mess of this or that, a person so lacking in focus and so game for anything that's bound to shock.

But an elderly person watching all this still can still keep his facility to understate: *'Dia ni karu sikik.'* To be *karu* is to be a mixed-up, unpredictable git; and *sikik* is a diminutive word. But to be *karu sikik* is to be just a little mean, bad or sad. It's a phrase with alarm bells and a red flag, used more in sorrow than anger, accompanied probably by a sad movement of the head from side to side.

Lèrè is surely at the root of it, a word that is sometimes heightened to *laghör* to denote carelessnes or disregard, normally of things religious. A *laghör* heads in the opposite direction when the call to prayer is made from the mosque. It may start as a casual neglect that soon becomes a habit, and then the person is no longer *lèrè* or *laghör* but something weightier than that: dancing at the club, gambling in the den, leering at girls at the bus stop; the true marks of a *laghör* gone to town, been through the passing-out parade. People would point and say, *'Hisy, dia tu waballaghör sunggoh!'*

Waballaghör is Arabic sounding, heavy like lead, judgmental to the hilt. It is *lèrè* gone bad, *laghör* with a college certificate; he is no son-in-law material, and is very, very sad.

Tepongs of Trengganu

HE WHO TIRES of *akök* is tired of Trengganu.

In Trengganu the *akök* is made in ceremony, with smoke billowing from dried coconut husks that heat the brass *akök* mould from above and below. The mould or *acuan* (add a 'g' to its end if you're a Trengganuspeak purist) is a clever device made in two parts. The bottom carries the embedded five-petalled flower that is almost two deep (inches that is, if you must know). The inner surface of its flat and eared top cover meets the bubbly *akök* ingredients as they simmer in the heat, its top outer surface carrying a top load of burning husks. In old-fashioned kitchens the entire contraption sits on the *tuku* that is normally made from three round stones the size of a kid's head, washed ashore and shaped by the motions of the sea. More coconut husks burn below the mould between the stone legs of the *tuku*. Mother stands watch all hour long so the *akök* will not burn away.

A good *akök* pops out of its mould at the right temperature, glowing goldenly for all to see, with its skin soft but not too crusty and its body dipping slightly when given the slightest pressure. In it is the yolk of duck's eggs, sugar and flour beaten with a beater that has a handle of brass and a coil of copper that runs round and round in a whirling way. And the sound that this springy copper coil makes as Mother beats the egg yolk, flour and sugar in a metal container is the sound of Ramadan as Hari Raya is drawing near.

Akök are also made in special moulds that turn them out in dainty sizes, each one deep in the middle and thinned out in its back and front with a thin rim running round its little boat shape. These are instant *akök* that disappear into a child in three or two mouthfuls, but they are a delight too, like their big sister below.

Then there's the boat-shaped *akök berlauk* that has a savoury centre, of chicken or meat and salt and spice. How Mother got them all in there I never knew. This *akök* has a slightly sweet carbohydraty taste on your first bite, but soon you're overcome by the spicy, bready flavour as you move towards its centre, which is boat-shaped, if you remember. I once had two of these *akök*s with a friend in our house as soon as we came back from *tarawih* prayers. On the third bite we spat out our mouthfuls with a loud 'Ptoooiii!' The *akök* was going ship-shape all right, but it was too late when we noticed the starchiness in its flavour and realised that it'd gone a little mouldy. But *akök*s give you litle fright if you treated them right. Why, I'm still here to tell the tale!

For the duration of the fasting month there are sweetmeat and savouries that are typically Trengganu. There's *hasidöh* which is not so much a *kuih* as a paste that comes embroidered in a tray. It has the consistency of dough laced with *ghee* and is often laid out flat in a dish. The top of this *hasidöh* is grooved out by a process called *cekik* that is either done with fingers or tweezers. In the grooves crispy bits of fried shallots are scattered to give the effect—if you study it from high above—of the formation of a crop circle. I've not been able to trace the provenance of this *hasidöh,* even if its name has a slightly Middle Eastern character. It is sweet and soft (but for its crunchy shalloty bits) and has the distinct characteristic of flour basted in rich *ghee,* then thrown into the heat of a thick brass pot and mixed and mixed with plenty of sugar.

The *hasidöh* is an adult 'thing' as we kids used to say, but in our hands it was pure putty. I had a cousin once, a boy even smaller than me, who took to this *hasidöh* thing and stuck it on our dining room wall. He became Mat Tèpèk (sticker) to us all his life, which wasn't long, I'm sad to say, for he died very recently.

So that's another *tepong* of Trengganu, but as *iftar*'s still a while away, I'll tell you of another: and that's *nèkbat* which sounds like the Arabic *ni'mat* meaning enjoyment when pronounced by someone with a heavy cold. *Nèkbats* are like little dollops of flavourless pastry, soaked in syrup of the heaviest density and is, as you may have guessed already, our dear sweet-toothed diabetic's dilemma.

These are *tepong*s, as I have said, that are made and baked in Trengganu to lighten the burden of our *puasa. Tepong* is a distinctly Trengganu word to describe our sweetmeats and savouries.

A Regular Kind of Guy

SITTING IN HIS SADDLE, Wan Endut (or Wang Ndok to us Trengganu people) looked every bit the regular soldier and only a shade out of the ordinary. He wore the General Giap pith helmet as he babbled incessantly about the enemy. These were mostly stray dogs of war that fed on the rubbish of Kuala Trengganu, forlorn animals that barked in the night, and during the daytime too. They wended their way from pillar to post, peering into overturned bins in back alleys, eyes darting here and there, always one step ahead of you.

Wan Endut had bones to pick with these stray dogs as he strapped his hat tightly to his chin while pedalling his daily *tèksi* from Pasar Tanjong to Batas Baru, from Ladang Titian to Atas Banggol in the heart of the textile district of Kuala Trengganu. If somewhere along the way you asked him for the time of day, he'd probably point you to the clock tower of Kedai Payang that kept its timekeeping haphazardly, clock faces pointing in many different directions. There were things you had to get used to in Kuala Trengganu—time was one. We had *jam waktu* and *jam Malaya*, one separated from the other by one hour. We also had cuckoo clocks that were just a tad askew; and *tèksi*s were trishaws if you had to call one in a hurry.

Wan Endut must've been demobbed at some early stage, though I don't know when or why. He was as tough as a nail and strutted about like the colonel, his heavy belt with gleaming buckle, sun hat tipped at a rakish angle, looking hither and thither. Then he'd twist his head a little to the side as though he had a tic, deliver some little philippic about the here and now, then move with another tic as his head twisted at another angle.

Some quiet afternoons when the passenger trade was a little slack, Wan Endut walked the streets in his heavy boots holding a piece of rope in hand for the little strays. But as the strays were always faster than a man in boots, Wan Endut was often left muttering by the side—a little tic here and a little there—about the state of his little world. Behind him was the Yen Tin Radio shop, opposite him the *surau* of Haji Mat of Kerinci, just ten paces from him, maybe, a grand old building that'd been the seat of a grand family before it had become the local Catholic Church and then was transformed into the Buddhist Association. God knows what it is today.

When strays were safely snuggled in their hiding places and the rickshaw-pulling business became too hot and sweaty, Wan Endut popped into our local *surau* and slung his khaki outfit on the bannister. He made a ritual of unlacing his boots. Then he stripped to little more than the *kaing ssahang* around his waist and doused his passions at the community well with the heavy brass bucket that hung on the cantilever.

I used to watch him from a safe distance—he suffered no fools gladly—as he disrobed from his *kaing ssahang* back to his army gear while still being able to tic and mutter some unhappiness of the day about wayward kids or the scarcity of stray dogs or his daily business of the *tèksi*. Then, fully clad but for his boots, he'd sit down with an old newspaper. Then began the Wan Endut ritual of wiping his toes, soles and heels with meticulous care, using the pages of bylines, news stories and sporting achievements that had popped hot off the press only the day before.

Having thus dried his feet—an old habit learnt from his jungle-trekking days in the army—Wan Endut put on his heavy boots, laced them up and 'tic'd his tic'. Then, with a little smile, walked the way that no stray dogs dared to go.

Phonographic Man

THERE ARE PEOPLE you don't remember yet can't forget.

My brother recently asked me if I remembered Cik Löh Sömböng. Listening to his description of the man, I began to wonder if he'd said *sömböng* or something else. Then I remembered; I was very grateful to him for that.

Cik Löh was a man we used to watch from afar but never spoke to, not because he was proud but because he had a very peculiar way. And he also carried a funny thing that made him look very odd indeed. Sometimes of an afternoon at the Masjid Abidin we'd see Cik Löh pulling out his bicycle from where he'd propped it up in the shade; at other times we'd see him cycle purposefully down the road, going somewhere that needed his call.

Cik Löh wore a *sarung pelikat*, a Malay *baju* and a turban wrapped around the skullcap on his head, and I seem to remember now that, like most men of his type, he also wore the loose Malay trousers beneath it all. On one of his handlebars was a peculiar contraption that dangled and sometimes almost scraped the earth when he took a tight turn. It was a tube with a bent end that opened and bloomed out gradually into a flower shape. This formed the open end of a speaking hole. We called it the *serömböng* to mean something that smoke came through or a contraption that you spoke into. Bhiku's coffee shop had a large *serömböng* jutting out of its upstairs window that blared out A. Rahman and R. Azmi or any old song that the DJ played of an afternoon through this public service radio 'horn' courtesy of the Information Department. Cik Löh's horn came from an old gramophone that he must've found among cobwebs in someone's hidden store.

Cik Löh used the horn in rural *suraus* that didn't have the benefit of electricity to blast out the *azan*s of the day. He probably placed his lips close to the base of his flower, and woke up babies and dozy men many times a day in Wakaf Tapai or some other far corner of rural Trengganu. We did not know who appointed him to be this itinerant megaphone man, or how far he travelled to spread his voice, but for him it was mission loud and clear.

Nasi on the Apör

FOR DEFTNESS OF THE HANDS you had to give it to Mök Söng.

Mök Söng sat behind her deep basket, round and woven from bamboo strips, lined with banana leaves and filled to the brim with *nasi dagang*. The steam from it rose and curled in the morning light, throwing more than a whiff of banana leaves scalding in freshly cooked rice, glistening with the fat of coconut milk, flavoured with the seeds of fenugreek and water from a well in Kampung Pantai.

Mök Söng scooped out more rice with her *södèk*, more steam escaping into the air, into the olfactory triggers of the awaiting crowd who were mostly her regulars. They looked, impatient to the core, at the plate of cucumber *acör*, cut into little fingers and soaked overnight in vinegar by the dainty hands of Mök Söng's daughter. They swallowed a little—*acör* did that even to grown men—as Mök Söng took her ladle to the enamelled basin of *lauk* filled with an orangey sauce of coconut milk, curdled in the swim with many other things: *asam gelugur* sliced and dried to a dark hue, *belimbing masam* pulled fresh from dangling in a tree, red chilli taken whole, thrown into the bubbly mix and stirred till it became soft and ready to release the seeds of fiery innards into the thick pot of Trengganu *tembaga*. But pride of place in this swirling mix was *Thunnus tonggol—ikan tongkol* in standardspeak, *ikang aya* in our native Trengganu.

The *aya* was a coarse fish in Trengganu, not normally chosen for our everyday meal by the ladies of our house who preferred the classier *tenggiri*. But as far as the *nasi dagang* was concerned, the *ikang aya* was de rigueur, a fish of choice whose excellence for this purpose was beyond comparison. Mother would first put it in water, then add salt and a slice maybe of *asam gelugur*. I'm sure Mök Söng did much the same as soon as her fish came ashore on the afternoon of the day before as she was nodding off after her afternoon tea.

The process was called *mmati air* which meant practically killing the flavour in the water. The blood of the tuna, the taste of the sea, the fishiness that could overpower, all these were leached in salt water and the *asam* flavour then left to baste in the pot till the ingredients were ready for the boil. In this first cooking, the bony parts of the *aya* also softened and became softer still when cooked again in coconut milk and all the ingredients that lent the mixture its taste and colour.

Nasi dagang aficionados knew this as *kerapöh,* the softened bony parts that gave their taste buds the added thrill. After scooping out the rice and putting in a dollop of fish and a tablespoonful, maybe, of the fishy sauce with its coconuty richness, pungent flavour and hint of tartness from the *belimbing* tree, Mök Söng would look up to the waiting customer. This was the window that waited for the obvious answer. 'Beri kerapoh sikik, Mök Söng!' the knowing would say. And Mök Söng would deftly scrape out bits of softened bones, parts of the tuna cheek or that tasty bit around the eye. Knowing when to butt in or how to respond to the question in Mök Söng's eye was the mark of the true cognoscenti.

You could stand there and watch all day Mök Söng's ergonomy in full flow; but you wouldn't want to do that as you had a shop to open or the office to go to, or school would start in just another half an hour and besides, you had people at home waiting for you (and the *nasi dagang*) around your table. And those who knew knew that, come eight o'clock, Mök Söng's basket would be empty of *nasi dagang* and her *bèsèng* drier than an iguana's back. But to recap, I'll try to itemise the deft movements of Mök Söng as best as I can remember: first she'd pick up the the moist rag to wipe the surface of the banana leaf, cut out to the right measure, then she'd ask you if you wanted your rice laid open on the *apör* or wrapped in a cone-shaped parcel called *kelösöng*. Then she'd reach out to the basket that was almost in her lap for the rice, and reach out to the basin of gravy and the fish that lay in there. Then she'd give you the *kerapöh* look before the *kelösöng* was finally sealed with a short spine of the coconut leaf that also served as the toothpick for your finale.

Eating your *nasi dagang* on the *apör* was the sign of a man in a hurry, and was the serving choice of the barrow boys in the fish market who came to Mök Söng at the first beep of the delivery lorries with sleep still dangling in their eyes. *Nasi dagang* was all set and matched and brooked little else besides. It was best left as it ought to be. To have your *nasi dagang* with a side dish of meat curry was the hallmark of a *göng* person, in Trengganuspeak, and to have fed it to your brood with some left-over fish from the previous evening's eat was infra dig, and shouldn't have crossed your mind at all.

Man of Oob

ON A COCONUT TREE along the coastal road of Batu Buruk in Kuala Trengganu were three letters arranged vertically to read: OOB. For a long time I wondered, as I cycled past it to and from school, what OOB meant vis-a-vis a coconut tree until someone pointed out that it marked the boundary for golfers swishing it out by the Kelab Cosmo.

'Out of Bounds' is an appropriate motto for the man who comes to mind every time someone mentions golfing in Trengganu. He started life humbly as Che Ngah Muhammad, clerk to Sultan Zain al Abidin III, but

Dato' Sri Amar Diraja.

285

later rose to the rank of Dato' Seri Amar Diraja, the chief minister. He was a Trengganu patriot, a devout man and a skilled negotiator who kept both the British and the sultans—first Zain al 'Abidin, then Muhammad then Sulaiman—constantly in check.

As chief minister he sat with another Malay judge (with a British adviser presiding) in the court of appeal where, as the historian Heussler noted with a Westerner's unconcealed irritation, 'he could be depended on to shave the fine points of Islamic law yet finer by the hour and to find reasons for opposing things the BA wanted to do.'

But it was on the golf course that the Dato' Amar made his lasting impression on the then British adviser, Jarrett, when the latter was out on the green with Sultan Sulaiman. They got distracted during the course of the game and completely forgot whose turn it was to putt. So the man they went to for wise counsel was Dato' Amar, and for this he finds a permanent place in my non-golfing heart for having given the golfers a long story about Solomon's [Nabi Sulaiman's] judgment when two women went to him claiming rights over the same child. Dato' Amar, said historian Heussler, concluded 'after a seemingly interminable wait that there was as much to be said on the one side as there was on the other.'

Trengganu was fortunate to be seen as too inaccessible and too economically insignificant to be worth bothering about by the two intervening powers of Siam and Britain. In the charming words of Heusserel, Trengganu was 'the never-never land of Malaya'. But even then Trengganu rulers and court officials were astute enough to have sensed British intentions from the outset. The governor of the Straits Settlements, Frank Swettenham, made no secret of his intention to directly take over Trengganu through negotiations with the sultan (with the Foreign Office already having one W.A. Evans waiting in the wings as adviser designate), but when he called on the Raja of Kelantan and the Sultan of Trengganu to get their agreement, the former accepted while the latter declined. Again, in Heussler's words:

'[C]ausing some embarrassment to Sir Frank, who was not accustomed to resistance from Malay royals, and to London, which had already found a man to serve as adviser.'

The British agent in Trengganu met with determined resistance from Sultan Zain al 'Abidin who refused to accept the 1902 British treaty with Siam.

Che Ngah (Dato' Amar as he then was) looked at the Johor state constitution and drew one up for Trengganu in 1911 to keep the British at bay. But this was power against the guile of the British, with their resources and experience in divide and rule. The British agent finally brought in the excuse of maladministration based, allegedly, on complaints from disgruntled Malay factions and some European miners—reason enough for them to bring a Commission of Enquiry to Trengganu.

And the rest, as they say, is history.

Sultan Zain al Abidin, who once said that he did not want to live to see Trengganu fall into British hands, had his prayers answered. He died shortly after the Commission finished its work. His successor, the young Sultan Muhammad ibn Sultan Zain al Abidin III, resisted attempts

Sultan Muhammad ibn Sultan Zain al Abidin III.

to bring him to Singapore to sign the hand-over treaty. He couldn't resist for long and when he did go, on 16 May 1919, he took with him four menteris (ministers) including our Dato' Amar, and seven council members, all opposed to the idea of British intervention in Trengganu. There the sultan's attempts to strike a favourable bargain with the British failed; the treaty was signed and, unable to suffer the humiliation, he abdicated just over a year later on 20 May, 1920 and lived in exile in Singapore.

Muhammad was succeeded by his brother Sulaiman who took the title of Sulaiman Badrul Alam Shah. Dato' Amar held onto his post as chief minister, trying his best to outmanouevre from within his old foe, the British, whenever he could. He frowned upon Brits who walked about in shorts, but complaints to the BA only brought the response that it was outside his (the BA's) remit. He was the *alim*, the learned man who saw himself as the upholder of religion. In this role, Heussler said, he was 'bent on stamping animism out of the people's souls with the white heat of cleansing Islam.'

In 1928 Dato' Amar had to travel to the *ulu* during the peasants' rebellion to make initial negotiations on behalf of the sultan. He refused British offers of help and brought with him a force of Malay police officers. It was the beginning of a complicated and sad incident in the history of Trengganu, one that caused Dato' Amar, the defender of religion in the face of colonial onslaught, to cross paths with another religious stalwart, rebel and saint, Haji Abdul Rahman Limbong.

And as history is full of delicious ironies, the two *alim*s, though now on opposite sides, had one thing in common: a distaste for the Brits and their colonial ways.

* * *

British Rule in Malaya, The Malayan Civil Service and Its Predecessors, 1867-1942 by Robert Heussler; Clio Press, Oxford, England, 1981.

The Bell and a Stick

THE MAN WITH the white turban wrapped around his red hat was our Mufti Sheikh Yusuf al-Zawawi. Egyptian and engaging, he was at ease with everybody and widely respected for his presence and learning. He leant on his walking stick as he looked around the Tanjong *pasar*.

I don't suppose the mufti of Trengganu in the present day goes to town anymore with his driver by his side and his handbasket of fish and fruit. But Sheikh Yusuf, with thobe flowing and driver in tow, looked at the array of fish laid out on the mat on the floor in the market and pointed at it with his walking stick. The fish seller, unmindful of the office of the mufti and the prospective customer in the flowing robe, grabbed hold of the stick and cast it unceremoniously away.

This was a story I was told by many elderly folk to illustrate the gap between foreign practicalities and Trengganu's delicate forms and ways. Even a man of religion was liable to make grave mistakes when it came to what we in Trengganu called *jjuruh* and its cousins *tertib terning* and *tamakninöh*. The irony is *tamakninöh* came from the Arabic *tuma'nina* meaning composure or calmness in prayer, but in Trengganuspeak it has taken on the extended meaning of 'being prim and proper'. Someone who's lacking in it, for example *takdök tamakninöh*, goes about hurriedly waving his stick, though I hasten to add that our mufti wasn't a man who was intentionally rude, just not totally immersed in our local ways.

'*Biar gök tamakninöh sikik wök! Tertib terning gök sikik!*' is a reproach from an elder to a very young person, or a *wök*, to be mindful, polite and right. As you've recognised, *tertib* comes from another Arabic word, *tartib*, meaning order. *Tertib terning* is what I call a ding-dong word. A *tertib* person knows the order of things and has the savoir faire that's born of good breeding, so his opposite would be *löklak*, a word I've also heard used in Kedah. Mat Löklak burns bread, trips on the cat, walks in front of elders without stooping down low and wears his *söngkök* with the edges aligned with his shoulder blades.

Here's the ultimate disapprobation for someone whose form is totally bad and manners absolutely out: '*Dök jjuruh haröh setabok harang!*' In other words, 'A person who is way beyond redemption.'

Now our Sheikh Yusuf al-Zawawi once shook his stick at Bukit

Putri and silenced the *genta* bell that'd been tolling for a good many years on the hill of our princess; and so it was that the bell was heard no more in the Ramadan months and on the eve and morn of Eid. His reason for silencing the chimes that brightened our festive months was because it was un-Islamic he said (and he could well have been right). For years Kuala Trengganuers felt the loss and mourned the silence and the emptiness of our *genta*-less Eids; but happily for them they still had the sonorous voice of Bilal Sa'id and the thunderous tones of Bilal Deramang that came down from the minarets from dawn to dusk to fill the emptiness in their hearts.

The voices of Pak Sa'id and Pak Deramang (Abdul Rahman) have long gone into the ethers of Hari Rayas past, and the *genta* is now perhaps forever silenced by the al-Zawawi stick, but I wish my Muslim readers a happy Hari Raya nevertheless: may your day be as sweet as the call of the *takbir* on this blessed Eid.

Cat Takes Nap

In *The Haji's Book of Nursery Rhymes*—a book I last saw many years ago in the window of a second-hand bookshop in Charing Cross Road, London—there is a nursery rhyme that translates as:

'Dang, dang kong,
Kucing dalam tong ...'

Of course, it's a translation of that familiar nursery rhyme:

'Ding dong bell,
'Pussy's in the well ...'

I can't recall many nursery rhymes from Trengganu that are spun around cats, but there are many feline-centred local beliefs. Bathe a cat for instance, and it will rain; the *hantu kucing* wakes up early in the morning from the *para*. We did not know what the ghostly cat did, nor why it spent the night sleeping in a bed of ash. But we knew that our cats had knotted tails because an ancestor of theirs once annoyed a tiger, so the tiger tied its tail in a knot and the knot got caught in the genes and was handed down to our present day cats. We also knew that cats bury their poo in the ground to hide their work from the tiger who'd probably be very annoyed if he trod on some. Wise cats, I'd say.

There were many cats around us in the fish market. *Kucing Körèng, Kucing Belang, Kucing Cicök* were the cats around the *kerepok* factories and around the well of our local *surau*, talking incessantly in cat language to Mök Song and Mök Nab, asking them to throw some fishy scraps or perhaps a freshly severed *kembong* head.

Körèng was your scruffy cat, with much mileage on the clock and an epithet adults used for little children with faces tarnished by heat and dust; *belang* was the striped one, not quite the tiger's coat but streaks in a prominent colour against a usually darker coat; the *cicök* was your Tabby that got its name from a textile pattern from Baghdad. But with all those cats in our midst I can't think of a word in Trengganuspeak (nor, for that matter, in standardspeak) to describe the sound of a purring cat. Perhaps it's because we don't pay them much heed when they are contented. But we do have the phrase *kucing kkarak* in Trengganuspeak to describe the dialogue that cats have with other cats before they lock themselves in a vicious embrace on the ground or in the mud. This is the *ggömö* that's done sometimes by their human counterparts.

Kucing jatoh anök was a phrase Mother used quite often to describe the restless pacing here and there of someone struck by a real or imagined anxiety attack—like a mother cat whose kittens have dropped from a higher nesting place, say the top of a cupboard. When the mother cat picks up the kitten in her mouth we call it *gömbèng*, which is gentler than the *kereköh* that we sometimes had to do when buffalo meat was *dök pök*, or especially tough in the pot. Then, of course, there's *kucing kurap* which is a mangy cat if you're a cat, but a term of abuse if you're not.

Return To Sender

BEFORE THE INTERNET blunted our pens and access to our address was via a letterbox, letter writing held more for us than present day emails.

There were pillar-boxes and postmen on bikes, and a human contact between deliverer and recipient that makes me ache for that beautiful film *Il Postino*.

In Kuala Trengganu our postman—we had one living next door to us named Awang Cèk, but he never delivered our letters—left our daily mail at the bottom of the stairs, inserted between the electrical wiring and wood panels. They were mostly bills and, occasionally, a postcard, but Eid al-Fitr brought a bigger bulk of mail from all over.

Malay letter writing is an intricate art, not least by the forms of address that we have to muster: *'Kehadapan Ayahanda yang dikasihi'* (*'To my beloved father'*) when writing to your beloved Dad; *'Bonda yang diingati serta dikasihi'* (*'My dear mother who is remembered and loved'*) to your dear Mum; followed by a series of good wishes, the most minimalist being, *'semoga berada di dalam keadaan sihat walafiat sentiasa'* (*may you be in good health always'*). We cherish the contents of penned letters, though nowadays we can hardly remember the contents of

Canai Bacaan.

emails. Part of the enjoyment of letter writing is the personal contact we have with its sender, the cursive hand contained within, the thoughts collected in a moment of joy, emotion or great sadness. It's as if the person is speaking to us personally. Indeed, in films, whenever a letter appears in close up, the voice of the sender will soon fill the air, reading the letter as if in conversation with the recipient.

Other joys also come with a letter: its tactile pleasure, the scent of perfume that some love-crazed paramour sprinkled on its page. Sometimes letters come registered and hefty in weight, to be signed for by the recipient with trembling hands. Is this the final note, a job offer, a postal order? That which plops out of an envelope is forever remembered, its memory sometimes shared and with it, perhaps, laughter, often at the expense of another.

Father never tired of telling us about our neighbour, his schoolmate, Ayöh Wang Mamat. Wang Mamat once fell a bit under the Trengganu weather, so he penned a letter to his teacher to explain his absence. At the end of the note he wrote in impeccable Jawi, *'Harap Cikgu pahang.'* *Pahang,* if you're not au fait with Trengganuspeak, is a state of understanding and not, in this context, our neighbouring state famous for its *joget.*

In his adult life Ayöh Wang found work in *kerepok* and brass, and from the number of times I stumbled on earthen jars hidden in the darkness beneath his house during games of *to,* I came to know that he was also a practitioner of the dark art of *budu.*

After he left school and his schoolmate Wang Mamak, Father moved on to the post office.

Those were the days when telephones and telegrams were under the same roof as the Pejabat Pos. I knew from stories that Father told that he was once a telephone operator. These were days when calls had to go through the operator at the exchange, and the stories Father told were harmless ones meant purely to amuse. One, I remember, involved a hilarious telephonic conversation between a very important man in Trengganu and his counterpart in a neighbouring state. Father also told us stories about his work and about a curious room called the 'Dead Letter Office'. Then he donned headphones and became a Morse code operator in the telegraphic wing of the post office. I don't think he ever sold stamps over the counter, though he was an avid collector with a small leather bag full of Empire stamps and first day covers that came through the post from a man named Dawood in Durban, South Africa.

I don't know where 'dead letters' went to, but I know that the 'live' ones that reached their addressees were often treasured and long remembered. I have in my possession many letters from Father, mostly in a sombre mood, written in beautiful Jawi over many pages of his writing pad. Father once told us about his father (our grandfather, Tok Wan) who gave A.E. Coope a hedgehog as a present before he left Trengganu. Then, a bit later, after the man Coope (compiler of an English–Malay dictionary) had had the animal well kept and perhaps truly stuffed, he wrote to Grandfather in his handwritten Jawi. The *landak*, he said, was *köhör sari köhör baik* (getting better by the day).

The charm of letters will not die even—especially—the old ones that bring back many scenarios and emotions to the reader. Recently, while looking through an old copy of *Kitab Canai Bacaan*—a Malay reader compiled by the scholar Za'ba (first edition printed 1925, 3,000 copies) that I bought from a second-hand bookseller—an old Jawi note fell out from its pages. It said:

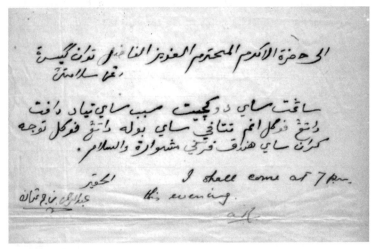

The note written by Abdul Rahman bin Haji Othman to Mr Guest that plopped out of my second-hand copy of Canai Bacaan.

294

'Sangat saya dukacita sebab saya tiada dapat datang pukul enam tetapi saya boleh datang pukul tujuh kerana saya hendak pergi mesyuarat wassalam.'

The sender of the note was one Abdul Rahman bin Haji Othman, a man who must have been of some importance judging by the *mesyuarat* that he had to keep. He was also an English-speaking sort of chap. As a subtitle to his Jawi note he also wrote in English: 'I shall come at seven this evening.'

I know from the note who the book once belonged to, as the note was addressed: *'Ila hadhrat al-akram al-muhtarim al-'aziz al-fadhil Tuan Guest, dengan selamatnya'* ('To the honourable Mr Guest, with greetings'). The note continues: *'Regrettably, six o'clock is out of the question, but I am able to come at seven o'clock as I am going to a meeting. Regards. Yours sincerely, Abdul Rahman bin Haji Othman.'* This would've been written in 1932 or later (the edition I have was reprinted in Singapore in 1932, 20,000 copies). It was sold by the second-hand bookseller Persama Store for sixty cents (sen). The note was still intact when the book was finally bought by us, so I'd like to guess that it was Mr Guest who spent the sixty sen at Persama all those years ago, kept the book handy on his writing desk in Malaya, and into which he

Song-request postcard sent to Radio Malaya.

inserted the note from Encik Abdul Rahman. On Mr Guest's passing the book, I guess, was consigned once again with the inserted note to a second-hand bookshop in London.

But thanks to another note from the past and to a lady from Kuala Besut, we are able to end this on a cheerful note. I found this postcard recently that leapt through time and space (and the radiowaves), and the dial of my steam-powered radio lit up once again with some joyful old notes.

Who nowadays goes to the post office to drop off a postcard to hear a song? 'Niza Bt Mohammad of Kuala Besut, what's cooking today? I'm sorry we can't play the song 'Senyum Dalam Tangisan' that you requested, but here's something to keep you humming, 'Cinta Sejati'. Keep smiling!'

On the request postcard, the lady requester from Besut, Niza bt. Mohammad of Kuala Besut, had asked for the song 'Senyum Dalam Tangisan' ('Tearful Smile') to be played. The producer had written on the card for another song, 'Cinta Sejati' ('True Love'), to be played instead.

Conference of Birds

ONE DAY, MANY YEARS AGO, our son came home from school with *kuau kepala puteh* and *kedidi, chiak perut merah* and *kelichap merah* all wrapped in transparent plastic. They were all in a long-out-of-print book, *The Birds of the Malay Peninsula, Singapore & Penang* that looked very delicate for its age. It was published by Oxford University Press in 1951 and purchased by a lady called Audrey Fairbairn in Singapore in 1954. (I know because she wrote her name, place and date of purchase on the flyleaf.) The book was a gift to us from our son's schoolteacher, and I've kept all the birds in their original wrap since the day our son brought them in, courtesy of Mr Inwood to whom I now once again say thank you.

Last week, while looking through a report of proceedings at the Old Bailey in London, I came across a passage about an indictment in 1830 against one John Pettet. Pettet—who was later found guilty—was accused of stealing one 'live tame fowl'. And it was the nature of the fowl that sent me looking for the book.

I found little about the 'Malay cock' in the book, though I presume that it could have been one of a variety of our *ayam hutan* or jungle fowl, or even *burung puyuh* or quail that, in Trengganu, was always connected with a gap in the teeth. *Ttendang ppuyoh*, or kicked by the quail, was how adults mocked a child who'd lost one or more teeth. But why a quail? Well, perhaps it was because, as my book puts it, 'the females are very pugnacious during the breeding season'. With a tendency to kick recalcitrant males in the teeth, perhaps.

During our frequent trips to Besut, where our grandparents lived, we were often surrounded by birds. Grandfather kept many *merpati* (see page 59) in elaborate cages, one of which was hoisted on fine days up a tall pole that he kept near the *rumah padi* (granary house). Another, I remember, was constantly cooing outside the window by Grandfather's reading table where he kept his *kitab*s and his correspondence, a corner I remember well as the best place to catch the morning light while trying to make sense of the adult world through news reports in *Utusan Melayu*.

The Birds of the Malay Peninsula, Singapore & Penang *by A.G Glenister.*

There were many birds above our heads in Kuala Trengganu, though we did not pay them much heed, perhaps because, being coastal kids, we had many other fish to fry. But on some days *murai* would sit by our well to pour forth a long story and Mother would stop her work to say, '*Bawök ssini berita baik, Cik Mura!*' ('Magpie, bring us the good news!').

Looking through *The Birds of the Malay Peninsula* I found another talking bird called, intriguingly, Brain-fever Bird. 'A frequent visitor to gardens, including mine at Ipoh,' the author says engagingly. A hawk-like bird with not an unpleasant voice, but wait:

'The call is a loud, melodious invitation to eat more froueet in an ever-ascending scale, repeated so frequently as to become irritating, particularly when it calls at night.'

To the Malays it is a constant wailing and clamouring for help. They call the bird, unsurprisingly, *burung mati anak*, meaning 'mother of dead chicks'.

I am especially pleased, though, to find in the book the *lang kangök* (the grey-headed fishing eagle, *Icthyophaga i. ichthyaetus*) which I thought was a fabulous bird, especially as we heard and imagined it so often from an adult-spun childhood poem that went:

'*Lang, lang kangök;*
Lang kangök...
....
......................,'

There are gaps in my memory, as you can see. This is because the 'fillers' were ad-libbed to suit the situation of the child. One ending that I can remember comes as the adult ad-libber pokes the child on the mat gently in the belly and says, in mock surprise, '*Dok ccongök atas tikör!*' ('Sitting pat on the mat!')

* * *

NOTE: For the Malay bird names in the opening paragraph I have retained their old spelling, as in the book.

Let Them Eat Cake

THE IDEA OF FOOD as a palliative runs through many cultures, from Jewish chicken soup to the piping hot *pisang bakörang* that Mother used to pull out from the fire to comfort us every time we had a fever. There were other items from the cooking pot that made their way into our domestic pharmacopoeia: *halba*, for instance, and ginger, and that appalling paste that came via many Indian tongues into our language as *inggu* or *hinggu*, otherwise known as asafoetida. In French, that most diplomatic of tongues, *inggu* is known as *merde du diable* or 'turd of the devil'.

Sometimes in our midst in Trengganu were kids with puffy cheeks glowing the brightest of blue. This signalled a malady that was known in Trengganuspeak as *bekök keng*, a swelling of the jaw also known as the mumps. A remedial paint that was a mixture of vinegar was applied to the cheeks to shrink the swelling. Indigo had the same effect, perhaps, as bells did for those poor lepers in days of yore. Then there was that cold poultice of dried tamarind soaked in cold water and pasted onto your forehead (with a shock that made you jump out of your skin) when you were fiercely burning with fever.

This last Ramadan, incapacitated by some virulent bug, I had a brief respite when a friend brought to me *lompat tikam*, which I quaffed down in one heroic, therapeutic dose as soon as we reached *iftar*. It made me feel a lot better. Then I got this email from someone I know as Abang Pin of Kemamang. It proved right the old Trengganu adage about cakes and their remedial powers:

'*Tapi rama örang kkabö Abg Pin, öbat diabetes ialah Tapè Ubi Kayu. Abg Pin cuba gök 2/3 kali, tapi kesang dök berapa sangat, sebab Abg Pin makang sikik—sa'mas je. Örang hök kkabör tu dia makang serial sekali makang. Abg Pin takut makang banyök, sebab makang öbat spital.*'

'Many people told me that the cure for diabetes is *tapai*. I tried it a few times with negligible results because I ate only fifty-sen's worth. The person who told me this ate a ringgit's worth at each sitting. I am reluctant to eat too much as I'm on hospital medication.'

I am, of course, stretching my definitions by classifying *tapai* as a cake, but the point I am trying to make is that there's nothing in Trengganu that cannot be taken on the pretext that it is medicinal. There are as many illnesses in our daily lives as there are foods that clash with pains and ague: *nangka,* for instance, is contraindicated for someone with muscular aches; any food that has gone through *irik* is to be kept away from someone recovering from *demang* for fear that he will suffer a *betang*; but then the patient himself or someone with a kindly heart will come forward to say, '*Dök apa èh, makanglah sikik, buat öbat!*' ('Never mind, just take a little as medication!')

When I told our Abang Pin in Kemamang of my happy tryst with the *löpat tikang* with a caveat that he, with his diabetes, should perhaps steer clear of this syrup-bathed angel, he popped back another email:

'*Balik ke löpat tikang, Abg Pin makang jugök, le ning örang jual ddalang bekah plastik hök bulat, seringgit sa. Tapi hök abang suka, Mèk Berèmbat tabor dengan tahi minyak di atas (kköleh sagu) yang dibuat oleh Mèk Munöh hök dudok dekat rumöh Mök Song, sebelah rumah Ma Wan Itam buat kerepok. Le ning ta'dök döh.*'

'Back to the *löpat tikang*, I do still eat it. Nowadays it is sold in round plastic tubs, at a ringgit each. But what I like is *mèk berèmbat* sprinkled with fried desiccated coconut, coconut shavings (*kkölèh sagu*, sago paste) made by Mèk Munöh who lived near the house of Mök Song, the neighbour of Ma Wan Itam, the *kerepok* maker. No one makes it nowadays.'

So there you have it in a brief paragraph: a short history of Trengganu cakes, a street map of our old *kampung* and a stout belief that cake conquers all. It nearly brought tears to my eyes.

Marital Omnibus

ONE DAY IN THE MID-1990s as I was standing in an open bus terminus in Valetta taking in diesel fumes and faint whiffs of *pastizzi*, I began to hear the distant cry of sweet *ananas* and Japanese pears. All that happened because of the association of things before me and things that lay in the depths of my mind; by meeting they produced overlapping memories.

In Malta there was unsettled dust that still blew in from the heat of the bus station in Kuala Trengganu, and the constant drone of ancient engines that pulled the yellow and red livery of the Trengganu bus company. Puffs of black and blue emitted from exhaust pipes turned rusty from lashings of monsoon rains and splashings of *teh tarik* from puddles in the muddy road to Jerangau. Some days we stood there among clusters of travelling people and street vendors, waiting for a bus that would take us to Jerteh or Marang. I remember the mellow scent of *kacang putih*, roasted and poured into thin dunce-cap paper funnels, and somewhere around the corner the sound and smell of bananas frying in oil that spat, grumbled and sizzled. These were memories wrapped in time and paper: paper *kacang putih* cones, and paper stubs from wads of tickets that had been audited and dumped into the big black bin of the bus company. We collected them to tear out during our own games, tickets in our own imaginary mode of travel.

How swiftly we travel in our memory. From the sound of bustling people and ancient internal combusters that pulled travellers in and out again of Valetta central, I was transported back to Kuala Lumpur in Jalan Melaka, to a smaller space but with a similar bustle of people, waiting and waiting for their desired numbers. Twenty-eight and thirty to Gombak, I think with the speed and imperfections of the Len Seng Company, no different then than the buses I was seeing now. And then that call again that took me so far away: the throaty cry of a gangly man, hunched by the weight of a metal tray on his head that sometimes dripped ice-cold water onto his workaday singlet as he waddled in his knee-length shorts that fanned out into a skirt with bulging pockets. '*Bolai, bolai ... nanas manis, manis,*' he said, enquiring eyes on the people who were waiting their turn to clamber onto the buses of Toong Foong or Len Bus Company, or the red buses that went, I think, to the further reaches of Taman Templar.

Then, we were new to Kuala Lumpur, where the sound of fruits and buses snarling like beasts in the dust soundtracked my after-school bus-waiting hours. It took me many more days of standing in Jalan Melaka before I realised that the *bolai* that preceded the sweet *nanas manis* in the man's peripatetic cry was *buah lai,* the Malay name for Japanese pear.

Valetta was many thousands of miles from Kuala Lumpur, and Kuala Trengganu further than both of them together; it seemed so then, at least in memory. But I knew that there was still something yet to unravel. Then, on old buses, came the tragi–comic life of that couple that we used to sing about in Kuala Trengganu :

'*Bas kömpeni*
Jatoh ddalang parit;
Kelahi laki bini
Berebut kaing carek.

Bas Kömpeni
Jatuh ddalang lökang;
Kelahi laki bini
Berebut ppala ikang.'

'A bus of the company
Has fallen into a ditch;
Husband and wife in disharmony
Fighting over a piece of rag.

A bus of the company
Has fallen into a drain;
Husband and wife in disharmony
Fighting over a fish head.'

The poetic form used here is, of course, the Malay *pantun*, quatrains that allude to matters in opening lines that have little or nothing to do with what follows. They merely act as *pembayang maksud*, or the route of allusion that leads to the matter at hand in the last two lines. To me, the *pantun* reflects the indirect nature of Malays in language and behaviour, and their constant awareness of things as parts of other things, even if the interconnectivity may not be so obvious.

In the *pantuns* above, the misfortunes of our Trengganu bus company (driving into the ditch in each instance) are used to connect two marital feuds—one over a piece of rag, another over a fish head, perhaps during a meal.

The Zen of Dok

BOREDOM IS AN ENGLISH TERM, and a recent one at that. The noun 'to bore' came aboard in the second half of the eighteenth century, and it was only in 1823 that Lord Byron* divided the world into the bores and the bored.

In Trengganuspeak—and I daresay in standardspeak too—we've been bored for as many years as the arm is long, but only in the sense of *bösang,* to mean 'I've had enough' of something, a noise maybe, or someone's constant nagging. But the idea of being bored from having nothing to do is a new one, imported from a Western fixation with instant gratification and the need to do something when nothing is being done, or to be moved by some manufactured outward stimuli because the moon, the sun, the shade, the trees and the chirping of birds aren't good enough. Suddenly *bösang* becomes an intransitive verb, a reason in itself.

This obsession with external stimuli has given rise to many weird and unwonderful things: a blaring video player on an express bus trundling down the motorway from Kuala Lumpur to Kemaman in the quiet of night; television sets blasting out in shopping malls, hospitals and recently, in London, one public library I went to had games blasting out from PCs when everything should've been still and quiet. It was to attract the kids and, irony of ironies, in a world of books that was the only way they could think of to keep them stimulated.

In Trengganu, *dok ssaja* is used to describe someone sitting quietly to one side, looking at passers-by or just chilling out. One better than *dok ssaja* is *dok mmetèk,* which is still not work but just adjusting picture frames on a wall, putting the finishing touches to the icing on a cake, patching up a torn sleeve or doing some other 'unimportant' work. But *suka mmetèk* is the love of intricate work: embroidery, needlework or designing a *kuih tat.* All these are within the ambit of *dok ssaja* in those after hours when boredom wasn't yet a word.

Hedonism's probably put paid to all that. *Dök léh dok ddiang* is often said of children, but adults too may suffer this predilection and an itch for something that rocks. *Dok ssaja* is more than just its opposite, it is meaningful rest from busy-ness, when the mind's set free to roam or rest and hands may move without deadline and for no set purpose. It was in moments like this, I suppose, that ideas struck and shapes like birds, prawns and even the simplest cube were woven from *palas* leaves, filled with rice and boiled into *ketupat*.

There are many varieties of *dok* in Trengganu: *dok mmikir,* or thinking; *dok mmenung,* or brooding; *dok ngitta*, just looking out of the window, not the more deliberate voyeuristic act; *dok ccökköh,* or just being there, sitting proud; *dok nnètèr,* hovering in a place with or without intent; and *dok ggedik,* or shaking your legs.

Then there's another kind of *dok* called *dok ssepèr,* wedged between other people or close to someone else and is probably the cousin of *dok ccetèk*; while *dok nnusuk* means to be in hiding, the opposite of that.

Dok is the diminution of standardspeak's *duduk*, to be doing something or to be seated and doing the not-doing (which is the real zen of *dok*). Someone I once saw pacing up and down said, when asked, that he was in the act of *dok*: 'Dok tengöh serabuk perok,' meaning that his stomach was all knotted up, and he was worried sick.

'Dok mmölèk,' advises a sage, 'live quietly in harmony, in peace.'

* * *

* 'Society is now one polished horde, formed of two mighty tribes, the Bores and Bored.' Byron, Don Juan, 1823.

Eating Your Words

THERE ARE WAYS TO EAT just as there are chairs for cats to scratch. Rice comes either on a plate, laid flat on the *apör* of banana leaf, wrapped in a conical *kelösöng* or laid out in a small punnet shaped from *daun pisang*. This is the same as the way of our beloved *tepong pelita*, though the punnet now, in step with time, is pinned over the folds with a stapler rather than toothpick sticks cut from the spine of a coconut leaf. The *tapèr* comes wrapped in a *tapèr* leaf, though its substance is tapioca— nothing to do with the leaf at all—that grows quietly in the earth. *Tapèr* is an ancient food that is sometimes made from fermented rice swimming in its own juice of sweetness and enough alcohol to make even the *lebai's* head swim in a daze. Teetotalism and *tapèr* are poor bedfellows, though I'll be chastised for saying that.

I learnt early on how eating was a part of us when, as soon the flooring was done in our refurbished *surau*, the chairman of works, Ayöh Wang Mamat, dropped everything and said to Father, his treasury head, '*Ning muak sepuloh bekah!*' ('This will take ten trays'). The area he was looking at was a wide expanse of floor, freshly planed and leading smoothly to the *mihrab*. This was a prayer place, and Ayöh Wang was already looking not only to the *solats* but also to the holidays and festivities of *mawlid, kenduri* and *bèkwöh,* and to the time when our South Indian shopkeepers would come and brighten up our place with their *qasida*. There'd be *nasi minyök* stirred in thick cauldrons that Ayöh Wang shaped out in his shed from brass. There'd be people from neighbouring *kampung*s, children going from place to place and dignified oldsters sitting six to a tray in the *surau*, ten trays all filled laid out into a wide space.

Children filled up the outer apron and bickered quietly under watchful eyes; and that was how we ate, and how we sat on days like that. This is *beradöng,* as we say in Trengganuspeak, to mean food all laid onto plates in fold-rimmed copper trays, soaked in tamarind juice and rubbed with ash till the yellow began to gleam, then laid in rows on the wall-to-wall *kaing seperöh*. *Seperöh* is a loan word from the Turkish *sofra* for dining table, but we just borrowed the word to give meaning to the cloth now spread on the floor to catch drips and crumbs as we ate.

In company we ate quietly to accusations of doing the *pölök,* which is hard to explain when your cheeks are all filled and puffed up—that's what *pölök* really is. The handmaiden of *pölök* is *kemang,* which is not altogether an active word: it simply states that food remains in your cheeks, stewing there quietly in your spit. *Kemang,* though, can be practised as an art, for example when you have a marble-sized boiled sweet that you want to keep secretly in your mouth. One sizeable pat on your back from a friendly lad and your *kemang* turns into a choke or *ccekèk*, as you would say if you could but you're too busy gasping and in the state of *belöhök* (spluttering).

In private you may eat as you please and whatever you like. You may *pua'* (a word that ends in a nasal note) your rice or *puèk* (spit out) the residues to your side. You may want to drink from a cup, but as you do not have a cup, you may want to feel free to *tögök* your Cola from its can as you sit and *asök* (stuff yourself). You'll have to listen to a chiding mother telling you of her son's plight to get the sense of this word, '*Dok asök jjugök lah dari takdi, döh dök sakit perok ba'ape?*' ('He's been stuffing himself all this time, are you surprised he's got tummy ache?')

This is makangspeak, or eating words. In derision, *makang* is downgraded into *ranggöh* which is one step above the more contemptible *kedaröh*. Sometimes it's emphasised as *bahang kedaröh*, an expression of extreme disapproval and often laced too with a curse; though *bahang* itself is sometimes used to describe an eating experience that's thoroughly enjoyed, '*Takdi aku bahang röjök, sedak sunggoh!*' ('I had that *röjök* just now, it's so good!') *Bahang* and *tibang* are identical twins in eating as in lascivious works.

All very well if you have your food and frolic, but left only with crumbs on the plate you may have to resort to *ggedik*. This *ggedik* is a cadging word, a child's ruse normally prefaced with, '*Mitök sikik gök!*' ('Gimme a bit!'). And then a 'ptoooi!' sound comes thundering back as your prey spits into his ice, his *kköleh* or *nèkbak*. What can you do about that?

There is, I think, a word for it, as you're left there, spirit flagging, *mulok nnèllèh* (salivating) and all that. It's that uncertain feeling of *kelak-kelak* (to be left high and dry).

Self and Other People

AMONG FATHER'S FRIENDS in the vicinity of Masjid Abidin was one called Che Ali Orang. He was *orang*, as I later discovered, because of his disconcerting speech that knocked you off your presumed place, requiring you, the listener, to re-orientate. He would say, for instance, *'Orang gi ppasör sebetör takdi,'* to mean 'I made a short visit to the market earlier'. He was, like many speakers of Trengganuspeak (and of many other 'speaks' too in the wider Malay world) reluctant to throw the directly personal pronoun of *aku* or *saya* into his conversation. Instead he replaced it with one that was totally unexpected.

'Orang kata döh takdi!' a mother would say when a careless child tripped over while running around the house. What's fascinating about this remark is that *orang* is used as a personal pronoun for emphasis, but it was Che Ali's insistence on taking it to an even wider embrace that earned him the amusing sobriquet.

Malays generally avoid identifying the self so overtly—unlike the 'I' of Indo-European languages—and are even more reluctant to address directly the 'self' of another person to whom he or she is speaking. *Saya,* or more familiarly *aku,* are, of course, used and understood in everyday speech, but Trengganuspeakers sometimes hide behind the collective pronoun *kita* for 'we' or *ambe* (lit. your servant). Someone would even refer to himself by name rather than use the pronoun 'I'. *'Mbong nök gi döh,'* is said by Embong of himself: 'I'm going now.' Likewise, a person speaking to Cik (Mr or Miss in Trengganuspeak) Embong would ask him, *'Cik Mbong makang döh?'* ('Have you [Mbong] eaten?') More confusingly, he or she may ask, *'Kita sapa bila?'* ('When did we [i.e. 'you'] arrive?'). *'Nök gi döh kita?'* asks a lady at the well of a child in school uniform, laden with a book-filled rucksack. ('Are we going [to school] now?')

Many years ago, a bored American insurance company executive named Benjamin Lee Whorf took up linguistics as a hobby and discovered that language does shape society. Society, it can be said, also shapes language—how a person thinks is reflected in how he speaks. If you ask a Trengganu person, 'What fruit is that?'—unmindful of Aristotle's A is A—he or she will reply, *'Hök tu orang panggil buöh ppisang, kang?'* Now is that an answer or a question? Or does it show an inner sense of modesty that makes this world look like an uncertain place? Haven't I seen that before in some philosophical works? This shyness about what Stuart Chase* calls 'the law of identity' (Aristotle's A is A) is also found among the Wintu Indians of North America. 'We say "This is bread" but in Wintu they say, "we call this bread",' says Chase. Again, ask a Trengganuspeaker, 'What is that?' and he or she will reply: '*Tu lah kita panggil ggènang.*' ('That's what we call *ggènang.*') Ask another for directions and the reply will most probably be, '*Kot tu lah kot!*' ('That's probably the way.')

But in one situation a Trengganuspeaker is certain about what he or she is looking for or thinking about. I've heard this said many times: '*Höh aku dok mmikir pasa nnatang apa takdi?*' [about some lost chain of thought], or '*Mana dia nnatang tu Mek?*' [about some lost things]. And here the lost physical object or abstract thought is referred to simply as *nnatang*, the beast. And that brings me to my all time favourite: '*Kita lupa dök setarang nök bawök nnatang tu!*' ('I damn well forgot to bring that beastly thing!') or its richer, fuller version: '*Kita lupa dök setarang nök bawök nnatang tu, döh nök wak guane setabok!*'**

* * *

* *Power of Words* by Stuart Chase, Harcourt, Brace & World, Inc., NY; 1954

** 'Drats, I forgot to bring that darn thing, can you believe that!'

As She is Spoke

Dök Léh Dok Lök

WHILE RECENTLY RUMINATING on the Zen of Dok (page 303), I noted how the 'o' sounds in Trengganuspeak could become problematic. It became more acute when my friend, SSS61, introduced *dök rök* in his comments (where the *dök* differed from the one in the topic of discussion). There are at least two 'o' sounds in Trengganuspeak: 'oh', as in our *dök* (short for *duduk*, previously *dudok* in standardspeak), and the 'o' sound that approximates to the English word 'or', as in *ök* (withstand) and *lök* (neglect). Seasoned Trengganuspeakers know where to switch the sounds, but it can be confusing even for veterans, as in Pök Ok's predicament below. In the past I've written *dak* where I meant *dök*, and this brought another confusion with *dak* (the 'ah' sound as in *kertas dak* that Mat Sprong found in the bins near Pejabak Jang Besor). To make a clear distinction in Pök Ok's plight I have used the umlaut (ö) for the 'or' sound, and will do so in future, where necessary, to set them apart. The sound of the unmarked 'o' will then be similar to the English 'oa' as in 'oath' or 'loath', or the Scottish 'Arbroath'.

Dok Tengöh Dök

'Pak Ok kaki kecök
Dia dok wak dök
Cakting-cakting
Tahang tu dok ök

Cari Mak Jeng Bbatu Burok
Nök mitök tulong urok
Bila ttemung tepak dudok
Dia pulök takdök setabok

Jjalanglah dia cakting-cakting

Cari bining keliling pusing
Nak mitök urok keting
Jjalang ddalang panah ddering

Pak Ok jerloh ddalang lökang
Sakit naik sapa ppingang
Adoh! Adoh! dia ngerrang
Ba'pelah nasibku ni sunggoh malang

Bila bini balik jengök
Tengök dia tengöh ggösök
Dia terus suka selök
Sapa dök buleh ök
Tulah, Guane gamök?'

The 'e' poses similar problems, as in 'Leh', the Trengganu diminution of the name Salleh, and the meeting of 'e' and 'a' sounds as in *keléh*. The latter, Trengganuspeak for 'look' illustrates another 'e' problem: the 'e' sound as in the English 'her' or 'per'. In old standardspeak spelling this used to be called the 'e' *tanda*, the marked 'e' or the 'e' with the little open bowl over its head 'e'. For my purpose I've left this 'e' ('her', 'per') alone. As for the two others I have adopted the French grave accent, è, to give a sound that is not dissimilar to the French '*père*', and the French acute accent for the e+a sound, as in the Trengganuspeak *dök léh* ('not possible'). In English this 'é' rhymes roughly with 'nay'.

The G-Spot of Trengganuspeak

IT IS HARD NOT TO form the impression that Trengganuspeak is a language in a hurry, eager to impress with little time for linguistic frills. It is the language of working people eager to push the boats out to sea, of ladies rushing off to market with baskets of fruits or trays of *pulok lepa* in banana-leaf wrappers still steaming from the fire. Anthony Burgess once said that the standardspeak sentence '*Seratus orang-orang perang*' evokes the noise and image of swashbuckling warriors marching to war. Now hear this in Trengganuspeak: *'Höh, budök ning, aku debök kang baru tau!'* Or this description of someone who's taken flight: *'Dia lari sapa kecik ppala!'* Both *debök* in the first sentence and *kecik* in the second have glottal-stop endings, making the former, *debo'*, sound just like the thump in the back that it's meant to be, for it is indeed a word with that ridiculous name, onomatopoeia. The second word, *keci'* describes so aptly with sound that visual effect of a fleeing person's head becoming smaller as he makes more distance from his pursuing beholder. 'He ran until his head began to diminish in the distance,' says the speaker.

One prominent characteristic of Trengganuspeak is, undoubtedly, its tendency to transform terminal 'n's and 'm's into a hard 'g': *makan/ makang, baham/bahang, bulan/bulang, malam/malang.* Another is its fondness for contractions: the standardspeak *pisang-pisang* or *mempisang* becomes *ppisang, bergolek* (standardspeak) becomes *ggölèk*, and *di pasar* (standardspeak) becomes *ppasör*.

The *kècek-kècek* in my blog title is, I must admit, a nod to standardspeak. It is meant to convey the idea of a light conversation, a soirèe maybe. This, at least, is the meaning that my worthy commenters are agreed upon, but applying the device of Trengganuspeak makes the word even more varied and interesting. *Kkècèk* on its own, for instance, may be just a contraction of the longer standardspeak version, *kecek-kecek*, with the meaning unaltered. But *kècèk* with the ungeminated 'k' can mean 'persuade' or, in its extreme form, 'bamboozle'. When a child is stubborn a friend will be asked to *'Gi gök mung kècèk dia sikik?'* ('Go and persuade him a bit, will you?' A seasoned politician will come not to *kècèk* but *nggècèk*, to bamboozle.

In a comment many moons ago someone asked what the word *kecek-kecek* is doing on a page on Trengganuspeak, suggesting that it is more widely used in Kelantan than Trengganu. Perhaps I should concede here that my blood has been coloured, in part, by the red-dye *ssumba* that seems to thrive in the sandy earth of my paternal grandparents in Besut, on the Kelantan–Trengganu border. But then again, *kecek-kecek* is used with the same meaning, even in those far flung islands of Indonesia where, in some of its even remoter parts, they also transform their 'm' or 'n' endings into the guttural Trengganuspeak 'g'.

Stressed Up Words

Gigi ggögèh, gguling-galök, ddènèr-pè are all stressed words that typify Trengganuspeak (or Kelantanspeak too, for that matter). They highlight the use of what's known as the *shaddah* in Arabic—stressed consonants that give you the feeling of a vertical take-off. In Malaysia the *shaddah* is more commonly known as the *sabdu,* which may be the *shaddah* spoken in a hurry or a corruption of it. In a circular way, my *Kamus Bahasa Melayu* defines *sabdu* with a little arrow pointing to *tasydid.* When I go to *tasydid,* I find another little arrow pointing to *sabdu.* '*Pi mai, pi mai ...*' ('Hither and thither ...') as they say in Kedah. '*Bila gi ssining dia suruh gi di nung, bila gi di nung dia suruh balik ssining pulök.*' ('When I come here they ask me to go there, when I go there they ask me to come back.')

The *sabdu* is a word connected with the *tajwid,* the proper recitation of the Qur'an, and has little relevance to standardspeak. But in Trengganuspeak you can't walk without stumbling on the *sabdu* or the *tasydid* and you have to give it due attention because it can change the meaning of a word. *Göcöh,* as you probably know, is a one-sided fight, but when it's *ggöcoh* it becomes two-sided. Likewise with *jalang* and *jjalang,* one's a noun and the other's a verb. So that's *sabdu* or *tashdid,* which is in fact related to *shaddah.* One is the stress on the consonant (*shaddah*) and the other's a word with the *shaddah* (*tashdid*).

In Trengganuspeak the *shaddah* is sometimes used to make a verb, as in *jjalang* (walk), as opposed to *jalang* (road). But mostly it's used to shorten words, normally those beginning with the prefix *ber-* attached to them in standardspeak. Here again, *jjalang* is *berjalan* in standardspeak, while *jalang* (standardspeak for 'prostitute') is someone you don't speak about—well, not in polite company outside Trengganu anyway. The stress also sometimes tells you that there's a preposition amiss, the *di* word. If you ask someone, '*Mana Mök mung?*' ('Where's your Mum?') and the answer is '*Ddunngung,*' then you know that she's in Dungun (*Di Dungun*). '*Duana mung beli nnatang ning?*' ('Where did you buy this thingymathing?'). '*Bbesut*' ('In Besut'). But to the question: '*Nök gi duane tu wei?*' ('Where're you going to?'), the answer could be, '*Ppasör.*' ('*To* the market.').

This, though, doesn't work all the time. You can't, for instance, say *Sselangor,* or *Ssingapura,* or *Ssumatra,* or *Pperlih;* and what the reason is for that I just don't know.

So the *shaddah* is used to indicate a verb, which is generally true; but safer by far is to say that it indicates that the word has been compacted because it can appear in *ppisang,* which is not a banana but another *buöh* that hangs from the branches of a big tree, is yellow and has stones the size of pebbles. My guess is that it was *pisang-pisang* in its earlier life. And if, in your childhood days, you've played *to nnusuk* you'd have been told by your team-mates to *nnusuk mmölèk,* hide yourself well. That's *menusuk* (hide) and *molek-molek* (well), a verb and an adverb, both having the *sabdu* or *shaddah.*

I was inclined to think, as I said before, that this device is found only in Trengganu and Kelantan, until I found this lovely sentence from a Bugis *toloq. Toloq* is a wonderful Bugis literary genre which embodies many literary conventions. Here's an opening line that caught my eye: '*Ala maressaq otaé ala kkédéq pabbojaé*' which is translated as, 'Faster than betel can be chewed, in the twinkling of an eye.' It's the *kkédéq* with the *shaddah* that caught my eye because we do that in Trengganu too: *kkedik mata* which is when you sit there blinking. '*Eh, budök ni dök tido lagi, dok kkedik mata!*' ('Hey, this kid's not asleep yet; he's fluttering his eyelids!')

Glossary

stdspk = standardspeak; Ar = Arabic; Eng = English

agar-agar: a versatile gelatinous seaweed used in Trengganu for making *beleda* [q.v] and by scientists for culturing germs

agar-agar kering: a sun-dried sweet with a crystallised sugar coating

aröng: of eggs, soft-boiled

AH: anno Hegirae / Hijrah

air: water

> *a. bah*, see *bah*; *a. ulu*, water from upstream, normally of *café au lait* colour; *a. pasang*, high tide; *a. suruk*, water flowing back to the river or sea, ebb; *a. sirap*, water sweetened with red-coloured, vanilla-flavoured sugar concentrate, sometimes drunk with the added flavour of condensed milk; *a. serbat*, a drink made famous by Ku Awang in Padang Malaya [q.v.]; *a. lamnid*, a clear drink allegedly lemon-based, bottled by a local company, now defunct. There's sugar, fizz and the occasional sighting of the local *cicök* [q.v.] in the bottle

ais: fr. Eng., ice

> *a. kacang*, a heap of shaved ice on a bed of *kacang* [q.v.]; *kabong* [q.v.] and *cendol*, sweetened with *sirap* (see, *air*) and condensed milk

akik: agate

akök: a Malay cake, basic ingredients of which are flour, sugar and eggs. Usually served during Ramadan [q.v.] in Trengganu

Allah: God

> *A. Yarham*, of a deceased person, from Ar. May Allah have Mercy on him/her.

ambe: stdspk. *hamba*, servant

apang: basically a cake made from steamed rice but Trengganu *apam*s are made from almost any steamable meal, from tapioca to sago; normally flat or flying saucer shaped, but not always; *a. ssakör*,

319

a spongy *apam*, muffin-shaped, nice if dipped in curry but not de rigueur; a veiled reference to the female pudendum

apit-apit: thin, crispy tubular sticks made from flour; sometimes used by children as edible straws for hot drinks

asam: anything sour, fruit or drink

a. gelugur; a fluted *asam* fruit, used as a flavouring; *a. keping, a. gelugur*, sliced and dried; *a. gumpal*, a Trengganu pudding of sago balls with a nutty centre floating in a coconuty sauce that's sweet or savoury

atap: the roof of a house or roofing material

a. nipah, atap material from palm fronds; *a. Senggora*, atap tiles brought back by the *perahu besar* [q.v.] that ply the waters between Trengganu and Senggora, Thailand

ayang: stdspk., *ayam*, chicken, fowl; *ccuri a.*, fowl stealer

azan: the call to prayer that can be done anywhere, not necessarily from the *masjid* [q.v.] or *surau* [q.v.]

ba/bo: fr. Eng., the light bulb

bah: flood

bah bberer: *bberer* is an onomatopoeia, originating from the sounds made by the bus parts that shook and trembled from the force of engine power

bai: fr. Hindi, Brother; *b. roti*, bread seller, fr. Punjab or Uttar Pradesh but mistakenly assumed to be fr. Bengal (hence also *roti Benggali*)

baju: dress or shirt; *b. kebaya*, figure-hugging blouse as worn by stewardesses on the airlines of Malaysia and Singapore; *b. Melayu*, loose waist-length Malay shirt, everyday wear, with the *kain pelikat* [q.v.] or formally with a loose trousers and a *sampin* [q.v.]

bangsawan: Song, intrigue, tears and joy, stuff of everyday Malay melodrama; sometimes mistakenly translated as opera

bangunang: building, fr. stdspk. *bangunan*

bata: stdspk., *bantal,* pillow (see *roti*)

batik: the art of lost-wax fabric printing, originally fr. Java; the *sarung* [q.v.] thus imprinted; common everyday wear for men and women in Trengganu; *b. lepas*, loose batik material, not sewn together at the seams

batu: stone; *B. Bersurat*, the famous Trengganu inscribed stone found in Kuala Brang; *b. giling,* the grindstone for grinding curry ingredients into a paste

bbadi: compete; *b. dang,* a children's competiton to see who will achieve something first; a game of chicken

bbaru: usu. *pohon* [q.v.] *bbaru* (stdspk. *baru*), a broad-leaved plant of the hibiscus family much loved by goats in Kuala Trengganu but not in Kemaman

bedil: cannon; *b. buloh,* cannon made from bamboo, fired normally during Hari Raya [q.v.]

belacang: stdspk. *belacan,* a foul-smelling sun-dried salted shrimp paste; the aroma of the shoreline of Trengganu from Kemaman to Seberang Takir in Kuala Trengganu

belebak: a banana pudding wrapped in the leaf of the same tree

beleda: jelly made from *agar-agar* [q.v.], of various colours, eaten when set or as a sun-dried sweet encrusted in sugar (*b. kering*)

belimbing: carambola or star fruit; *b. masam,* a tart ovoid *asam* [q.v.] fruit used as flavouring.

belinjau: a bullet-shaped thin-shelled fruit covered in soft skin, *Gnetum gnemon*; eaten boiled, or flattened and sun-dried into *kerepek* [q.v.]

beluda: see *roti*

bendang: rice field

benteng: rampart; a concrete wave breaker that juts into the water in the *kuala* [q.v.] of the Trengganu from the customs jetty, reputedly Japanese-built during the Occupation; an edifice as mysterious in the psyche of Trengganuites as the obelisk in Kubrick's *2001: A Space Odyssey*

beris: raised sandy earth

berkawöh: (cooking) in a caludron

berönök: a pudding made from sago, coconut, sugar and colour.

beseng: fr. Eng., basin

betang: stdspk., *bentan,* a relapse in illness

binjai: a mango-shaped fruit called the Jack (*Mangifera caesia*), with buff rind and an unpleasant smell; an adult food, its whitish flesh sliced and added sometimes to *budu* [q.v.] to give it a sweet–sour flavour

bismillah: [Ar.] in the name of Allah

bölör: blind or very short-sighted; *selör b.*, clumsy and very awkward movement; a person with such attributes

bomoh: a shaman, hired for healing or casting spells. Sometimes a man dressed in a singlet and *batik sarung* [q.v.] stands behind the goal in a Trengganu vs. Kelantan football match. The man's head is usually wrapped in thought and *batik lepas* [q.v.]; he is the team's *bomoh*.

bubor: broth or gruel; *b. lambok,* a broth made usually during the fasting month, its main ingredients being rice, *pucuk paku* (wild fern shoots) and *budu* [q.v.]

budu: fish fermented in salt in earthen jars

bukit: hill; *B. Putri,* a landmark historic hill overlooking the harbour of Kuala Trengganu on which hangs the *genta* [q.v.] and tales about a fairy princess called Tuan Putri

bulan puasa: see *puasa*

buöh: fr. stdspk., *buah*, fruit; *b. manjikiang*, small red fruits of the *pinang gatal* [q.v.], causes itchiness when rubbed on the skin, has laxative properties; *b. gömök*, 1. a pudding made from sago floating in coconut milk; 2. A *kör* [q.v.]; *b. guling*, 1. marble 2. candy

ccuri: fr. stdspk., *mencuri,* to steal; *c. ayang* (see *ayang*)

cèndöl: takeaway *c.* is often taken home in a clear plastic bag with the *c.* swimming in its coconut-milk sauce. For some this adds to the ambiguity of the *c.* because of the single *c.*'s resemblence to an overgrown tadpole. Its green colour and shape lends credibility to assertions that this gruel is inspired by the bogey of its ailing inventor. In recipe books *c.* is said to be the result of squeezing a blob of cooked rice flour through the *c.* sieve

cengal: a hardwood much valued in house construction, *Balanocarpus heimii*

cerak: (also *cirak*) a mini aqueduct fed with water from the community well of a *surau* [q.v.]. Users of the *cerak* cleanse themselves by unplugging narrow tubes in the body of the duct; the bungs are usually made from coconut husk

ceranang: a Trengganu salad made from blanched *kangkung* (*Ipomoea reptans*), sliced eggs, bean sprouts and fried tofu. It is eaten with dollops of peanut sauce preferably under the watchful eye of Mök Mèk in the back of the Chee Seek bookshop in Kampong China

che: (also *cik*) in Trengganuspeak and spoken stdspk. *che* is used as honorific for male and female people. On the east coast *che* is also the polite term for one's mother

cicök: stdspk., *cicak;* the gecko lizard chirping upside down on the ceiling in the night, a bane to flying insects and people down below as its droppings, shaped like dark exclamation marks with the dot emphasised in white, fall everywhere. Even new homes built in extreme isolation have the *cicök* chirping from their rafters. Where do they come from, I wonder?

cik: (see, *che*); *c. ru*, an insect that lives in sandy soil, the Ant Lion, a myrmelrontidae, (Greek, *myrmex,* ant, and *leon,* lion)

cirak: see *cerak*

cokelat: fr. Eng. chocolate but also embraces sweets generally in T'gnuspk; *c. nnisang*, a sweet made from coconut sugar and wrapped in scraps of old newspaper; *c. ra*, a mint-flavoured sweet, *ra* (a nasal word) being the up-your-nose sensation of the mint

cot: a grab or a touch

dacing: a weighing scale

dam: the game of draughts, with the 'board' normally etched into the floor of the *wakah* [q.v.], and the pieces made from the tops of *air lamnid* bottles (see *air*)

daun: leaf; *d. kesum, Persicaria odorata (Lour)*

dedök: rice polishings

delima: ruby

demang: stdspk., *demam,* fever

dök pok: stdspk., *tak empok*, not tender

durian: fr. *duri*, thorns, hence, *durian*, a (fruit) of thorns. A fruit much prized for its taste and powers, and hated for its odour. Banned by most hotels and airlines. Anthony Burgess once described the enjoyment of it thus: 'like eating custard in a lavatory'.

enjut: when a contraption bobs up and down, as in a see-saw, it is said to *berenjut* in stdspk., i.e. it is doing the *enjut; e-e papan*, the up and down movement of a plank; *e-e semut*, a game played by two players that involves pinching the top side of each other's hand while singing a song about biting ants. As it is a game usu. played by adults with very young children, it has no discernible purpose or conclusion except to keep the children amused

gambir: an extract from the *Uncaria gambir* leaf that comes in flat, thin discs, chewed with *siréh* [q.v.] leaf; *g. China*, red, sweet discs that come in paper tubes, made in China for children's delectation, containing probably fruit extract and sugar

geduk: stdspk., *beduk*; a big drum used in the *masjid* [q.v.] or *surau* [q.v.] to alert worshippers before the formal call to prayer

genta: also *geta,* a big brass bell that hangs on Bukit Putri. The *genta* was used during the Ramadan fasting month to signal *iftar* [q.v.], and even earlier than that, it was an amok alert for the people of Kuala Trengganu. The *genta* ringer requires strength, good eyesight to walk in darkness on the unlit hill and gall

gertak: (also *gertök*), bridge, normally a wooden structure

ggarék: fr. Ar. *maghrib*, the time for dusk prayer

gerbang: see *pintu*

gok: an enclosure for animals, usually under the house

gömök: see *buöh*

gulai: Malay curry

guni: sack made from cloth or jute; hence the Eng. 'gunny sack'

hamis: the sweaty smell of a goat

hampas: (also *apah*) residue, say of shaved coconut once it has been pressed for its milk

hantu: ghost, spirit; *h. kangkang*, a supple, naughty ghost with a very wide stride that reputedly hangs out after midnight from the Pintu Gerbang (see *pintu*) of the Istana Maziah at the foot of Bukit Putri

hari: day; *h. raya*, there are two in the year: *h. raya puasa*, the feast day to mark the end of Ramadan [q.v.], and *h. raya haji*, during the month of hajj; the Eid festivals

hasidöh: a sticky sweetmeat concoction of flour, *ghee*, sugar and pandan [q.v.], stirred for a long time in a thick brass pot over a wood fire which is usually in a shed in the compound of the house during Ramadan [q.v.]. Sliced shallots, crisply fried, are scattered over it before it is served

hati sökma: a Malay sweet

hizb: fr. Ar. litany; *hizb ul bahr*, the famous *Litany of the Sea* for travellers, composed by the Sufi Sheikh al-Shadhili

hun: a unit used to measure the length of nails in Trengganu. Windstedt says that *h*. means a share or 1/100 tahil in Chinese

iftar: time for the breaking of fast in Ramadan [q.v.]

igal: coil of rope placed on the Arab headdress on formal occasions to keep it in place.

ikang: fr. stdspk., *ikan*, fish; *i*.ddukang (stdspk., *belukang),* a catfish usually found in the bay area, *Arius macronotacanthus*; *i.* cerlong; *i.* cerming; *i.* yu, shark; *i. kembong*, mackerel

imam: a person who leads the Muslim daily prayers, no matter where it is done

irik: vigorously stirred

Isha': the last prayer of the night, usually at around eight o'clock

istana: palace

jam: clock or watch

jama'ah: (also *jema'ah*) fr. Ar., a group of people, usually in a congregation

jambang: fr. stdspk., *jamban*, lavatory

jambu: a name given for an assortment of fruits; *j. air*, the water apple *Eugenia aquea*; *j. butir banyök*, the many seeded *jambu*; *j. golok*, the cashew

Jawi: now normally used to mean the Arabic characters with adaptations for Malay sounds such as the hard 'g', 'c' and 'ng'. Fr. Ar. orig. which meant 'people of Jawa'. Malays from the archipelago were once widely known as *Orang Jawi* in the Malay-speaking Arab world which, believe it or not, did exist, and probably still does now

jelebi: a very sweet Indian sweet of syrup trapped in brown-coloured tubes coiled into whorls and deep fried

jering: a foul-smelling pod that is boiled and eaten with shredded coconut, excess of which can lead to kidney failure

junjong: to carry something on the head

kabong: a fruit-bearing palm, *Arenga saccharifera*, source of palm sugar, *gula k.*; *buöh k.*, translucent, white seeds of the palm, sweetened and used in *ais kacang* (see, *ais*)

kacang: a bean; a word generally used to describe peas, beans and pea-sized nuts (e.g. groundnut, *k. tanah*)

kaing: fr. stdspk., *kain*, material for clothing or the *sarong* [q.v.];

k. pelikat, a sarong usu. with checked pattern, widely worn by men at home or for going to the *masjid* [q.v.] or *surau* [q.v.], said to have originated in Pulicat, India (see also *sarung*); *k. bèlong*, orig. brightly coloured synthetic parachute material but stripped and sold for clothing; *k. ssahang* (see, *ssahang*)

kambing: goat; *k. nerök*, billy goat usu. foul smelling (see also *hamis*)

kampung: the heartland of the Malay soul, the village

kanciperat: a thin inner garment, a t-shirt buttoned down to the middle of the chest, usu. worn by hajis or men as casual wear. Imported fr. China usu. under the brand name of Pagoda

kangkong: see *ceranang*

karong: sack, made from fabric or plaited fr. *mengkuang* (screwpine) leaves

kati: a measure of weight, approx. 1.5lbs

kaya: a spread made from eggs, flour, sugar and coconut milk and flavoured with pandan [q.v.]; *r. kaya* (see *roti*)

keda: fr. stdspk. *kedai*, shop; *k. kopi*, coffee shop, café, K. Bbunga; the Flowered Shop, a famous grocery store on the *gertök* [q.v.] in Kampung Daik, Kuala Trengganu; K. Payang, the shopping centre and fish market in the centre of Kuala Trengganu famous for its four-sided clock tower that simultaneously showed the times of at least four parts of the world, but no one knew where (or why)

keladi: calladium

kelèndar: fr. Eng. calender

keleper: pouch

kelong: a structure built in the water for trapping fish

kemunting: a fruiting shrub; *buah k.*, its fruit

kerepok: boluses of fish, salt and sago flour rolled into long sticks, boiled in a cauldron and eaten dipped in chilli sauce, as is or fried. This is *k. gètèl*, *k. göndè* or *k. dèkör/lèkor*. When sliced and sun-dried, it is known as *k. kering* (dried *k.*) or *k. keping* (*k.* pieces) fried and served with a chilli dip. This is the famous Trengganu fish cracker (*k. ikang*)

kerèpek: a cracker that is not made from fish (*kerepok*) is kerèpek, e.g. *k. mminja* (*belinjau* [q.v.])

ketupat: rice, glutionous or plain, cooked in leaf packets and served on feast days

kicap: soy sauce

kijang: Barking deer, the state symbol of Kelantan

kitab: fr. Ar., book

kölöh: a low-sided open water tank in the *masjid* [q.v.]or *surau* [q.v.]
for worshippers to do their ablution before prayer

kopiah: skullcap

kör: a throwing object, used in games

kota: fort; rampart

kuali: wok

kubur: grave, burial place

kuih: cake, sweetmeat. Generally described in Trengganuspeak as
tepong

ladoo: an Indian sweet

lampu/lapu: lamp; *l. panjang*, the fluorescent lamp; *l. lat*, the winking
lighthouse; *l. pam*, a pressure lantern much used in Trengganu houses
prior to electricity

landak: hedgehog

lastik: a slingshot made from strands of rubber bands, attached to the Y
of a tree branch

lebai: a pious person, usu. dressed in a haji's skullcap and tailed
headwrap; *buat l.*, Trengganuspeak for someone who pretends to be
innocent or uninterested in temptations around him

lègèr: barrel

lekak: stdspk., *lekat*, stick

lembèk: soft; *l. lutut,* feeling weak at the knees

lembing: spear

lempok: durian [q.v.] cake

lompat: jump; *l. tikam* (lit. jump and stab) a soft, sticky Trengganu cake
with a name that's hard to fathom

lötèng: storey; the upper floor of a building

maghrib: see *ggarék*

majalah: fr. majallah [Ar.], magazine

mamak: South Indian Muslim, predominant in the catering trade.
Inventor of the *pasembur* (a kind of *röjök* [q.v.]), the *Mee Mamak*
and exponent of the *téh tarik*

mandalika: district

manjikiang: see *buöh*

masjid: fr. Ar., mosque, where the weekly Friday prayer is performed in addition to the five daily prayers. cf. *surau* [q.v.]

mata-mata: lit., eyes (fr. *mata*, eye); policeman

mee: noodles; *m. halus*, the fine noodle, vermicelli; *m. kasör*, the regular egg noodles; *m. kkuöh*, noodles served in gravy; *m. Jawa*, noodles served in a peanut-based soup which, contrary to its name, is unknown in Java; *m. bandung*, another type of noodle, with meat-based gravy, also uknown in the town of its purported origin, Bandung in Indonesia; *m. Mamak*, a popular fried noodle, prepared/inspired by the *mamak* [q.v.] with constant banging of the *kuali* [q.v.]; made by itinerant vendor or from a street stall

melatah: has been described as Eskimo hysteria, a sudden involuntary movement (dancing, doing the *silat* [q.v.]) or uncontrolled speech (vulgarity, etc), usu. by old ladies at the slightest instigation (loud, unexpected encounters, a prod in the tummy). This hysterical outpouring of ideas not normally expressed in polite company is often accompanied by interesting word association, usu. linking random words with the genital area

menarik: see *nnarik*

mengkuang: leaf of the screwpine, dried into strips and used for plaiting into baskets, mats or hats. There's confusion extant between this (*pandan berduri,* the screwpine, that is found in Trengganu coastal areas) and the pandan used as a food flavouring

menuang: see *nnuang*

menteri besar: chief minister

merpati: pigeons

mesyuarat: formal meeting

minyök: oil; *m. sapi, ghee*; *m. nyör*, coconut oil

mök: stdspk., *mak*, diminuition of *emak*, mother. Hence Mök Cik (lit. Small Mother) is Auntie. Mök is usu. used with the senior woman's shortened name, e.g. Mök Jöh, which is translated as Auntie Jöh, or another epithet that tells about the woman, e.g. Mök Ngöh, an auntie who's a middle child in her family, Mök Long, lit. 'Auntie Eldest', etc.

murai: magpie

musim gelora: *musim* is from the Arabic *mausim* meaning 'season' that also begot the word 'monsoon'. *Gelora* refers to the sea in a bad mood

musolla: see *surau*

nak: stdspk., *nakal*, naughty

nasi: see *nasik*

nasik: (also *nasi*), in conformity with stdspk; cooked rice; *n. hapör,* rice and accompanying dish served on coconut leaf as plate; *n. dagang,* a sepcial east coast rice, cooked then steamed in coconut milk and eaten with coconut milk-based curry usu. of tuna fish; *n. benör,* plain rice; *n. ulam,* rice mixed with finely cut herbs and served with *budu* [q.v.]; *n. kapit,* rice compressed into a slab, diced and eaten usu. with peanut sauce

nasi kapit: see *nasik*

nasi minyak: Trengganuspeak, *nasi minyök, ghee* rice

nèkbak: spongy unsugared pastry soaked in syrup, eaten usu. during Ramadan

ngilla: to laugh hysterically and loudly

nipah: a palm tree, its leaf is used for making *atap* [q.v.]; *Nipa fruticans*

nira: a juice tapped from the palm; fermented, it turns into toddy

nnambang: fr. stdspk., *penambang*, a ferry boat

nnarik: stdspk., *menarik*, a mould-making stage in brasswork, when the wax-dipped mould is placed on a spindle and the excess wax trimmed with a blade before it is covered with clay

nnuang: stdspk., *menuang*, a stage in brassware making, after *nnarik* [q.v.], when molten brass is poured into the mould to replace the wax

nobat: royal musical ensemble of string and wind instruments that emit strange haunting sounds

nyiur: coconut; *n. kömèng,* very light dud coconut that has no flesh inside; a dip is carved into the outer husk for the *n.* to be used as a headrest on the floor of the *wakah* [q.v.]

orang: people; *O. Darat,* people of the interior, derog., country bumpkin; *O. Judöh,* labourers in the port of Jeddah in Saudi Arabia, a term used by Mother—based on her experience from a sea journey to Jeddah—for someone who is clumsy and uncouth

palas: a species of palm with fanning leaves, *Licuala spp.*; leaf used for wrapping *ketupat* [q.v]

pah: Trengganuspeak for 'until'

pandan: The *pandanus* family. The leaves of the screwpine, *Pandanus tectorius*, are used for making mats, baskets, hats, etc. The smaller-leaved *daun p.*, *Pandanus odorus*, is used as food flavouring and colouring, and as an effective air freshener in cars

pantai: beach

pantun: Malay quatrains where the two opening lines merely act as hors d'ouvres before the following concluding lines; in a stanza is reflected the indirect nature of the Malays and their knack for seeing connections in things that are, to the world, unconnected (see *pembayang*)

paruh: the beak of a bird

pasar: market

paung: see *roti*

pawagam: cinema; acronym of PAnggung WAyang GAMbar

paya: a swamp or marsh; P. Bunga, an area in Kuala Trengganu that has no *paya* nor *bunga* (flowers)

payang: a fishing boat

pedas: hot

pejabak: stdspk., *pejabat*, office

pekasam: fermented fish

pelayaran: travels

pelesit: a female ghost fond of gobbling up little children; *belalang p.*, the *p.*'s familiar in the shape of a cricket. Thanks to people with long fingernails, we know the *p.* because it is often said that so-and-so has *kuku* (fingernails) *panjang macang* (as long as) *pelesit* (the pelesit)

pelikat: see *sarung* and *kaing*

pelita: an oil lamp; *p. ayang*, an oil lamp on a tall stand with the wick uncovered, used by night-stall vendors in the Tanjong market

pembayang: that which gives an imagery, a reflection; *p. maksud*, that which reflects a meaning, the two opening lines of the pantun [q.v.]

penambang: see *nnambang*

penyu: turtle

perahu: boat; *p. besar*; lit. big boat, the sailing boat of Trengganu;
   p. jalur, dugout canoe

perösa-er: the fast in Ramadan and other acts connected to it

perut ayam: circular pieces of flour rolled and cooked into flat white
   discs, then basted in a pure white sauce that is neither sweet nor
   savoury

petai: strong-smelling, almond-shaped green beans of the *petai* pod,
   Parkia speciosa

petik: to strum or flick something; *p. mata*, a children's game that
   involves flicking out a short stick from the ground with a longer stick
   and hitting it away from you

pikul: to carry a heavy load on the back; a hundred *kati* [q.v.]

pinang: specifically, areca nut, but generally, any hard-stoned fruit of
   the palm tree; *p. gatal*, small reddish fruit of a species of palm that
   has soft fleshy skin around a small hard stone

pinas: a cargo boat (see also *perahu*)

pisang: banana; *d. pisang* (see *daun*)

pitu: stdspk., *pintu*, means both 'window' and 'door' in
   Trengganuspeak but only 'door' in stdspk; *p. gerbang*, the archway

pohong: stdspk. *pohon*, a tree, a plant, e.g. *pohong jarök*, castor oil
   plant

Pök: father; also used to mean uncle, as in Pök Mat (Uncle Mat), Pök
   Cik (lit. Small Father) hence, uncle (see also *Mök*)

pölök: to stuff food hurriedly and greedily down the throat

pondok: madrasah

pontianak: banshees

ppayang: stdspk., *tempayan*, earthen water jar, usu. found at the foot of
   the stairs of a Malay house

ppiöh: stdspk., *kopiah*, skullcap specifically, hats generally; *p. lembèk*,
   lit. soft cap, skullcap; *p. hitang,* lit. black hat, i.e. *söngkök* [q.v.]

puasa: fast; *bulan p.*, the month of Ramadan [q.v.]

putri: princess; *p. mandi,* a cake made from glutinous rice, usu. green in
   colour and mixed in scraped coconut

putu: cookie made from rice flour or peanuts as in *p. kua* and *p. kacang*
   respectively; there are also wet *putus*, as in *p. beras* and *putu ubi*,
   both steamed and made from rice and tapioca meal respectively; cf.

apam [q.v.]

qasida: fr. Ar., poem

raka'at: one movement in a *solat* (formal prayer), beginning from the standing position, standing with a prostration

Ramadan: the month of fasting (see *puasa*)

rasa: feel, taste

rèmpéyék: a crispy disc with embedded fish (white bait) or peanuts. A savoury cracker, fried, with a funny name; a favourite snack of TV addicts

rengas: a large tree, *Gluta renghas*, with beautiful wood containing a blistering sap; *buöh r.*, fruit of the *rengas*, washed ashore during the monsoon months in Trengganu but avoided because they cause itchiness

rödat: a Trengganu performance art, hard to fathom but much enjoyed by the populace

röjök: 1. stdspk., *rojak*, sometimes a vegetarian salad with a tart, biting sauce; sometimes a mixture of the vegetarian and carnivorous, the latter consisting mainly of cows' lungs and chicken meat. Winstedt said it was 'vinegar salad' but he was in Kemaman and never ventured to the stall opp. the post office in KT to savour the *röjök* of Pök Dé which was simply a breathtaking plate of meat, veg and a secret sauce; *r. betik,* made from shaved green papaya and vinegary, fishy sauce. The most famous exponent of this was Mök Téh Spring in Tanjong; *r. katèh,* made from the cartilaginous cow's heel, in very vinegary hot sauce

2. reference to an admixture of anything and everything, usu. derog

rökök: cigarette; *r. Arab,* a rich, sweet stick made from flour, *ghee* and eggs; *r. daung,* long, thin cigarette rolled from dried palm leaf and laced with a thin thread of tobacco from the pouch

rönggeng: a song and dance movement; a predilection towards which is a sign of misspent youth

rösök: stdspk., *rosak,* ruined, spoilt

roti: bread; *r. bata,* plain bread baked in long tins with the result looking like a long row of terraced houses; *r. canai,* flat fried bread, invented reputedly by the *mamak* [q.v.]; *r. beluda,* the Trengganu muffin; *r. kaya,* sliced bread eaten with the *kaya* [q.v.] spread; *r. keras,* hard, short bread stick, enjoyed by children who use them as drinking straws for sucking up hot drink

saf: the line formed by worshippers in a formal Muslim prayer at the *masjid* [q.v.] or *surau* [q.v.]

sahang jatuh: Trengganuspeak for *saham jatuh*, falling shares

sahur: the last meal taken before starting the daily fast during Ramadan [q.v.], usu. taken just before the dawn prayer

samping: cloth worn as a short skirt around the waist over the Malay costume

sarung: material, usu. *batik* [q.v.] or *pelikat* [q.v.] worn by men and women in the manner of a long skirt

sawah: see *sawöh*

sawöh: padi field, stretching as far as the eye can see, replete with birds, water buffaloes, the farmer's hut and trees in the distance. A scene in the mind of many bucolic artists

selalu: contrary to its stdspk. meaning of 'now', 'this very moment', it means 'always' in Trengganuspeak

selasih: the seed of holy basil, *Ocimum basilicum*, used as a flavouring and for its aesthetic quality (the seeds transform into dark-eyed little tadpoles when soaked) in drinks

selèndang: a cloak, veil or scarf

semayang-bang: the act of prayer and what comes with it

serambi gantung: hanging verandah

Trengganuspeak: Malay language as she is spoke in Trengganu

selèndang: short material worn by ordinary village women as head covering, or as a plaid by stylish folk

selèpang: stdspk., *selimpang*. Sewn material, usu. a *sarung* [q.v.] worn as a sash; same as *samping* [q.v.]

semutar: long, colourful material that men wrap around their heads during daily work. An art form in Kelantan, workaday wear in Trengganu

Senggora: a source of terracotta tiles for Trengganu houses, reputedly from a town in Siam (Thailand)

serban: the haji's head gear; also worn by non-hajis for respectability; *Tok Aji S.*, a Trengganu cake of glutinous rice wearing a soft, brown hat made of eggs and coconut sugar

silat: a Malay art that combines self-defence and dance

singgang: a basic dish of fish cooked in a thin sauce flavoured with ginger, *lengkuas* (galangal), salt, whole chilli and a little *asam* [q.v.]

siput: snails

siréh: a leaf widely chewed in the *kampung* with a dab of lime (*kapur*), and an extract from the *Uncaria gambir* leaf

sömböng: proud

söngkèt: Trengganu brocade

söngkök:the Malay hat

ssahang: a piece of rag worn by men and women when bathing at the community well; also used to describe everyday wear

suji: a cake, prob of Indian origin

sukun: bread fruit

surah: fr. Ar., chapter

surau: a small prayer house, usu. in a community that also serves as a its centre. Most daily prayers are performed there, but not the Friday congregational prayer.

surung: the front part of a house that juts forward

tahajjud: late night supererogatory prayer, usu. performed during a break between sleep

tajwid: the art of proper recitation of the Qur'an

takbir: the citation of the Arabic phrase '*Allahu akbar*', 'God is Great'

tanglong: a paper lantern

tanjong: cape; *ujong t.,* the edge of the cape, land's end; T. Pasar, a part of Kuala Trengganu bounded by the Pantai Teluk and Ujong T. The birthplace of this book

tapai: sweet, fermented tapioca, wrapped in *tapai* leaf

tarawih: series of prayers done after *Isha'* [q.v.] during Ramadan [q.v.]

tarhim: pre-dawn wake-up call to the faithful, before the *azan* [q.v.]

tasawwuf: Islamic mysticism

taukeh: towkay

téh: fr. Eng., tea, drunk without milk; *t. oh,* with; *t. susu*, usu. with sugar and condensed milk; *t. tarik*, a fierce concoction of very strong tea (usu. tea dust) drunk with sugar and condensed milk, and aerated by throwing the mixture in the air, usu. done by the *mamak* [q.v.]

tèksi: fr. Eng., taxi. In Trengganuspeak it is also used for trishaws *teluk*: bay

tembusu: (also *temusu*), hardwood, *Fagraea spp*

temucut: (also sometimes *kemucut* in Trengganuspeak) love grass

tepong: see *kuih*

tengkojoh: the rainy season

terendak: a conical hat worn by farmers and market vendors. It is made from dried palm leaves

teringat: lit. remembering. A longing word that has one foot in fact, another in fiction

tibb: fr. Ar., a book of potions and medical prescriptions. The most famous of this is the *Taj ul Mulk*

tikör: a mat, usu. made from *mengkuang* [q.v.]

timba: a dipper usu. made from recycled metal from cans, for bailing water from a well. Trad. made from palm spathe, *timba upéh*

titiang: bridge

tok: a title of respect for an elderly or learned male person, male or female. Specifically, grandfather or grandmother. Also used as a deferential title for feared animals, e.g. Tok Belang, the Striped Tok, for tigers; *t. peraih*, the middleman, esp. in a fish market; *t. mudéng*, the man who circumcises boys.

töngkang: a barge

topi jjambul: pomponed hat

ttua: from stdspk., *tua*, old

ttuke: stdspk., *toka-toka*, rayfish. (see also *ikang*)

ubi: any edible root; *u. kayu*, tapioca

ujong tanjong: the water's edge

ulam: herbs that are eaten raw as accompaniment to rice and other dishes

ulu: lit. the source of a river, upstream; derog. term for someone who is ignorant or awkward with the modern appurtenances of life; *air u.* (see *air*); *orang u.*, (see *orang*); *buöh u.* (see *buöh*)

umrah: a minor pilgrimage to Makkah, done outside the Haj season

ustaz: religious teacher

wajik: a sweet made from glutinous rice cooked in milk and sugar of the coconut, and *pandan* [q.v.] flavouring

wakaf: see *wakah*

wakah: fr. Ar. *waqf*, a pious foundation. An open, roofed platform built as a place of rest in the countryside or along the beach on the east coast. A meeting point in the *kampung* [q.v.]village

wali: saint

zabib: raisin

zamrud: emerald

zikir: (also zikr) fr. Ar., devotional chanting either in solitary or in a group